Christ and the Moral Life

LIBRARY OF THEOLOGICAL ETHICS

Other Books in This Series

Basic Christian Ethics, by Paul Ramsey
Christ and the Moral Life, by James M. Gustafson
Christianity and the Social Crisis, by Walter Rauschenbusch
Conscience and Its Problems, by Kenneth E. Kirk
Economic Justice: Selections from Distributive Justice *and* A Living Wage, by John A. Ryan
Ethics in a Christian Context, by Paul L. Lehmann
Feminist Theological Ethics: A Reader, edited by Lois K. Daly
The Holy Spirit and the Christian Life: The Theological Basis of Ethics, by Karl Barth
Love and Justice: Selections from the Shorter Writings of Reinhold Niebuhr, edited by D. B.
    Robertson
The Meaning of Revelation, by H. Richard Niebuhr
Morality and Beyond, by Paul Tillich
Moral Man & Immoral Society, by Reinhold Niebuhr
The Nature and Destiny of Man: A Christian Interpretation (2 vols.), by Reinhold Niebuhr
Radical Monotheism and Western Culture: With Supplementary Essays, by H. Richard
    Niebuhr
Reconstructing Christian Ethics: Selected Writings, by F. D. Maurice
Religious Liberty: Catholic Struggles with Pluralism, by John Courtney Murray
The Responsible Self: An Essay in Christian Moral Philosophy, by H. Richard Niebuhr
"The Responsibility of the Church for Society" and Other Essays by H. Richard Niebuhr, edited
    and with an introduction by Kristine A. Culp
Situation Ethics: The New Morality, by Joseph Fletcher
The Social Teachings of the Christian Churches (2 vols.), by Ernst Troeltsch
The Structure of Christian Ethics, by Joseph Sittler
The Ten Commandments, by William P. Brown
A Theology for the Social Gospel, by Walter Rauschenbusch
Treasure in Earthen Vessels: The Church as a Human Community, by James M. Gustafson
War in the Twentieth Century: Sources in Theological Ethics, edited by Richard B. Miller

Christ and the Moral Life

James M. Gustafson

With a New Preface by the Author

WESTMINSTER
JOHN KNOX PRESS
LOUISVILLE · KENTUCKY

BJ
1251
.G87
2009

First published by The University of Chicago Press, 1968

This Library of Theological Ethics edition published by Westminster John Knox Press, 2009

09 10 11 12 13 14 15 16 17 18—10 9 8 7 6 5 4 3 2 1

www.wjkbooks.com

Cover design by Lisa Buckley

♾ The paper used in this publication meets the minimum requirements of the American National Standard for Information Sciences—Permanence of Paper for Printed Library Materials, ANSI Z39.48-1992.

PRINTED IN THE UNITED STATES OF AMERICA

Library of Congress Cataloging-in-Publication Data
Gustafson, James M.
   Christ and the moral life / James M. Gustafson.
       p. cm.—(Library of theological ethics)
   Originally published: Chicago : University of Chicago Press, 1968. With new pref.
   Includes index.
   ISBN 978-0-664-23295-5 (alk. paper)
   1. Christian ethics.   2. Jesus Christ—Significance.   3. Jesus Christ—Ethics.
   I. Title.
   BJ1251.G87 2009
   241—dc22
                                                                    2008022120

Westminster John Knox Press advocates the responsible use of our natural resources. The text paper of this book is made from at least 30% post-consumer waste.

To my beloved, Louise

Contents

Library of Theological Ethics

General Editors' Introduction

The field of theological ethics possesses in its literature an abundant inheritance concerning religious convictions and the moral life, critical issues, methods, and moral problems. The Library of Theological Ethics is designed to present a selection of important texts that would otherwise be unavailable for scholarly purposes and classroom use. The series engages the question of what it means to think theologically and ethically. It is offered in the conviction that sustained dialogue with our predecessors serves the interests of responsible contemporary reflection. Our more immediate aim in offering it, however, is to enable scholars and teachers to make more extensive use of classic texts as they train new generations of theologians, ethicists, and ministers.

Volumes included in the Library comprise a variety of types. Some make available English-language texts and translations that have fallen out of print; others present new translations of texts previously unavailable in English. Still others offer anthologies or collections of significant statements about problems and themes of special importance.

We hope that each volume encourages contemporary theological ethicists to remain in conversation with the rich and diverse heritage of their discipline.

ROBIN W. LOVIN
DOUGLAS F. OTTATI
WILLIAM SCHWEIKER

Preface to the Library of Theological Ethics Edition

In 1996 a symposium, *Christian Ethics: Problems and Prospects*, was published that consisted of twenty-one articles by my former students. The fact that very few of the essays focus on traditional theological subjects is one measure of changes in the field of Christian ethics since the time that *Christ and the Moral Life* was written.

This Preface is not the place for impressionistic observations and interpretations of various changes, not to mention evaluation of them. Traditional theological ethics was not my only teaching and research interest during the period of this book's gestation. I taught courses in social ethics in which students studied not only books and articles in social ethics by Christian writers but also publications by secular social scientists that represented contemporary contributions to social policy discourse. My thrust was to break through Protestant satisfaction with "middle axioms" that avoided coming to grips with the institutional and empirical details of, for example, welfare policy and economics. One of my major lecture courses was Recent Christian Social Thought, the syllabus of which itemized publications from all traditions, the ecumenical movement, and even journals and books coming from the United Kingdom, India, and other parts of the world. Like others of my generation, engagement with important contemporary publications in moral and social philosophy became more important. I became as learned as possible in the contemporary theological ethical literature from Europe while at the same time being critical of the narrowness of subject matter and perspective. At Lund University I read dissertations and listened to disputations in ethics which, for example, analyzed Luther's teachings on marriage with no attention to changing family structures and processes in Western industrialized countries.

Theological ethics, however, continued to be at the core of my teaching and research with both ministerial and doctoral students. At Yale Divinity School

I lectured on systematic Christian ethics from 1962 until 1970 when I was asked to leave that faculty. The focus on a constructive Christian ethics atrophied after I moved to the University of Chicago, though there my lecture course on Introduction to Theological Ethics exposed students to the systematic analytical agenda I had developed to interpret typical writings from various traditions, including Orthodox Christian and Jewish. At both Yale and the University of Chicago I conducted seminars on theological themes that are crucial to ethics. We studied selected important writings from the history of the Christian tradition, from biblical documents to important contemporary treatises. Examples of topics are Love, Sin, the Use of Scripture, Law and Gospel, Nature and Grace, and comparisons of writings of Thomas Aquinas and Karl Barth on a whole series of issues.

In *Christ and the Moral Life* the themes in each major chapter demonstrate the inseparability of theology and ethics in the Christian tradition. Indeed, the themes meld into each other and are internally related both as ideas about theology and ethics and in the experiential religious and moral dimensions of Christian life. (The chapter headings are not a typology; in a typology themes are consciously compared with each other to highlight the distinctiveness of each. H. Richard Niebuhr's *Christ and Culture* is the most widely known typology in Christian ethical literature.) Theological ethics is a discipline in which ideas from both domains are seen, developed, and related to each other. Faith, or piety, and morals are experiential, and while correlated with ideas about theology and ethics, require a different focus of attention. For example, I always stressed that Karl Barth's articulation of an ethics of the command of God was not merely ideational, biblically, theologically, and philosophically grounded, but clearly a matter of deep religious conviction. I think that Karl Barth really believed that he "heard," at least sometimes, specific commands of the gracious living God.

Only after several decades of thinking about theology and ethics, and faith and moral activity, was I ready to publish my own deepest intellectual, spiritual, and moral convictions about the interconnections I studied with students. *Ethics from a Theocentric Perspective* was the result, rightly divided in two volumes between theology and ethics, and ethics and theology. Since I had never lectured on what was published in that book, the outcome was a surprise even to some friends and students. Obviously, my own views hinted at or expressed in *Christ and the Moral Life* were significantly changed in *Ethics from a Theocentric Perspective*. There is, however, a deep continuity between the two books, and I could not have written the latter without having written the former and over the years studied more broadly and deeply the Christian theological tradition as well as other literature related to ethics and the moral life. The crucial difference between the two books is the great expansion of the publications and experiences I was compelled to incorporate, and changed criteria of judging the intellectual and religious adequacy of theological ethics. Given my understanding and experience of our modern world, and given knowledge from secular disciplines that interpret the same activities and events that theology does, theological ethics has to go beyond the margins within which I wrote *Christ and the Moral Life*.

I believed at the time I wrote *Christ and the Moral Life*, and still believe, that the study of theological ethics requires as much knowledge and understanding as possible of the Bible and the traditions of Christianity. The theology and ethics of the prophetic books of the Jewish Scriptures are important, but so is the legal casuistry of Deuteronomy and Leviticus as examples of how moral life was to be lived in fidelity to Yahweh. The Gospel narratives and teachings of Jesus depict a paradigm of Christian moral life, but 1 Corinthians and Romans 6–8 are also very important. The New Testament as a whole is worthy of more study than current scientifically informed accounts of moral and faith development. To study Augustine, Thomas Aquinas, Bernard of Clairvaux, Luther, Calvin, Anabaptist authors, Jonathan Edwards, Schleiermacher, Karl Rahner and others, as contributors to theological ethics, is more important than keeping up with many of the current books in the field. William Law's *A Serious Account of a Devout and Holy Life* is as important for the study of Anglican theological ethics as Richard Hooker's *Of the Laws of Ecclesiastical Polity* and K. E. Kirk's *Conscience and Its Problems*. To know the manuals of moral theology used in Roman Catholic seminaries to train priests on how to enumerate sins and grade the offenses of the penitent is as necessary to understand Roman Catholic moral theology and life as is St. Thomas's "Treatise on Virtue" and "Treatise on Law." Bernard Haring's *The Law of Christ*, which I first read enthusiastically in German in the Lund University Library, is more important for understanding twentieth-century Christian ethics than is knowing the differences between my late colleagues, Paul Ramsey and Richard McCormick, SJ, on the principle of double effect. Classic studies of themes in the history of theological ethics, such as Ernst Troeltsch's *The Social Teachings of the Christian Churches*, Anders Nygren's *Agape and Eros*, Kirk's *The Vision of God*, and H. Richard Niebuhr's *Christ and Culture*, can guide critical and constructive analysis through great texts in the tradition, and also contribute to the shaping of students' own thought and life.

To reread the major themes about the person and work of Christ used to organize *Christ and the Moral Life* makes clear to me again how some controversies and arguments in the literature of Christian ethics have distorted the richness and complexity of Christian thought and life. Calling attention to "misplaced debates" has always been part of my academic vocation. I refer to publications which make a case that Christian ethics are situation ethics rather than ethics of principles, virtue ethics rather than rule ethics, or that biblical ethics are deontological ethics. Each such emphasis, or exaggeration, implies (if it does not specifically develop) a larger context of beliefs and concepts that cohere with it. Just as the chapters in this book demonstrate that different christological themes suggest different emphases in Christian ethics and in Christian moral life, so different choices by theologians of ethical theory imply different religious beliefs and experiences. If not necessary inferences, at least plausible ones can be drawn about theological themes that correlate with the ethics. There are also tacit, if not explicit, assumptions about human nature and activity, social institutions and processes of social change, and physical/biological life of which humans are a part and in which they participate. For example, an argument for the idea that Christian ethics are character or virtue ethics implies some correlative beliefs about doctrines of justification and sanctification, about the work of the Holy Spirit, or about some processes of human socialization and views of human choice that can be naturalistically interpreted.

A constructive, or systematic, interpretation of theological ethics does not require a balance of the christological themes, nor a hyper-theory that makes all aspects of ethics cohere at a highly abstract, or generalized, level. An integrating theme ought to be defended, and which brings all aspects of ideas into some coherence without reductionism. In *Ethics from a Theocentric Perspective* I proposed an integrating theme that articulates not only a personal outlook and conviction but which I propose as fitting for Christianity in our contemporary personal, social, and cultural circumstances. Any chosen theological or ethical theme is selective and can be criticized for what it does not emphasize or ignores. Each of the themes in *Christ and the Moral Life* has provided a focal point for ideas about Christian theology and ethics and for the religious and moral experiences of communities and traditions. But, inherently, none of the themes excludes incorporation of others; ethics based on justification by grace and faith alone can include an ethics of discipleship, as Joseph Sittler so eloquently proposed by saying that "the shape of the engendering deed" is the pattern for Christian moral life. The grand cosmic process of redemption of all things in Orthodox Christian ethics is related to ways of Christian living in which ethics of virtue and of rules also play a part.

Preferences for one integrating theme or another develop in the religious and moral convictions of different traditions and communities. The moral life and teachings of Anabaptist communities and traditions are distinctive and currently adapted in other Christian churches, for example. The reasons for the continuation or the adaptation of any historically identifiable tradition cannot be simply historical, but show its religious and ethical importance for Christianity in particular times and places. An example is Bonhoeffer's *The Cost of Discipleship*, which is universally appealing but which developed in a very particular historical and ecclesial condition.

There will always be a variety of ideas about theological ethics, and a variety of ideas about Christian moral life. For many reasons this is the case. The Scriptures and Christian tradition are too rich to be simplified into one theme universally valid for all Christian communities and all historical conditions. Different elements from different sources will be drawn upon as persons and communities try to live and act faithfully. The moral, political and social, cultural and intellectual contexts change, and in responsible participation richly different biblical and theological resources will be drawn upon. This is incontrovertible and easily demonstrable from even the most recent history of theological ethics and moral activity. Conditions of social and political oppression evoke emphasis on the Christian message as liberating, and draw upon preferred biblical and historical sources both for backing and authorization and to orient polemics against theologies and ethics that are judged to be oppressive.

Perceptions of loss of Christian particularity and identity in a historical period or a particular culture can evoke an emphasis on the distinctiveness of Christian faith and morality. Variation will continue because of the richness of the literary sources of Christian life and thought.

Variation will continue as different intellectual and cultural events and circumstances come to the fore. The more vivid experience of religious and cultural diversity that is part of life today throughout the world focuses more attention on the relations between Christian theology and life, and the life and thought of other religious traditions. Academic books and articles about theological ethics often engage the current most important philosophical and cultural interpretations of ethics and social life. For example, I could show how existentialism was replaced by analytical philosophy and that in part by virtue theory and a renewed pragmatism in my own professional lifetime. New knowledge from the many sciences describe and explain personal life, social relations, and the natural world which can either be ignored by theological ethics, or be confronted as significant for the ideas and practices of Christian life and thought.

Christ and the Moral Life invites readers to appreciate the depth, richness, and variety of modes of theological ethics and moral life present in the tradition and by inference in the current thought and life of Christian communities.

RIO RANCHO, NEW MEXICO
AUGUST 16, 2007

In memory of Louise Roos Gustafson, died 4 September 2007

PREFACE

THIS BOOK EXPRESSES A LIMITED INTENTION ON MY PART. I HAVE stated in the opening chapter that there is one central question: What claims for the significance of Christ for the moral life do theologians explicitly make or apparently assume? This question is at once both vast and confining. It is vast in that the tradition of Christian theology and ethics is vast; I have only dipped in here and there to deal with writers I have found to be significant for the ways in which they have answered the question. It is vast in that it raises theological questions that could move one into every area of Christian theology: Christology, the doctrine of God, the doctrine of man, the nature of revelation, the authority of Scripture, the doctrines of justification and sanctification, and many more. The subject of "moral life" suggests as vast a spectrum of considerations as does theology: it opens the way for philosophical, theological, psychological, sociological, and political perspectives. It suggests a great variety of practical moral questions faced by persons today, and in previous generations. Obviously this book does not deal with all of these matters; some are left out completely, some are barely touched upon, some are dealt with in depth.

The question is at the same time confining. I deal specifically with the claims made for "the benefits of Christ," and with theories of the person of Christ only to the extent necessary for each chapter. I deal with "moral life" largely in terms of the personal existence of individual men, and do not develop views of men's action in the world, their relations to social structures, their involvement in particular moral issues. Materials from moral philosophy have been absorbed into the ways in which I state and follow through on certain questions, but I have not developed extensive annotations about these philosophical sources. Nor do I address the philosophical question of whether moral values can exist without the existence of God. No attempt has been made in this book to use social scientific materials and theories, as was the case in *Treasure in Earthen Vessels: The Church as a Human Community.*

Readers who are caught up in the discussions about how Christians ought to make moral judgments will find that this book was not evoked by that or any other current debate, though inferences can be drawn from it for such a debate. To some extent the question that is central to the book is a question many people are not asking today in their celebration of secularity. Thus for some persons the book might appear to be irrelevant—which is to condemn it in this decade. I would suggest that the question of this book, however, is implicit or explicit in all Christian ethics worthy of that name, that it is a question worth asking, and that persons who think about Christian morality ought to ask it. The reader is invited to prescind many questions and issues that are of highly popular and current interest and engage with me in a process of theological ethical analysis and reflection. "Analysis" and "reflection" are carefully chosen words here. Although the direction of my own thinking is disclosed in the ways in which I analyze the thought of others, and in my reflections upon the significance of their thought, I do not intend to provide a systematic Christian ethics in this book. The last chapter is constructive in character, but is confined to the ways in which I would go about answering only the question that is central to the book.

Theological ethics always invades territories where other scholars reign. I am acutely aware of issues that can be raised by experts in theology, moral philosophy, the history of Christian thought, biblical studies, and other fields. But I make no apologies for not having dealt with all the questions in the terms in which specialists in these fields believe they have to be dealt with. Ethical inquiry has its own relative autonomy, and as long as the ethicist is reasonably clear about what questions he is asking, and why he is asking them, he has a right to press them on to materials that have not been shaped by these questions. Some distortions might well result, but I doubt if they are any more serious than the distortions that appear to the eyes of the ethicist when other writers exercise their right to move into the field of Christian ethics. Christian reflection simply has to take place in the conversation between various fields; I hope this book can be seen as part of the ongoing work of the intellectual life of the community of scholars and doers.

It is difficult to cite all those persons and institutions to whom one has accumulated indebtedness for a project that has been as long in the making as this one has. The initial research, and some of the first-draft writing was done during a leave provided by the generosity of Yale University and John Simon Guggenheim Memorial Foundation in the academic year 1959–60. In the spring of 1963, I ventilated the general statement of the issues and the materials of two chapters in seminars with faculty members and graduate students at Duke University under the auspices of the Gurney Harriss Kearns Fund. Invitations to give lectures at the Theological School of Dubuque University and at the Pittsburgh Theological Seminary (Elliott Lectures) provided the occasions to develop the last chapter. My colleagues in a theological discussion group that meets in New Haven responded with proper critical acumen to what is now Chapter V. For four years I conducted a seminar on the topic of this book, and a number of friends among my students and colleagues have from time to time read portions of the manuscript, or all of it, and have made helpful critical comments. To name all those whose intellectual companionship and personal friendship have had various effects on this book would require much too extensive a list for this preface; I mean to belittle no one's contribution by citing only the late H. Richard Niebuhr, and Julian N. Hartt. The latter also shared administrative responsibilities with me for three years in such a way that I had more time for thought and writing than would have otherwise been the case. Various persons have assisted in the typing; I mention only Mrs. Edith Reemsnyder who added some work on this book from time to time to her duties as Secretary of the Department of Religious Studies at Yale, and Mrs. DeAnn Martin who skillfully and swiftly typed the complete final draft. Mr. Stanley Hauerwas and Mr. James Childress assisted extensively and intensively in checking references and proofreading.

In addition to Louise, to whom I have dedicated this book, Karl, Greta, John Richard, and Birgitta Maria have sustained me with the love and delight of family life during the years this book has been developing.

JAMES M. GUSTAFSON

New Haven, Conn.
April, 1968

I $\rangle$ A STUDY IN ETHICS:

A Statement of Procedure and Method

THE QUESTIONS ASKED IN THIS BOOK ARE QUESTIONS OF ETHICS. THE materials upon which these questions are pressed are primarily theological writings. The most fundamental question asked is this: *What claims for the significance of Christ for the moral life do theologians explicitly make or apparently assume?* In pressing this fundamental question upon the materials, I have begun the analyses with the issue that is most centrally personal to every conscientious moral person; namely, the query, "What ought I to do?" To begin with this not only puts the reader in a stance with which he can easily identify himself, but it also is a question that yields other questions when it is pursued. To begin with this "level of moral discourse" is to provoke questions at other levels of moral discourse.[1] In proceeding to answer the moral question of "What ought I to do?" one is likely in one way or another to press on to the three questions that form the basic structure of this book. One is likely to ask, "What criteria, principles, models, or values do I turn to for guidance in proceeding to answer the personal moral question?" One is likely to ask, "How is my answer to the personal moral question conditioned or determined by what I have become and am as a person?" This is to ask a question about the nature and character of the moral self, the question of

[1] I have found it useful here and in other writings to turn to Henry David Aiken's "Levels of Moral Discourse," in his *Reason and Conduct* (New York, 1962), pp. 65–87, for one procedure for sorting out the questions. I do not strictly apply Aiken's pattern here, but there are affinities with it, as there are with the way in which William K. Frankena states the questions of ethics in his succinct and very valuable *Ethics* (Englewood Cliffs, 1963).

1

"moral psychology" as some philosophers call it. If one is of an
inquiring speculative bent, one is likely to press on to a question like
this: "What is the nature and locus of value, of the good? What
powers and beings, places and things are sources of moral goodness,
and thus can be relied upon?"

These three questions seem almost to be intrinsic to ethical inquiry
as one reads not only the analytical work of the philosophical
inquirer, but also as one reads the more hortatory persuasive writing
of those who are trying to bring their readers to a particular moral
point of view. In some ethical writings more attention is given to one
of these questions than to the others, but often the others are
touched upon if not fully developed. In Aristotle's ethics, for example, the concentration is on clarification of the *telos*, the end that
all men seek for its own sake and not for the sake of anything else,
and upon the formation of the self, the virtues, that are likely to
make that end attainable. Eudaemonia, or well-being or happiness, is
that end, and once stated it can become a criterion in actual experience for the governing of conduct. "What ought I to do?" is answered in part by "Seek your well-being in all things." This end,
however, is not arbitrarily selected; its designation is the result of
Aristotle's analysis of human behavior, so it is in accord with man's
nature. In a sense, then, Aristotle is answering the question of the
locus and nature of the human good by saying that its locus is in man
and its nature is his well-being. But it is clear that Aristotle does not
assume that one finds his happiness in a primitively natural way;
indeed, there is a training and discipline of the self that makes it
attainable. Thus he expounds the virtues, the qualities of the character of the self, that are necessary for the attainment of the good.

Scholars who have dealt with the history of Western ethics also
point to the persistence of these three questions. Henry Sidgwick, in
his "General Account of the Subject" indicates that writers on ethics
deal with the good of and for man, with the principles and duties
that govern his behavior, and with the faculties of human action.[2]
The similarity to my three questions is evident. In his *Critique of
Previous Ethics*, the theologian Schleiermacher indicates that three
formal concepts are used or dealt with in all ethical systems, and that
in a particular system one of the three tends to be the integrating or

---

[2] H. Sidgwick, *History of Ethics* (6th ed.; London, 1931), pp. 1–11.

dominant one. These are the concepts of duties (*Pflichten*), virtues (*Tugenden*), and the good (*der Güter*).[3] These are parallel to the questions I have indicated: the specific criteria of judgment and action, the character of the moral self, and the nature and locus of the good.

One need not have these questions set *a priori* by a historian or philosophical analyst of ethics. If one reads critically and carefully a work in ethics with the question "What issues is the author trying to address and resolve?" something like these three are likely to come to one's attention. A basic assumption and contention of this book is that the issues which concern theologians who write about ethics and morality are no exception to these questions. The basic methods and procedures of theological ethics are no different from the methods and procedures of other ethics. This is true in both the critical analytical task of the analysis of literature in Christian ethics, and of the types of appeals made normatively and persuasively by those who exhort or commend Christian conduct.

There is no unique method or procedure for the theological analysis of morality in general, or for Christian morality in particular. This is important enough to be reiterated, for there is some obfuscation of the point in some theological writings. There are theologians who assume or claim that not only the content, but the form and method of theological ethics are unique. Such assumptions and claims are unwarranted, as the subsequent chapters of this book demonstrate. There are different appeals made in answering these three questions of ethics. The ultimate locus of the good is claimed by some to be God, who has revealed himself in Jesus Christ, rather than in man himself, or in nature. The Christian moral self, it is claimed, is moved by God's grace, or by the presence of the Holy Spirit in man, rather than by natural moral sentiments or by well-schooled and disciplined virtues. Jesus Christ, or God's will, is the norm of conduct, rather than man's happiness, for many writers on Christian ethics. But the questions themselves are imbedded in the claims; the issues dealt with are formally the same as those dealt with by other writers on ethics. Thus the method of analysis is common to all ethics, and theologians who self-consciously analyze the worth of

[3] Friedrich Schleiermacher, *Grundlinien einer Kritik der bisherigen Sittenlehre* (2nd ed.; Berlin, 1834), pp. 129–79.

other theologians, or systematically develop their own theological ethics deal with the issues that are present in all ethical analysis.

When Christian writers in a more homiletical and hortatory mood seem to evoke or commend Christian morality or Christian behavior, however that is detailed by them, they also follow the lines of these questions. There may be an appeal to the gracious benevolence of God known in his creation and redemption of the world. This might evoke a loyalty to him, and a gratitude to him as the infinitely rich source of life and goodness, which not only gives a "reason" for being moral, but some impetus to be moral in a certain way. There may be an assurance that one can become a certain kind of person, one who is inwardly free from preoccupations with self-interest and who is lovingly directed toward meeting the needs of others. There may be appeals to certain models of conduct, such as the person of Jesus Christ or the lives of the saints. There may be appeals to normative principles of ethics, such as the commandment of Jesus to love the neighbor as the self. Insofar as preaching or other activity in the Christian community is ethical, it tends to try to evoke responses that follow the lines of these three questions of ethics.[4]

These three questions of the good, the moral self, and the criteria for judgment and action form the three parts of this book. Chapter II deals primarily with the way in which some theologians see the significance of Christ in answering the ontological question of ethics, the question of the nature and locus of the good. Chapters III and IV show how claims are made for a change in the moral self as a result of Christ's sanctifying and justifying work. Chapters V and VI treat the ways in which Christ has been commended as the pattern or example for the moral lives of Christians, and the ways his teachings have been commended as criteria for the judgments that Christians make. Although I believe Schleiermacher is correct in observing that for a particular writer, one of the questions or concepts is dominant and the others are integrated into it, I have not followed that suggestion out as a principle for ordering this book. Such a procedure might yield a typology of ethics, a typology of the ways that Christ's work affects morality, and thus a typology of theologians as they organize their theological ethics around one of the three questions or concepts,

---

[4] I have worked this out more completely, yet still in a relatively sparse outline, in an essay, "Theology and Ethics," in Daniel Jenkins, ed., *The Scope of Theology* (Cleveland, 1965), pp. 111–32.

comparable to H. Richard Niebuhr's widely known typology in *Christ and Culture.*[5]

This book is neither a typology of ethics nor a typology of theologians who have written about ethics. Rather, it is a study of ways in which theologians have answered the questions of ethics as I have formulated them in this chapter. Since some writers have addressed themselves to all three questions, their materials recur for analysis in each basic part of the book; others appear in two parts of the book. Yet, since some of the writers more prominently and centrally concentrate on one of the questions, their work is either more prominent or exclusively dealt with in one part of the book. Thus Karl Barth's work is analyzed more in Chapter II, "Jesus Christ, the Lord Who Is Creator and Redeemer" than in the other two basic parts of the book, though it appears in them as well. Thus John Wesley's work comes to attention in Chapter III, "Jesus Christ, the Sanctifier" and is not used elsewhere, though it could have been.

The formation of a typology of theological ethical writings requires a certain distance from the material that I have tried to avoid. One has to deal with writers' works as wholes, making generalizations about them that are of a very high level. There is raw material for typologies in this book.One could have designated the three sections as the three offices of Christ, as these have been used in the theological tradition. The first part could be worked out as the ethics of Christ the King, the second as the ethics of Christ the Priest, and the third as the ethics of Christ the Prophet. One could have decided under which of these designations the central or dominant tendency of Barth's or Calvin's or Newman Smyth's theological ethics most appropriately fit after having given an ideal delineation of each type and its relation to the other two. But typologies, as the sophisticated literature on the method of ideal types shows, involve exaggerations and simplifications of what is present in any particular instance of the type. And if they are used heuristically the analyst would make them function as benchmarks for pointing out salient features of particular materials as well as the ways in which they are divergent from the ideal construct. Such work is extremely useful both as a way of managing divergent materials, and as a way of highlighting crucial distinctions and issues.

[5] H. Richard Niebuhr, *Christ and Culture* (New York, 1951).

In distinction from a typological approach, I have chosen to stay closer to the texts in this work, and to show how interpretations of the significance of the work of Christ are believed to entail certain consequences for the moral life. If "entail" is logically too strong a word (and it is not one used by writers of materials used here), it may be more proper to say that I have shown some of the inferences drawn for morality from some ways in which beliefs about Christ have been stated. Another way of stating the basic concern of the book is this: "What relationships are claimed or assumed between religious beliefs and life grounded in Jesus Christ, on the one hand, and the morality of the people who hold those beliefs and share that life, on the other hand?" This is an issue that is only now beginning to tantalize philosophers of religion, and moral philosophers.[6] It involves many difficult and intricate problems, such as the general relation of religion and morality, the movement from theological assertions to moral assertions, from statements about what Christ is and does to statements about what men are and ought to do, and others. Much closer and more detailed work needs to be done on particular crucial texts in particular authors than is done in this book, and I will be most grateful to those who undertake such publication. While this book is not as general as a typological approach would be, on the one hand, it is not as refined and detailed as a philosophical analysis of arguments could be, on the other hand. Instead its main body is an effort to draw an ethical map that indicates the ways in which the relations of theological affirmations about Christ to moral life are disclosed in a great variety of the literature in theological ethics. It should result in a specification of issues in particular materials and in the field of Christian ethics in general if its intention is reasonably well fulfilled.

Thus the bulk of the book is critical exposition of materials that illustrate the basic issue of each main section. The critical intention is

---

[6] The work that William K. Frankena has done is the most significant. See his chapter: "Love and Principle in Christian Ethics," in *Faith and Philosophy*, ed. Alvin Plantinga (Grand Rapids, 1964), pp. 203–25; also his section "Religious Ethics and Existentialism" in his part of *Philosophy*, by R. M. Chisholm, Herbert Feigl, *et al.* (Englewood Cliffs, 1964), pp. 420–35. While some of the essays in Ian Ramsey, ed., *Christian Ethics and Contemporary Philosophy* (New York, 1966), are very helpful, its utility is severely limited by the absence in all but one or two essays of any reference to any of the literature of Christian ethics.

at least threefold: to see what stresses and strains are present in the consistency of particular materials; to indicate the particular ways of working present in various materials by comparing them with each other; and to judge the contributions and limitations of materials in the light of the author's own norms pertaining to the ways in which Christian ethics ought to deal with the issues.

The latter critical intention suggests a number of problems of its own. One is the relation between critical ethical work, including what some now call "meta-ethics," to normative ethical work, the positive affirmations about both the content and the method of ethics that one would defend as adequate. This book is primarily an exercise in criticism, an effort to disclose and to lift to objectivity the thought patterns present in the materials. Once disclosed, these patterns can be argued about from various points of view and on various grounds. There are many facets to the works used in this book, and not all of them are equally developed or criticized; some of them are only alluded to or suggested. The ways in which authors use Scripture— their assumptions about its authority, their selectivity in references, and their interpretations of it—are often alluded to, but not dealt with in detail. The Christologies at work are subject to the critical scrutiny of the systematic theologian; this task is not part of the conception of the present work. Views of the self implicit and explicit in materials receive more critical attention than do Christologies. A fuller explication of the beliefs about the nature of God that are present in the authors' works would be required if this were a more extensive anaylsis of "God and the Moral life"; I have confined myself to statements about the *work of Christ* just as I have confined myself to the ways in which that impinges upon man's *moral* experience. The effort to disclose patterns of thought has then clear limitations with respect to both the content of the authors' works and the kinds of questions addressed to them.

The evaluations that occur in the book testify to the fact that I have not only an intellectual curiosity about the issues, but a commitment to the task of resolving them as well. They are expressions of my own efforts to think constructively as a theological moralist or as a moral theologian. I believe, within a commitment to the faith of the Christian community, that there are more and less adequate ways of stating the relation of Christ to the moral life. The measurements of adequacy, if fully developed here, would have to be as many as there are facets of the problem itself—theological criteria for judging a Christology, logical criteria for judging the relation claimed between religious belief and moral judgments and actions, empirical criteria for judging whether claimed significance of Christ for moral life actually is valid, and many more. And I am willing only to say that a view is "more adequate" with respect to all these reference points, never that it is right or wrong.

Thus in the analytical critical task there is a movement that both reflects normative concerns and moves toward them; normative both with reference to the content of the ethical (in this case what one is willing to say about Christ and faith in him that is important for morality) and with reference to the ways in which Christian ethical thinking needs to be done. This normative constructive concern is a long-range one that I hold, and persistently work at in various ways and various writings. It is not executed in this book in a systematic and complete way. In the last chapter, however, I have ventured a sketchy preliminary statement that is limited to the concerns of the questions of this book. I have lined out an approach limited to Christ in its *theological* reference (there is more to theology than Christ), and limited and incomplete in its moral reference to certain aspects of moral selfhood. I have not superimposed the language that is constructively useful to me there onto the chapters of critical analysis in a schematic way, although it is present throughout. The last chapter, "Christ and the Moral Life: A Constructive Statement" chronologically came out of the work of the previous chapters, and could be written only after the others had been well formed. Yet some readers may wish to look at it first to see more succinctly stated a perspective that informs the rest of the book.

It is not part of the task of this book to address as a philosophical problem the relation of meta-ethical work to normative work. I am acutely conscious that the two tasks are distinct, and that I engage in both in this book, and I believe I am aware of the occasions when I move from one to the other. Thus the question of the book shifts from "What claims are made for the significance of Christ for the moral life?" to "What claims can be made, and how can they be explicated, from the point of view of the author?" Since the way in which I proceed to answer this question is based on the use of certain ideas such as disposition and intention, a final comment needs to be made about the approach of this book as a study in ethics.

In its constructive final chapter, and in the evaluations made through other chapters, I am using an understanding of moral experience that is not itself derived from "revelation" or even from theological writings. Such a statement is not worthy of much attention except for the fact that it runs counter to the stated procedures of theological ethics as these are given by the writer to whom more attention is given in this book than any other, namely, Karl Barth. Part of his great revolution in Protestant theology and ethics was directed against the formation of views of man, how he knows God and his commands, independent of the revelation of God in Jesus Christ itself. In the *Church Dogmatics,* II/2, where he stipulates the task of theological ethics (developed at greater length in the next chapter of this book), Barth surveys various positions in theological ethics with his critical acumen fixed on the views that are held of man and consequently shape the ways in which men can hear the command of God. The Thomist view as well as Wilhelm Herrmann's *Ethik* and other "Neo-Protestant" writings are subjected to the charge that a philosophical view of man, developed independent of God's election of all men in Jesus Christ, is formulated which in turn determines the way in which the command of God is known. If, for example, one views man in terms of intellect, will, and appetite, and as part of the order of nature in which beings have tendencies to fulfill their ends, God's grace and his command will have to be understood as received through this preconceived view of man. This is to limit God's freedom, and not to understand the "real" man, since he is understood only in his relation to God. Since man and ethics are to be determined by God's election of men in Jesus Christ, Barth wishes to sweep out such views of man, and establish one that is grounded in revelation. Thus not only one's view of man, but the task of theological ethics is to be governed by revelation, and not by independent views of man or of ethics.

Clearly this book is written from a different perspective. It assumes that questions of ethics, Christian or any other, can be established on the basis of both general human experience and reflection on literature in the field. It assumes that the Christian thinker is not violating his integrity as such when he examines theological ethical materials from the standpoint of such questions as this chapter has stated. It assumes that one can properly evaluate writings in theological ethics from other criteria than those established in and by revelation. When a constructive proposal is made in the last chapter, the key terms used are not drawn from revelation, or even theological literature. This is done out of the conviction that any significance of the work of Christ for the moral life takes place through such aspects of selfhood as disposition, intention, and judgment that are common to all men. Thus some of the points used in the critical analysis in the end become normative in my attempts to make constructive Christian ethical proposals.[7]

I have not, in this book, developed systematically all the aspects of my understanding of man as moral actor, as responder and initiator in a social-historical process. This task would have expanded the last chapter to book length in its own right. In that chapter, however, I have cited some of the principal materials that inform my efforts in this regard. As what is used in this book is subject to the charge of methodological error for normative theological ethics from Barth's position, so an even more elaborate statement would be also. If it is not to claim excessive dignity for what I have done here, I might well construe this book in terms of the subtitle of H. Richard Niebuhr's *The Responsible Self*,[8] a study in "Christian Moral Philosophy." Indeed, what I have proposed, in indicating how the critical analytical method and task become a basis for the normative task, would make it necessary to say that no sharp line can be drawn between Christian theological ethics and Christian moral philosophy. The movement of the book is from a study of the claims for the significance of Christ for moral life that theologians make or apparently assume to a brief statement of the claims I believe can be made, and how I would propose to make them.

---

[7] An earlier draft of this chapter consisted primarily of a defense of this procedure against theological objections that can be raised against it. I am now convinced that such an elaborate defense is not so important, for the polemical lines of ethics and theology have rapidly shifted. A theological defense of the right to work in the way this book does could be made, but to make it would in its own way surrender a point; namely, the independence of the language and questions of ethics. Even if it were made, I am sure it would make no actual difference to the way in which specific analyses of this book are developed.

[8] H. Richard Niebuhr, *The Responsible Self, an Essay in Christian Moral Philosophy* (New York, 1963).

II 〉 JESUS CHRIST,

The Lord Who Is Creator and Redeemer

He is the image of the invisible God, the first-born of all creation; for in him all things were created, in heaven and on earth; visible and invisible, whether thrones or dominions or principalities or authorities—all things were created through him and for him.

COLOSSIANS 1:15–17

. . . and he has put all things under his feet and has made him head over all things for the church. . . .

EPHESIANS 1:22

Therefore, if any one is in Christ, he is a new creature; the old has passed away, behold, the new has come.

II CORINTHIANS 5:17

He was in the beginning with God; all things were made through him, and without him was not anything made that was made. In him was life, and the life was the light of men.

JOHN 1:2–4

What ought we to do? . . . In Him the realization of the good corresponding to divine election has already taken place—and so completely that we, for our part, have actually nothing to add, but only to endorse this event by our action.

KARL BARTH, *Church Dogmatics*, II/2, p. 540

11

I may bid him [each peasant and beggar in the land] rejoice, and give thanks, and sing merry songs to God who made him, because there is nothing created which his Lord and Master has not redeemed, of which He is not the King. . . .

F. D. MAURICE, *Theological Essays* (1957 ed.), p. 123

The point of departure for Christian ethics is not the reality of one's own self, or the reality of the world; nor is it the reality of standards and values. It is the reality of God as He reveals Himself in Jesus Christ.

The problem of Christian ethics is the realization among God's creatures of the revelational reality of God in Christ. . . .

DIETRICH BONHOEFFER, *Ethics* (1955 ed.), pp. 56–57

AN ANSWER TO MAN'S MORAL QUESTION

The morally serious Christian asks in the midst of his concrete responsibilities and opportunities, "What ought I to do?" One answer he hears from theology is, "That is the wrong question. You cannot know what you ought to do, or can do, until you acknowledge what has been done for you and for the world. You must turn to Him who is the source, power, and goal of personal life and history. Jesus Christ is the starting point; Jesus Christ the Incarnation of God, Jesus Christ the judgment of God, Jesus Christ the elect of God, Jesus Christ the victor over sin and death. Jesus Christ is the reality of moral life. He objectively rules, he is the King and Head of every man. He reveals God; in Jesus Christ we know the nature of creation (for all things are created in and through him); we know the nature of redemption (for he has brought all things under his feet—principalities, powers, death, and sin); and we know the fact of our new creation. What you ought to do is bear witness in your action to what has been done. Walk in the light. What you can do is express in your moral life the power of Christ who reigns within and without. Actually, really, everything has been done. Evil, sin, death, have been, indeed *are* vanquished. Now you still have some moral conflicts, but finally they are more apparent than real. There is evil in the world, and we must not forget that, but really it has been overcome and is no ultimate threat. You still do what you ought not to do, and do not do what you ought to do. But even though you are not sinless, you are free from the power of sin: you are a new creature, really, even if you seem to be still the old one. Christ is Lord. In Christ all is created, in him all is redeemed. This is so; this is *Reality*. Live this reality. (We cannot tell you, live *as if* this is so; this suggests that it is hypothetical, indeed a useful fiction.) Actualize, realize this reality!

"What should you do? No one can tell you precisely, but in general—be affirmative, be open to life, be joyous. Surely you will worry about what is required of you; you will see conflicts in your responsibilities and opportunities. But do not let these overcome you. God has said 'Yes' to man, to creation. Live in the sense of God's 'Yes.' Christ is King over all. Indeed, Kant once said the right words, though he based them on the wrong principles. He said 'Trust your own understanding.' He had the Enlightenment view of man in mind. As a Christian, you can say, 'Trust in God, and act in the light of your knowledge of him as you meet each new day.' There is still God's commandment and law to be obeyed. But what used to be a stark and fearful command is now a free permission. What you once did in fear you now do in joyous love."[1]

This way of answering the moral question of the personal "ought" proceeds by claiming that the right question is, in a sense, the question of the "good," and that the answer to that question can be found in Christ. The characteristics and implications of this answer need extensive exposition. Its relation to other affirmations about the moral life of man qualifies its simplicity when taken in isolation. The unity one can create in this thematic answer becomes diversity, first through analysis of its theological foundations, and then through its ethical implications.

SOME THEOLOGICAL IMPLICATIONS

CHRIST IS THE REALITY

For those who answer the moral question in this way, *the Reality* of the Christian life, indeed of life, is Jesus Christ. He rules; he has overcome sin and death. Such a statement requires a reversal of the

[1] The reader must remember that this is a composite answer, drawing from several sources as they touch on this point. We are taking one theme to see its significance; this theme is never the exclusive one, even in the writings that make it central. Authors who agree on the importance of the main point sometimes arrive at it by different paths and disagree about its implications.

direction in which ethical reflection generally goes, and particularly that of American Christian ethics. It requires a transposition of man's viewpoint on the questions of the ethics. The morally serious man usually senses first of all the immediacy of obligation and possibility. He assesses the concrete situation: the threats to human welfare, his self and its power and limits, the facts and figures, the persons and the powers, and the definitions of possible right and good. He is concerned to define the temporal good. Primary attention to Christ, the Creator and Redeemer, reverses this normal order. The concrete reality is Christ. Christ is no abstraction, no contentless form or idea, no object of historical curiosity. His power is more real than the power of the state, of economic resources, of personal influence. His being is as real as, or more real than, the being of institutions, of persons, of my good will, and of the experiences of the senses. The goodness of his love is more real than the love of children for grandparents, husbands for wives. His judgment is as real as that of one's own conscience or a court of law. We are new creatures in him; we are members of his body; his spirit dwells within us. These are statements of fact, not poetic metaphors or the archaic language of a prescientific age. Jesus Christ is the key fact, the central fact, the controlling fact of our lives and of events in the world. Matters of moral action find their proper perspective only when grounded in Jesus Christ. The objective reality of the Christian moral life is Jesus Christ, Lord of Creation, King and Head of every man.

Theologians who affirm this centrality of Christ for ethics often arrive at this position in different ways, and mean by it different things. For Karl Barth, it might be more accurate to say that God is the center and determinant of moral life. But God is no vague or general power; he is a person. He has elected Jesus Christ, Jesus Christ stands between God and man, "Himself God and Himself man, and so mediating between the two."[2] Jesus Christ is both the electing God and the elected man. He is both the Reconciler and the reconciliation. Our knowledge of God rests exclusively in him; "the Father is the Father of Jesus Christ and the Holy Spirit is the Spirit of the Father and the Spirit of Jesus Christ."[3] God has said his "Yes" to man in Jesus Christ; he has chosen to be for man in him. Our

---

[2] Karl Barth, *Church Dogmatics*, II/2 (Edinburgh, 1957), p. 94.
[3] *Ibid.*, p. 115.

knowledge of this divine yes-saying, this divine choice, is in Christ. Barth affirms this on the ground of faith, the authority of Scripture, and of his interpretation of it.

If our knowledge of God through Jesus Christ is determined by him, so also is our conduct. Right conduct for man "is determined absolutely in the right conduct of God. It is determined in Jesus Christ,"[4] for Christ is the electing God and the elected man in One, he is the sanctifying God and sanctified man in One. All men are elect in Jesus Christ. "There is no humanity outside the humanity of Jesus Christ. . . . There is no realization of the good which is not identical with the grace of Jesus Christ and its voluntary or involuntary confirmation. For there is no good which is not obedience to God's command."[5] What we are to do has already been done, in Jesus Christ. When we obey, we obey one who has already fulfilled the obligation, who has been obedient for us. Jesus Christ is both our commander and our enabler; he requires what is to be done and he empowers us to do what he requires.

In Bonhoeffer's case, as in Barth's, an extended interpretation of his ethics would require a careful delineation of the nature of God's action in Christ. Both are theocentric in their ethics, but God reveals himself exclusively in Jesus Christ and thus, for both, the theocentric interpretation of the moral life becomes Christocentric. Bonhoeffer suggests that Christian ethics "speaks of the reality of the world as it is, which possesses reality solely through the reality of God." The reality of God has manifested itself in the world. The answer to the question concerning the nature of God and the world, however, is "designated solely and alone by the name Jesus Christ. God and the world are comprised in this name."[6] Bonhoeffer cites Col. 1:17 for biblical evidence. Ethics, then, is an inquiry directed "towards the way in which the reality in Christ, which for a long time already has comprised us and our world within itself, is taking effect as something now present, and towards the way in which life may be conducted in this reality."[7] The ethical life is conformity to reality; that is, conformity to Christ in whom both the reality of God and the reality of the world are known. The moral life of man has its center in Jesus

4 *Ibid.*, p. 538.
5 *Ibid.*, p. 541.
6 Dietrich Bonhoeffer, *Ethics* (London, 1955), p. 61.
7 *Ibid.*, p. 62.

Christ. "One thing is needful: not to hear or to do, but to do both in one, in other words to be and to continue in unity with Jesus Christ to be directed towards Him, to receive word and deed from Him."[8] Christ is the goal and source of the Christian life.[9]

F. D. Maurice expresses a different temper in his Christocentricity. He was driven to it in part in reaction against an "evangelical theology" which seemed to him to make sin the primary point in interpretation. He was moved by a German review of his *Kingdom of Christ* to write. "I cannot believe the devil is in any sense king of this universe. I believe Christ is its king in all senses, and that the devil is tempting us every day and hour to deny Him."[10] In *The Kingdom of Christ* he wrote, "we look upon the Incarnation, the Resurrection, and the Ascension of our Lord, as declaring him to be really and actually, not nominally or fantastically, head of the universal kingdom. . . ."[11] Christ has established a universal kingdom. The Bible convinced Maurice of this, but the Bible was not the sole source of sustaining authority. Reflection on the nature of the family, the nation, and the universal humanity leads to a confirmation of Christ's Kingship. From the point of view of the knowledge of Christ's Kingdom, in turn, each of these levels of human community can be rightly valued.[12] Thus the moral life is a witness to Christ, in the life of the world. It is the actualization in history, society, and personal existence of the divine constitution of life, known in and through the victory of Jesus Christ.

The reality of Jesus Christ has widespread implications for these authors, several of which bear elaboration. It means that nothing in

---

[8] *Ibid.*, p. 170.

[9] This Christocentric theme is widespread in contemporary European Protestant ethics. See Alfred de Quervain, *Ethik*, Part I, *Die Heiligung* (Zollikon-Zurich, 1946), p. 34, where he states that preaching, action, and admonition all are grounded in Jesus Christ. "He stands in the center of theological ethics, that is, the doctrine of sanctification. We go out from him, and we return to him." See Jacques Ellul, *The Presence of the Kingdom* (Philadelphia, 1951), and *The Theological Foundation of Law* (New York, 1960), in which he develops a theory of law from Christocentric premises. Two works that draw heavily from the Christocentric premise, but work out the ethics more through the doctrine of the Holy Spirit are N. H. Søe, *Kristelig Etik* (5th ed.; Copenhagen, 1962), and Henrik van Oyen, *Evangelische Ethik*, I (Basel, 1952).

[10] Frederick Maurice, ed., *Life of F. D. Maurice*, Vol. I (London, 1884), p. 450.

[11] F. D. Maurice, *The Kingdom of Christ*, Vol. II (London, 1958), p. 150.

[12] *Ibid.*, Vol. I, pp. 227–57, and *Social Morality* (London, 1893), *passim*.

heaven and on earth is exempt from his Lordship. Christ's victory means that grace is more real than sin. Christ's objectivity and power mean that it is he who acts, and not we ourselves.

Christ Is Lord of All

Nothing is exempt from the Lordship of Christ. In contrast to the interpretation found in Lutheran theology, here his work as the Redeemer is not sharply distinguished from the work of God the Father as Creator. Creation and redemption of *all things* are through the *one* person, Jesus Christ. Nor is the sphere of his Lordship confined to the Church as the people of God. It is not confined to the personal life of piety, and to faith in contrast to the life in the sphere of vocation, or institutions. He is Lord of the state and the economy, the family and personal life. His Kingdom is the true constitution of all of life. The action of man is to witness in the world to the universal Lordship of Christ.[13] Christ is Lord of the community that acknowledges his Lordship, the Church, and he is also Lord of the community that denies his Lordship, the world. There is no left and right hand of God, that is, God working his strange works of love through his law in creation (i.e., in the state, economy, etc.) and his proper works of love through the gospel of Christ in the Church. Rather, the law by which institutions in the world are ruled is the form of Christ's work. All of life is under Christ's rule, not partly under the devil or partly under the law of God (in contrast to the gospel). This is true even if it has not been fully actualized in history and personal life. Christ is Lord of all, though different institutions have different functions in him.

The striking character of this point of view can be seen when one observes particular patterns of human life. Government, for example, has been legitimated from various assumptions. For some thinkers it is based in the social and political nature of man, and reflects the law of nature. For some, it is based upon man's inability to keep order voluntarily and reflects a need arising out of man's sin, or man's "brutish" nature. For some, government is the work of God's ordering action, the historical and social mask of God's law. For con-

[13] Since the various meanings of Christ for the moral life of a person are elaborated in a later section of this and subsequent chapters, at this point we confine the discussion of Lordship over *all* to those areas often considered to be "secular," e.g., nation and state, economy, and other institutions.

temporary Christocentric ethics, however, the true basis of government is Jesus Christ.[14]

The basis for this assertion lies in the favorite Christological texts of men who stress this point of view, e.g., John 1:3, I Cor. 8:6, Heb. 1:7, and Col. 1:16–17. Bonhoeffer develops the relation of Christ to government around these and similar passages. Government, as part of "all things," is created *through* Christ, the mediator of creation; he is the mediator between earthly power and God. Only in Jesus Christ does it have its essence and being, for all created things consist only in him. The goal of government, like all things, is directed toward Jesus Christ; its purpose is to serve him. As the possessor of all power in heaven and on earth, he is the Lord of government. Through the atonement Christ has restored the relation between earthly power and Christ.[15] "Government is deputyship for God on earth. It can be understood only from above."[16] Moral common sense asks, "What does this mean for the order of my government?" Bonhoeffer draws only very general inferences: "That form of the state will be relatively the best in which it becomes most evident that government is from above, from God, and in which the divine origin of government is most clearly apparent." This tells us little as yet about what form accomplishes this purpose. That state will be relatively the best in which "its power is not endangered but is sustained and secured (*a*) by strict maintenance of an outward justice, (*b*) the right of the family and of labor, a right which has its foundation in God, and (*c*) by the proclamation of the gospel of Jesus Christ." Finally, that state will be relatively the best "which does not express its attachment to its subjects by restricting the divine authority which has been conferred upon it, but which attaches itself to its subjects in mutual confidence by just action and truthful speech."[17]

In the collection of Barth's writings published as *Against the Stream*, and other of his pastoral moral tracts, one finds this Lordship

---

[14] A very good discussion of the theological ground of the state is that of Gunnar Hillerdal, *Gehorsam gegen Gott und Menschen* (Göttingen, 1955). Chapter V is an exposition of the Christological theories of the state in Barth, Ellul, and de Quervain. Hillerdal defends the Lutheran order of law and gospel as the principle for understanding the state. His argument with the Barthians and others is finally on the grounds of exegesis of the New Testament.

[15] Bonhoeffer, *Ethics* (1955 ed.), pp. 300–3.

[16] *Ibid.*, p. 297.

[17] *Ibid.*, pp. 316–17.

of Christ over state, economy, foreign policy, etc., expressed in relation to concrete events. He rejects the idea that the state is a product
of sin, and instead claims for it, as for the Church, the function of an
order of redemption. This is not to say that the state is free from the
possibility of becoming demonic; Barth's participation in the German
Church struggle of the 1930's is enough in itself to free him from
such illusion. But even in claiming too much for itself it cannot
escape being in Christ's service.[18] In the famous essay "The Christian Community and the Civil Community," a more inclusive sphere
of reality than the "state" is included, i.e., the whole of civic life.
Here government, like other aspects of life, is seen to be a sign of the
Kingdom which is the hope of man in the redemptive work of God.
The civil community has the same center as the Church, i.e., Christ,
or existence within the gracious election of God in creation and
redemption. Thus it can reflect "indirectly the truth and reality
which constitute the Christian community."[19] The state is not
"redeemed," but it serves the God of grace, the God who is for man.
The Church ought to pray for the state, and to keep it ever mindful
of its purpose under God, whose gracious work in Christ establishes
the nature of justice. And what ought Christians to do? They ought
to seek in all the natural problems of life those ways which make it
possible for "the active grace of God, as revealed from heaven, [to
be] reflected in the earthly material of the external, relative and
provisional actions and modes of action of the political community."[20] For Barth this required one response against the Nazis and
another against the Communist domination of Hungary, East Germany, Czechoslovakia.[21]

[18] See "Church and State," in Karl Barth, *Community, State, and Church*, ed.
W. Herberg (New York, 1960), p. 111.
[19] Karl Barth, *Against the Stream* (London, 1954), p. 33.
[20] *Ibid.*, p. 34. The image of concentric circles with Christ as the center, and
the Church and the civil community around him merits more extensive comparison with F. D. Maurice than can be given here. Cf. Maurice, *Theological Essays*
(London, 1957), pp. 276–77, "The world contains the elements of which the
Church is composed. In the Church, these elements are penetrated by a uniting,
reconciling power. The Church is, therefore, human society in its normal state;
the World, that same society irregular and abnormal. The world is the Church
without God; the Church is the world restored to its relation with God, taken
back by Him into the state for which He created it."
[21] See, for example, "Letter to a Pastor in the German Democratic Republic,"
in Barth and Hamel, *How to Serve God in a Marxist Land* (New York, 1959).

The family, like the state, serves the Lord who is Creator and Redeemer. For Maurice, the human relationships in family can be a means by which Christ's love is made known to man. We are born into social relationships which reveal to us the ultimate relationships in the spiritual constitution of the world in which Christ is Lord. Our sonship with parents discloses to us that "There is a root below me. There is an Author of my existence."[22] It teaches us the nature of authority. Marriage testifies to an existing relationship into which a couple enters; it shows us our incompleteness without the other and our dependence on each other. It engenders trust, which is as essential to the order of life as is authority and obedience.[23] The reality of our experience testifies to the reality of God's relationship to us, as the Bible makes clear to Maurice. Abraham, for example, interpreted the fact of his relation to God through the feeling of his human relation; in turn he could fulfill his familial relations by his acknowledgment of the higher relation. "That there is a God related to men and made known to men through their human relations, this was the faith of Abraham."[24] Maurice's conviction of the possibility of movement back and forth from knowledge of life in the family to knowledge of life in the family of God was personal, and not merely speculative. In a letter to his mother, for example, he wrote his thoughts about the love of his family for him. He had worried about returning their love, and thus could not acquiesce in it. "We must learn to dwell and delight in the thought that others are infinitely better and kinder than we are, and then this delightful feeling of affection comes and breeds in the heart. Does this not apply, too, my dearest mother, to our heavenly relation?"[25] Yes, because all things are summed up in Christ, "all relations acquire significance and become felt as actually living and real when contemplated in Him."[26] Indeed all things are in Christ; when we acknowledge this we feel his power in our relations in the family. Christ is the center, the Lord of the family. When we deny this the true order of family life is disrupted; love is replaced by antagonism. We are to live in the light of

[22] F. D. Maurice, *Social Morality*, p. 22. Differences between Barth and Maurice are discussed below.
[23] *Ibid.*, p. 44.
[24] *The Kingdom of Christ* (1958 ed.), Vol. I, p. 238, see also pp. 242–43.
[25] *Life of F. D. Maurice*, Vol. I, p. 130.
[26] *Ibid.*, p. 131.

the reality of the divine order of life, summed up in Christ and his reign, in family as well as in nation.

The reign of Christ is not actual in every detail and circumstance of life. We do not live in the Kingdom of God. His reign over all things is not a *state* of life. Rather, while he is King of all, and while all things serve him, the confrontation with sin and evil continues. But there is a sure foundation in the struggle. The imagery of the decisive battle of a war having been won has been used to describe the situation. Ultimate victory is no longer in doubt, but the "mopping up" operations must continue until the end. Christ has won the decisive battle.

CHRIST IS THE VICTOR OVER SIN

To affirm the victory over sin and evil, and yet to retain a moral seriousness about the dilemmas of moral life is not as great a problem as some critics of this point of view sometimes think it is; its resolution may be in more personal terms than logical ones. Perhaps, however, the critics are correct: it may finally relegate sin to a shadow status, and underestimate the objective reign and power of evil. But against the critics can be quoted a number of hard biblical texts, which make cosmic claims for Christ, and which cast the moral life into an affirmative confidence about the long range and consequently the immediate course of events. Have we not died with Christ, and are we not alive to God in him, and thus free from sin? "For sin will have no dominion over you, since you are not under law but under grace" (Rom. 6:14). Christ sits at the right hand of God "with angels, authorities, and powers subject to him" (I Pet. 3:22).[27]

"What ought we to do?" we ask again. Maurice seems to answer, "Live in the assurance that 'an abyss of love . . . is deeper than the abyss of death,'[28] 'that there is a depth in His love below all other depths, a bottomless pit of charity deeper than the bottomless pit of evil.'[29] 'You have such a righteousness. It is deeper than all the iniquity which is in you. It lies at the very ground of your existence.

[27] Cf. Amos Wilder's discussion of the validity of interpreting principalities and powers in terms of an ethical character in "Kerygma, Eschatology and Social Ethics," W. D. Davies and D. Daube, eds., *The Background of the New Testament and Its Eschatology* (Cambridge, Eng., 1956), especially pp. 527 ff.
[28] Maurice, *Theological Essays* (1957 ed.), p. 323.
[29] *Life of F. D. Maurice*, Vol. I, p. 529.

And this righteousness dwells not merely in a law which is condemning you, it dwells in a Person in whom you may trust.' "[30] Man ought not to regard himself primarily as a sinner; the prior fact in reality is the forgiveness of sin. Maurice writes in his book on the Johannine Epistles, which has the subtitle "A Series of Lectures on Christian Ethics": "There is selfishness, there is separation from *thy* brother, there is the very essence of sin in that thought. St. John strikes at the root of it when he says, '*Your sins are forgiven for His Name's sake.*' You are not looked upon as a sinful race, you are looked upon as a race of which Christ the Son of God is the head. . . . We have no right to count ourselves sinners, seeing we are united in Him. We become sinners when we separate from Him. . . ."[31] We ought to be and do what we really are; we ought to walk in the Light, witness to the reality of the gracious forgiveness of sins.

"That man is against God is important and must be taken seriously," writes Barth. "But what is far more important and must be taken far more seriously is that in Jesus Christ God is for man."[32] Sin, death, the devil, and hell are "works of God's permissive will which are negative in their effects." "Even in these God's knowing and willing are gracious. . . . Even the enemies of God are the servants of God and the servants of His grace." Indeed the enemies of God cannot be known unless they are known "in the service which they render as instruments of the eternal, free and immutable grace of God." God is gracious and not ungracious "even in His permitting of sin and the devil, even in the terrors of death and hell. . . ."[33] The world of Satan is a shadow-world. God has elected man in Christ; Christ who is the Judge takes the place of the judged, and man is fully acquitted of sin and its guilt and penalty. "Thus the wrath of God and the rejection of Satan and his Kingdom no longer have any relevance for [him]."[34]

[30] *Theological Essays*, p. 62.

[31] F. D. Maurice, *Epistles of St. John* (London, 1893), p. 110.

[32] *Church Dogmatics*, II/2, p. 154. Professor Gustaf Wingren from a strong Lutheran orientation has directed a significant part of his critique of Barth at this "shadow" character of sin and evil. See *Theology in Conflict* (Philadelphia, 1958), pp. 117 ff.

[33] *Church Dogmatics*, II/2, p. 92.

[34] *Ibid.*, p. 125. See also pp. 170–71. "The possibility of existence which evil can have is only that of the impossible." But it must have that status, for the

What God has done for man, then, is to bring him into a new freedom. It is a freedom that exists because God has chosen man. It is freedom from the dominion of sin and evil, and thus freedom to be obedient only to the will of the gracious God, freedom to obey Christ. Since we still live in history, we still confront in ourselves and in the world that which appears to be an autonomously working destructive power. But its reality is the reality of a shadow, the reality of a nonbeing whose only reality is based in its function to oppose being in creation. But evil and sin no longer paralyze us; they do not evoke fear or anxiety, they do not create moral hesitation and indecisiveness, for more real is the victory over sin and death and Satan. *The* reality is God-for-man in Christ. "Therefore 'to become obedient,' 'to act rightly,' 'to realize the good,' never means anything other than to become obedient to the revelation of the grace of God; to live as a man to whom grace has come in Jesus Christ."[35] We are to walk in the light "which lighteth every man." Christ is Lord of Church and cosmos. This is the primary datum of ethics—not the reality of sin, hell, death, and the devil.

The fact that we remain sinners, and evil is real in the world, keeps us from claiming anything for ourselves, from depending on our own merits. Indeed, we are not the ones who act; we are the means through which the objective power and goodness of God acts. This is another inference drawn from the theme of the Lordship of Christ.

GOD, NOT MAN, IS THE SOURCE OF MORAL ACTION

Man's moral question is answered by first looking to the Divine Person at the source of his creation and redemption. This does not answer all questions, but by relating ourselves to Christ we are in the right Light, in the proper perspective for viewing ourselves and for viewing the world of moral claims and possibilities. We see institutions as grounded in Christ's election, or in his Lordship; we see

---

glory of God would not shine without a shadow. "The only autonomy and status that evil can have is that of a being and essence excluded from the divine economy and rejected by it—the autonomy and status of the non-being which necessarily confronts and opposes being in the realm of creation, but which has its basis and meaning only in this confrontation and opposition, only as the spirit of constant negation."

[35] *Ibid.*, p. 539.

ourselves as forgiven by the Redeemer of the world who has con-
quered sin, death, and evil. This does not tell us precisely what to do,
nor does it assure us that any worldly measurement of good will judge
us righteous. We are, nevertheless, to act in obedience to Christ, and
in conformity to his established Kingdom.

But, in this perspective, care must be taken against claiming for
ourselves any moral worth, insight, or goodness. The words of St.
Paul command attention, for they are painfully clear, "I have been
crucified with Christ, it is no longer I who live, but Christ who lives
in me" (Gal. 2:20). To be sure, an eschatological sophistication must
be used in interpreting such a text, for St. Paul sets life within the
two aeons,[36] the age of this world, and the eternity which exists and
in which this world will be fulfilled. And such a text must be set in
the context of the whole of Paul's theology, for he, like most Christians, including Barth and Maurice, does not lose sight of man's sin
and rebelliousness, his pride and "sloth" and "misery" (Barth) even
in the life of faith. With these and other qualifications, however, the
text still points to our being the instruments of a person who is
objective to us. The good is objective to us.[37]

"No one is good but God alone," said Jesus. Barth reminds us of
this in the course of defining a good action. "Man's action is good in
so far as it is sanctified (*geheiligt*) by the Word of God, which as
such is also the command of God." "Man's action is good insofar as

[36] See Anders Nygren's *Commentary on Romans* (Philadelphia, 1949), in
which this is a keynote. See also Reinhold Niebuhr's exegesis of Gal. 2:20 in *The
Nature and Destiny of Man*, Vol. II (New York, 1943), pp. 107 ff.

[37] On this point there is wide agreement between theologians who center their
view of man in Christ, the Creator and Redeemer, and those who make a
distinction between the creative and governing work of God, on the one hand,
and the redemptive work, on the other. E.g., Luther's conception of man in his
vocation as being a mask of God makes God's law the real power and director of
human activity. The suggestive imagery of the mask leaves many questions
unanswered. See G. Wingren's theology for contemporary use of this notion:
Luther on Vocation (Philadelphia, 1957), and *Creation and Law* (Philadelphia,
1961). Niels Søe echoes Barth to some extent in his insistence that a work is
good not because of either our motive or its consequences, but because it is God
who works it through Christ and particularly through the Holy Spirit, *Kristelig
Etik* (5th ed.), pp. 128–37. Nygren's conception of *agape* has the same objectivity. The issues for ethics involved in this exclusive objectivism of the good are
discussed further in various sections of this text. Contemporary theologians take
refuge in it in order to avoid the pitfalls of pietism and of liberal Christianity's
assumptions about experience.

he is the obedient hearer of the Word and command of God."[38]
Theological ethics "will regard the revelation of the grace of God as
so true—so very much the revelation of the actual involvement of
man—and the work of grace as *so powerful*—so very much the
decision which God has already made about man—that, whatever
attitude man may take up or however he may act in relation to God's
command, it necessarily understands him as *actually determined* by
God's command, as altogether oriented by it objectively."[39] Command is not meant to imply only an objective requirement on the
part of another. The commander is the Creator and Redeemer; he is
the same one who permits us to obey, who brings us to the freedom
in which we freely execute by his grace that which he requires of us.
Our action is a part of a wider field of action, God's action in electing
us, in commanding us, in redeeming us. Our action thus is by no
means the center of the field. We respond in faith and obedience to
God in Jesus Christ.

An important avenue into the objectivity of our new creation with
its implications for the Christian life is through the doctrine of
Christian baptism. The Pauline literature makes important claims for
what occurs through baptism; we die and rise with Christ, we are
engrafted into his body. The fact that the early church was perplexed
by postbaptismal sin is a witness to the seriousness with which they
took the sacrament. For F. D. Maurice, the objectivity of righteousness, its independence from our own merit and worthiness, is
grounded in our baptism. Righteousness is not our own property and
can never become such. Baptism proclaims this. We partake in
Christ's righteousness. In principle, then, any notion of self-righteousness or of claim to righteousness is false. Rather, it is man's right
and duty "at all times to turn to Him in whom they are created,
redeemed, justified." Only in this trust do we "rise above our
enemies."[40] We are to "exhibit the fruits" of a righteousness which

---

[38] *Church Dogmatics*, III/4 (Edinburgh, 1961), p. 4. Cf. a summary statement in de Quervain, *Die Heiligung*, p. 25. "When we speak of the action of the
Christian, it is not an action which glorifies man, nor the Christian, but Christ
and his work. Christ, according to Scripture, is our righteousness and sanctification." "Faith is . . . obedience to what God has done for us."
[39] *Church Dogmatics*, II/2, p. 523. Italics added.
[40] Maurice, *Theological Essays* (1957 ed.), pp. 149–50. See also *The Kingdom
of Christ*, Vol. I, pp. 283–84, and *Life*, Vol. II, p. 152.

can never belong to any man in himself but, rather, is possible because "our Lord came among men that he might bring them into a kingdom of righteousness, peace, and joy," "a kingdom grounded upon fellowship with a righteous and perfect Being."[41]

Certain implications for the moral life from this theological transposition of the moral question have been briefly suggested. The conviction that the first question is not "What ought I to do?" but "What has been done for the world and for me?" must find its way back to man again.[42] The moral question remains for the Christian. "All right, I believe in what has been done for me in Jesus Christ. I believe he is Reality, the Lord of all things, the resurrected victor over sin and death, the source of all action. In the light of this what ought I to do? Many claims are made upon me; many possibilities exist; I feel responsible for the sphere of life, great and small, in which I am involved as a parent, a citizen, a worker. What ought I to do?" What have these theologians to say?

SOME ETHICAL INFERENCES

A Critique of Ethics

One inference that has been drawn from the central conviction of Christ's Lordship in creation and redemption is that a critique of ethics itself, or at least of certain kinds of ethics, is necessary. Ethics as written and practiced in culture and the Church makes many false turns; different types of ethics make different mistakes. Ethics normally is concerned with the temporal good, and therefore makes judgments about the moral value of the immediate consequences of action. Christians know that the temporal good is not the sole locus of the good. God is the determiner of the good; God in whom the past with all its historical injustice and suffering is governed and redeemed, in whom the present with its uncertainties about the future and its bondage to the past is made free, in whom the open future is governed and ordered. Christ frees us from preoccupation

---

41 Maurice, *The Kingdom of Christ*, Vol. I, p. 256.
42 For an American affirmation of this point, see Paul Lehmann, "The Foundation and Pattern of Christian Behavior," in John Hutchison, ed., *Christian Faith and Social Action* (New York, 1953), pp. 97 ff., also *Ethics in a Christian Context* (New York, 1963), pp. 74 ff.

solely with the temporal good. The claim is made that he frees us from "ethics."

Ethics is often concerned with the proper formulation of the moral law and its appropriate application to particular instances. Christians know that Christ has redeemed men from bondage to the law. It is charged that concern for moral law and its use tends to make man into God; man becomes the manipulator, the one who orders life. Attention to Christ, the Reality, convinces us of the living, dynamic character of *his* presence, of a Lord who is ruling in every moment and event. Man does not direct the course of events in complete autonomy by his definitions of what really is, or what ought to be. The living, ruling King, Christ, is the Lord of events. We are obedient to a Person, and not to a code or an ethical principle. Thus Christ frees us from legalism, from false assumptions about the ultimate nature of morality, from casuistry, from "ethics."

Ethics sometimes looks first at the goodness of the moral man, and assumes that the moral order of life will bear the good fruit of his actions. It is concerned with the cultivation of the cardinal virtues— justice, temperance, wisdom, and courage. It is concerned to establish a harmonious and therefore right relation between appetite, intellect, and will. Or ethics defines goodness in terms of the good will. Christians have added faith, hope, and love to the virtues. Pietists have sought to ferret out evil desire through introspective self-examination and the converting power of grace. Or modern men have tried to free man from the guilt that has arisen in his relations to others so that he may be the superabundant personality, creating and evoking the good. Others have tried to educate men out of false values and desires into true ones. It is claimed that faith in Christ, the Creator and Redeemer, eradicates the primary presupposition of all these expressions of self-centered ethics, namely, that goodness, or moral value, or rightness has its source in the character of man. Preoccupation with man cannot avoid the grossest form of sin, i.e., trusting in oneself or in man for the order and improvement of life. Its assumptions are not verified in human experience and, worse, are contradictory to the message of the Bible. It is God who acts in the course of events; it is God who is revealed as the Creator, Redeemer, and Governor of life. The focus of attention on the object of faith (and faith includes knowledge) inverts ethics. It abolishes the

absorption of man in himself as the source of good. Christ frees us
from "ethics."

The critique of ethics is never as drastic as the language in which it
is made would sometimes lead one to think. Some theologians are
adept at making a new broom sweep so clean that they must extract
some of the refuse out of the trash can again. A lot of "ethics" that
is criticized is brought back in again under other auspices, another
name, and from a new point of view. Thus, e.g., biblicistic legalism
and casuistry are abolished in the name of the freedom given in
Christ, and in the name of the immediate concrete character of the
command of God. But in Christ obligation becomes "permission"
and the Bible norms become useful for "practical casuistry." Nonetheless, from the center of attention on Christ, on his reality and
power, ethics and ethicists are chastened; their limits of power,
insight, and faith are exposed.

There is wisdom in Bonhoeffer's limitation of ethics and ethicists.
"An ethic cannot be a book in which there is set out how everything
in the world actually ought to be but unfortunately is not, and an
ethicist cannot be a man who always knows better than others what is
to be done and how it is to be done. An ethic cannot be a work of
reference for moral action which is guaranteed to be unexceptionable,
and the ethicist cannot be the competent critic and judge of every
human activity. An ethic cannot be a retort in which ethical or
Christian human beings are produced, and the ethicist cannot be the
embodiment or ideal type of a life which is, on principle, moral."[43]
Only the haughtiest ethicist will feel condemned by this chaste
statement; most ethicists would hardly claim more for themselves
than can be claimed within its fence.

Far more extreme in his attack is Jacques Ellul, who wishes to set
forth the Christian life as a sign of the new covenant in a revolu-
tionary world in an apocalyptic mood. He accuses, in a rashly inclusive manner, "all Christian ethics or sociologies or politics" of aiming
at a "kind of 'Christian conception' of things: they want to have
'good' institutions, 'good' morals; they want to know what is 'the
good' in every situation." Christian ethics, he says, tries to see to it
that Christian conscience is not too shocked by the condition of the

---

[43] Bonhoeffer, *Ethics*, p. 236. Barth quotes this passage with approval in *Church
Dogmatics*, III/4, p. 10.

world. Ethics becomes the bridge between the world and the Kingdom of God. All this "is in reality the most anti-Christian position
anyone could possibly adopt."[44]

Barth's critique of ethics is far more subtle than Ellul's. Its subtlety
lies in both its comprehensiveness and its careful redefinitions in the
light of his own convictions. If one begins with Barth's answer to the
ethical question, much of traditional ethics is at once superfluous but
useful, unnecessary but convenient. "The grace of God *is* the answer
to the ethical problem." "The man Jesus . . . does not *give* the
answer, but by God's grace He *is* the answer to the ethical question
put by God's grace." Our sanctification, the claim of God upon us,
our "pre-determination" to "self-determination" is that we freely
obey God, God's judgment upon us, and his command in the actual
concrete situation—all these take place in Jesus Christ.[45] This being
the case, what happens to other points of view on the nature of
ethics?

The clearest, most general answer is that ethics is not autonomous,
but is part of the doctrine of God. "We cannot act as if we had to
ask and decide for ourselves what the good is and how we can achieve
it; as if we were free to make this or that answer as the one that
appears to us to be right."[46] In trying to work out an answer for
ourselves we try to escape from God's grace. This makes the usual
conception of ethics coincide with the conception of sin, for sin is
denying God. The questions of the law or good or value, or standards
for judging human action, of the truth and knowledge of the good—
these are no problems in Christian ethics immanent in the doctrine
of Divine Election. The man who "obediently hears the command of
God is not in any position to consider why he must obey it."[47] In
contrast to "apologetico-theological ethics," "theological ethics has to
accept the fact that it must not believe in the possibility and reality
of a general moral enquiry and reply which are originally and

---

[44] Ellul, *The Presence of the Kingdom* (Philadelphia, 1951), pp. 14–15. He
continues his attack on "morality." The object of true ethics is to "manifest the
gift which has been given us" (p. 82). The Bible and Ellul's certainty about
what the actual judgment of the return of Christ means for economies, technics,
etc., become the guidelines for the moral life, however.

[45] *Church Dogmatics*, II/2, pp. 516–17.

[46] *Ibid.*, p. 518.

[47] *Ibid.*, p. 522. The whole discussion is found on pp. 509–42.

ultimately independent of the grace and command of God. . . ."[48]
The important words here are "ultimately independent," for finally
nothing is "ultimately independent," and therefore nothing is finally
excluded. In the beginning and the end, the grace and command of
God are so central and universal that much of the same moral
reckoning characteristic of normal moral inquiry comes back
within theological ethics. As we have seen, there is finally *no* humanity outside Christ's humanity, and *no* realization of the good that
is not identical with the grace of Jesus Christ.[49] Barth's analysis of
"What ought we to do?" within the hearing of the command of God
and within God's gracious election testifies to the inexorable confrontation with moral reflection regardless of the theological framework. The answer does not come, in Christ, as a self-evident moral
intuition, any more than it comes through legalism, a formal conception of the good, the categorical imperative, the conscience, or some
formal conception of the will of God, the Kingdom of God, the
righteousness of God, or the love of God.[50] The requirement of God
is concrete and specific. This, according to Barth, is what "ethics" has
not really understood: the *concreteness* of the commander, the command, the person commanded, and the situation in which the command is given, and above all the fact that all of these are determined
in Christ, though determined so that we freely obey the determination.
Finally, we must trust our own understanding, as he told the
Hungarian youth in 1948.[51] But this does not imply blind reaction to
every immediate event and pressure. Barth, like believers in natural
law, Kantians, pietists or any moral man, labeled or unlabeled, cannot
get away from the problem of moral reckoning in spite of his denial
of an independent validity to ethics.[52]

[48] *Ibid.*
[49] The plain question to be asked from the point of view Barth says we cannot
have (but it seems we do have!) is: What difference to our moral action does his
intellectual reformulation of the problem of ethics make? In effect he does not
allow the questions generally called ethical the right to be independent of grace.
But since nothing is independent of grace we have them back again. See, for
example, his section on "The Sovereignty of the Divine Decision," *ibid.*, pp. 631
ff., esp. 643 ff. We return to this problem below.
[50] See *ibid.*, pp. 664–69 for Barth's critique of formalism in ethics.
[51] *Against the Stream*, p. 60.
[52] Since we have previously discussed F. D. Maurice in this chapter, it is
essential here to indicate why he is excluded from this section. The reason lies in
his quite different attitude to ethics in general. His lifelong battle against closed

Thus the critique of ethics is never as radical or as complete as it at first appears to be. The crucial point on which it turns is important, that is, the preoccupation of usual ethics (even when the language of the Church is used) with moral reality as if nothing of significance had occurred in Jesus Christ. One can state a positive side of this. If one begins and ends with and in the Creator-Redeemer, if he is the reality who commands and makes possible our free obedience at once, and if he is grace manifest in man, then many of the preoccupations of ethics are ruled out or made trivial. In Christ the ground, the criteria, and the power to act are all given really and concretely to the person who is responsible. The critical question comes at this point: How is Christ present? What language is used to elaborate the central affirmation? What language, principles, and ideas does one use to express the reality in terms related to the moral life? How are legalism, intuitionism, formalism, pietism, and natural law avoided? But a further general ethical consequence of the affirmation of the Reality of Christ must be defined before the specific implications for moral action are considered.

AN AFFIRMATION OF THE WORLD

A common reputation of such theologians as Augustine, Calvin, and Barth has been that they are sad men preoccupied morosely with man's sin and evil in the world. And even F. D. Maurice has been associated with a "Moral realism," often called "Christian realism," which enjoins us to be wary at all points against the triumph of evil. But in each of these men of reputed darkness, there is an overwhelming shaft of light, in their sadness a victory of joy. They all share in what Perry Miller has described as a "cosmic optimism" that he found in the Puritans. Words of St. Paul express this affirmation of life and the world—"For all things are yours, whether Paul or

---

systems had as its reverse side his openness to insight from whatever source he met. All error contains some truth. He could be open to ethics because of Christ's Lordship and the universal character of the spiritual constitution. A general English Platonism and an unsophisticated view of the law of nature are closely bound to his view of Christ's Lordship. Here the cleavage between his thought and Barth's assumes the proportions of an abyss. But the abyss is partially closed. Via his route he has an openness to the world that Barth also has via the route of denying the independence claimed for ethics and then finding much of what is denied within Christ's election. For Maurice's absorption of "human morality" see, e.g., *Social Morality*.

Apollos or Cephas or the world or life or death or the present or the future, all are yours; and you are Christ's; and Christ is God's" (I Cor. 3:21–23).

Dietrich Bonhoeffer, in spite of his involvement in the struggle against the power of evil historically manifest in Nazism, could write a text for this assurance: "The reality of God discloses itself only by setting me entirely in the reality of the world; but there I find the reality of the world, already always sustained, accepted, and reconciled in the reality of God."[53] The reality of the world is already and always *sustained, accepted,* and *reconciled* in God. Or F. D. Maurice could say in the context of a discussion of non-Christian religions, "we shall say boldly to all people among whom we go, 'The devil is not your master, he has no right to your worship; the God in whom is light and no darkness at all, has claimed you and the whole creation for His own.' "[54] God in whom there is no darkness has claimed man and the whole creation for his own.

The starting point in God's gracious creation, preservation, acceptance, and reconciliation of all things is not only an idea deduced from textual comparisons in the sacred document. It is an affirmation of faith in its most positive and inclusive terms. This is personal belief and trust; it is knowledge. It is the truth from which one views his anxious and sinful self and the accumulations of sufferings and evil in the world. It is the truth from which one sees his own joy and forgiveness, and those elements of peace and welfare that occur in history. Thus God who has already reconciled the world, and claimed it for his own is the ground on which one firmly stands, from which one sees the world. This can only mean an affirmative, grateful, hopeful response to events of moral significance. It will seek the affirmation of the good above the destruction of evil, and the possibility of reconciliation before the commitment to a deadly struggle. It will provide a sustaining conviction of hope, of ultimate rightness, of the triumph of God, and therefore of righteousness and goodness in even the darkest and most desperate crises of life. An openness to the world and its manifold possibilities of good for man is a consequence of the conviction that "all things are yours, for you are Christ's and

---

[53] *Ethics*, p. 61, but the translation used here is the more forceful one of Charles West, *Communism and the Theologians* (Philadelphia, 1958), p. 344.

[54] *Religions of the World*, pp. 238 ff., quoted by A. R. Vidler, *The Theology of F. D. Maurice* (London, 1948), p. 44.

Christ is God's." Technology, urban life, social mobility, African nationalism, Indian socialism, American social tensions—all things are fraught with potential goodness, for Christ claims all these things. He is their Creator and Redeemer, and men are called to his service.

The openness and affirmative character of the world, when experienced as the reality God has reconciled, can be seen in contrast to a view that is determined more by man's sin. The weight of emphasis is delicate, but important. No sophisticated Christian theologian denies the reality of grace; to do so is to deny the reality of God. Nor do any deny the reality of sin and evil, for to do so is to claim for history that which exists *de jure* and not wholly *de facto*, that which has the reality of promise, and not a promise totally fulfilled in history. But if the delicate weight lies to the side of the reality of sin and evil, the moral life becomes a resistance battle, a defensive action. One never sees a good without stressing that it is a corrupted good; never a historical possibility without noting fully its moral ambiguity and possibility of evil. One never looks to himself without mistrusting his response to God and the world, without confessing his confused motives, his partial knowledge of the moral situation, his biases. Man is justified and sinner, but it is morally wiser to stress the latter against the former. The world is reconciled and yet evil; to trust in reconciliation will lead to illusions about the world and maybe to moral and social catastrophe. It is wiser to be wary of evil.

Both sides become open to the world, but with different relations to it. One accepts it joyfully and with full possibility of its goodness, the other accepts it as a necessity and understands that the children of light must be as wise as the children of darkness to preserve good against evil. The conviction of Christ's power of redemption for men like Barth and Maurice thus leads to a "cosmic optimism," to an openness and hopeful relation to men and the historical situation. Such faith colors moral action throughout, from the center to the edges. The God in whom is light and no darkness at all has claimed us and creation for his own.[55]

[55] Readers will note a caricature of Reinhold Niebuhr's theology in the paragraph of comparison. We return to the questions formed here later. Charles West notes affinities between the implications of Barthian theology and Niebuhr's theology for ethics, and suggests that the latter is really a Barthian, p. 14, *Communism and the Theologians*. I cannot concur in this, for they come to an "empirical ethic" from quite different standpoints, and with quite different interpretations of what they see. The affinities are noteworthy, though, and raise the

"What ought I to do? to be?" Clearly—be what Christ has claimed for you; rest your action on his action. Acknowledge his victory. Be open to the world in hope and joy. Be affirmative. But moral man longs for more precision in his answer. Indicative is prior to imperative, yes. But what are its consequences for the definitions of action?

DIRECTION WITHOUT LEGALISM

A central conviction developed from a study of Barth and others can be stated in this way: Moral life is in response to a Person who has acted and continues to act, to a reality which is personal, and not to the definitions of a person or definitions of what is the ground and the obligation of moral seriousness. Or: A Person enables us, commands us, directs us, chastises us, preserves us, judges us, redeems us, sanctifies us; and the same Person acts and speaks in and through the events in which we participate. Thus the proper analogy to moral life is not to be found in legal ideas, but in personal relations. The Person is not any random charismatic personality, he is Jesus Christ, the Lord of a Universal Kingdom, the Reality in which the reality of the world is established, the Commander, Justifier, and Sanctifier of our lives. Thus the element of definition and precision which is forthcoming for Christian moral life is a specification of the meaning of Jesus Christ, and inferences drawn from man's relation to him. Criteria of moral guidance must be derived from him, or from the implications of his being the center of life, the source of our knowledge of God, and of real man.

From Jesus Christ, however, comes no single specific inference for moral life. The language used to give direction to moral action depends upon what other elements are united with the Lordship of Christ. One stress is on his command and its concreteness. Another is on the "third use of the law," that is, on the prescriptive and instructive use of the Bible for Christian life. Another relies more upon the illuminating power of the Holy Spirit. Or, the call to discipleship is introduced. These various emphases are not mutually exclusive, and more than one can exist in the writings of the same man.

---

interesting question of the extent to which a theological framework for moral action is mere ideology in a Marxist sense, i.e., provides a socially acceptable (in the Church) justification for actions really grounded in other motives.

COMMAND BECOMES PERMISSION

One general inference drawn from fixing Christ's Lordship so centrally in Christian ethics is a qualification of an ethic of obligation to a commandment. Command becomes permission. At least it is qualified by the "permission" character of man's relationship in faith to what God has done for him. We can do, we are permitted to do, we are free to do freely what we must do, what we are commanded to do, what we are required to do. This is a consequence of the precedence of God's indicative over his imperative, of God's gracious action over evil and man's sin, and Christ's victory through resurrection over the power of death. Command does not become permissiveness; it becomes permission. God enables man to do freely and thankfully what He requires him to do. The subtlety of the relation of permission and command is seen in historical and personal terms more easily than in terms of formal logic.

The Old Testament foreshadows the clarity of this double character of Christian morality given in the revelation in Christ. The exodus, the crossing of the Red Sea, is temporally and in other respects prior to Sinai and the giving of the Decalogue to Moses. In both Deuteronomy (5:6) and Exodus (20:2) the first words of God are, "I am the Lord your God, who brought you out of the land of Egypt, out of the house of bondage." Then comes the law. The testimony to God's action in delivering his people out of oppression rings out again and again in the Old Testament. It is because of God's goodness, historically made known in the freeing of the children of Israel, that they ought to, and do, obey his commandment gladly. The memory of that event is as important as the memory of the law itself.

The New Testament is the story of the new covenant, the new act of God for and with man. It reveals the depths of God's love, his "Yes" to man, in Jesus Christ. Moral life is grounded in this Love, in this "Yes." Men are able to do freely and gladly what is required of them because God has freely and gladly given himself to men in Christ. And the history of Christian ethics is marked by various expressions of the relation of permission to commandment. "What is enjoined with threatenings under the law of works, is granted to belief under the law of faith," wrote St. Augustine.[56] Calvin could praise Christian liberty as highly as Luther. Christians "do not observe the law, as being under any legal obligation; but that, being liberated from the yoke of the law, they yield a voluntary obedience to the will of God."[57] This is so because men participate in Christ, the Lord. Luther's theses in his famous essay on the same topic stressed the doubleness of obligation and permission. "A Christian man is a perfectly free lord of all, subject to none. A Christian man is a perfectly dutiful servant of all, subject to all."[58]

This permission to obey can be claimed from theological grounds that are, in precise definition, different from each other.[59] But its wide acclaim testifies to its centrality in Christian belief and action. It is of particular importance within the theme of Christ the Lord who is Redeemer and Creator, for the affirmative, positive character of life in this view is unusually clear.

Bonhoeffer wrote that "the commandment of God is the permission to live as man before God." It is permission; "it differs from all human laws in that it commands freedom." "The impossible becomes possible, and that which lies beyond the range of what can be commanded, liberty, is the true object of this commandment."[60] The consequences of this "permission" character of the commandment are two-fold. First, the permission "is still always *God's* permission." This means that man cannot in his liberty act according to his own choice, free from any external authority of God's commandment, and free from obligation to God. He can now live as man *before* God, that is, he can now live freely in his whole life (not merely his moral life) within the will of God. More specific is the second consequence, namely, that by the permission of God man is made free from the "crossroads" character of life. "He is not everlastingly striving for the right decision. He is not always wearing himself out in a conflict of duties. He is not continually failing and beginning again."

[56] "The Spirit and the Letter," 22, in Augustine, *Later Works*, ed., Burnaby (London, 1955), p. 211.
[57] Calvin, *Institutes*, III, 19, 4, Allen trans. (Philadelphia, n.d), Vol. II, p. 79.
[58] Luther, "A Treatise on Christian Liberty," *Three Treatises* (Philadelphia, 1943), p. 251.
[59] We return to this question under the headings "the Justifier" and "the Sanctifier."
[60] Bonhoeffer, *Ethics*, p. 248.

"It does not make man a critic and judge of himself and of his deed, but it allows him to live and to act with certainty and with confidence in the guidance of the divine commandment." Worry over purity of motives, constant self-questioning, "the glaring and fatiguing light of incessant consciousness"—these have nothing to do with God's commandment. Rather, God permits man to live and to act freely not only in the normal sequence of daily life, but also in the "great, agitated and intensely conscious moments of crisis in life."[61] Man has the right decision behind him; he can live with the liberty of God's permission before him. In Bonhoeffer's ethics, the command which becomes permission frees one to be obedient to God in every circumstance of life. The God who permits also claims obedience in the world of which he is the Redeemer and Creator.

The same double character of the moral life in relation to God is developed extensively by Karl Barth.[62] In his characteristic way of twisting and turning words to extract new meanings and implications from them, he gives us the axis on which his discussion turns. "Obligation—the obligation of the real command—means permission. That was the first point. But the second is that permission—the permission which is the proper inmost form of the divine command —also means obligation."[63] Right obligation is true permission, and right permission is true obligation. Such propositions make no sense when developed from the common usage of the key terms. They only make sense, Barth assures us, when seen in the faith of the Church, "The propositions of Christian ethics are propositions of Christian dogmatics."[64] The key presupposition is a tautology—grace is grace; or to make the first term synthetic, and thereby more meaningful: the sanctifying grace of the command of God is grace. "The fact that God gives us His command, that He puts us under His command, is grace."[65] The immediate result of this statement is the double character of permission and obligation: the obligation of this command is at the bottom permission, and this permission is properly obligation. At this point our interest is in the first part, i.e., the

[61] *Ibid.*, p. 250.
[62] Barth, *Church Dogmatics*, II/2, "The Form of the Divine Claim," pp. 583–630.
[63] *Ibid.*, p. 602.
[64] *Ibid.*, p. 603.
[65] *Ibid.*

consequences for moral life of the "permission" character of the command.

The permission of the obligation is not the permission we assume to be ours out of a natural free will, according to Barth. The assumed natural permission can be seen in the story of the fall. "And the woman saw that the tree was good for food, and that it was pleasant to the eyes, and a tree to be desired" (Gen. 3:6). The final consequences of the chain of events begun by Eve permitting herself to take the fruit is that "man permits himself to renounce the grace of God. He permits himself to be set up as one who knows good and evil and therefore as judge over both."[66] And he thinks he is free and happy.

The real permission, established in the gracious election of man in Jesus Christ, is, rather, the granting of a very definite freedom. It is his gift to man, giving of himself so that we might live with him in peace and joy. We live as those who accept as right what God does for us. We are freed from harassment, self-doubt, and anxiety. Fear and anxiety "are obviously the direct opposite of what the New Testament describes as freedom and of what we have described as the permission given to man by the command of God."[67] Rather than wallowing in concern about appropriateness of our decisions, the definition of the goodness and evil of their consequences, introspection and worry, we are given to see "that in itself and as such the command of God is a festive invitation."[68] Let us remember the epitomy of all apostolic exhortation, "Rejoice in the Lord always; again I will say, Rejoice" (Phil. 4:4). "How can any part of what Paul demands of Christians be rightly done if in the first instance it is not done with joy, as an 'ought' whose seriousness lies at bottom in the fact that it is a 'may,' something permitted?"[69] This is how the command of God speaks. "Do this, because in so doing you may and will again live of and by My grace." "Do this, because in Jesus Christ you have been born anew in the image of God. Do it in the freedom to which you have been chosen and called. . . ."[70] Imperative is the action of indicative; command is permission—the Christian life is

66 *Ibid.*, pp. 593–94.
67 *Ibid.*, p. 598.
68 *Ibid.*, p. 588.
69 *Ibid.*
70 *Ibid.*, p. 587.

rejoicing, freedom, peace. Live out what God has done! In so doing
God is obeyed.

ACTION OF THE CHRISTIAN IS CONCRETE

Christ permits and thus commands specific actions in the immediate situation in which man lives. Jesus Christ, the Redeemer and
Creator, is the living person whom we meet when we turn inward
and when we turn outward. Such is Barth's claim. Our action in
freedom is possible because of what God has done graciously for man
in freedom. As actors, persons, we are solely dependent upon this
source of our action. Looking inwardly through the self, then, we
finally (or perhaps first of all) focus on Jesus Christ. He permits us to
live. Looking outwardly through the world we also finally (or perhaps
first of all) focus on the same Jesus Christ, the same gracious action
of God. It is Christ who rules the external circumstances of life, it is
Christ whom we meet speaking, ordering, redeeming, preserving,
commanding, in every concrete moment and situation of life. There
is no concrete action which is not in relation to what God is doing for
man in his gracious work; and there is no divine grace that does not
impel concrete action.

The comparatively serene and eclectic Maurice, as we have seen,
finds Christ ruling through personal relations, through the nation and
the Church, by ascending and descending the ladder from the human
relationships to the divine. This view would be odious to Barth and
Bonhoeffer, for while it is Christocentric in one sense, it begins with
natural experience rather than with what the Bible says about Christ.
It also avoids the dramatic, personal language of "speaking" and
"hearing" so central to Barth. Maurice can say that Christ's grace is
concretely met in the love of parents for children, and Christ's
chastising rule in the authority of father or of state. The requirement
upon the Christian is to acknowledge and show forth the divine
ground of human relationships in every specific context of life.
This means avoiding ideological schemes for moral reconstruction,
such as doctrinaire socialism, while at the same time lending support
to objectives of socialists in specific situations. It means no identification of Christianity with Demos, with radical democracy, but participating in democratic struggles insofar as particular objectives witness
to the spiritual constitution of the human community ruled by

Christ.[71] But for Maurice the historical specificity of the place of obedient witness to the reality of Christ does not become the kind of rallying point in the system of ethics that it does for some of our contemporaries on the continent of Europe.

In Barth's interpretation of marriage we have one instance in which concreteness is stressed. As in the relation of parents and children and other human situations, he seeks to avoid all forms of legalism, idealism, and formalism. This rules out various common preoccupations. For example, God's command is free from systematic definitions of the "essence" of manhood or the "essence" of womanhood. Thus in marriage we are not concerned about how close the union fits ideal essences of each sex or some ideal essence of marriage itself. There are in God's command no formal standards of the marriage relationship which in detail define what the common life is to be. The command of God will always set man rightly in his place and woman in hers. In each situation, each task, each conversation, their functions and possibilities take on particular, distinctive, but proper character where life is lived in obedience to God.[72] Indeed, marriage is instituted for a concrete man and a concrete woman. The wife is the partner of the man not in the form of woman or wife in general, not in the form of an idea of the wife, certainly not as the Virgin Mary, but as the specific, concrete wife. So also a man is the partner of the wife not as some essence, nor as the ideal man, nor as the "heavenly bridegroom," but as real man who is called to be bound to a specific individual woman.[73] Each marriage is instituted by God; there is no essential form of marriage into which a man and wife move.[74] Each marriage is a particular act of particular people.

The concreteness of moral life is seen by Barth to be an implication of the concreteness of God's election of man in Christ, of the

---

71 The tentativeness of the relation to socialism can be seen, e.g., in *Life of F. D. Maurice*, Vol. II, pp. 33–36; for comments on democracy (of which he was suspicious) see *ibid.*, pp. 128–32, p. 497 (a letter evoked by the assassination of Lincoln with comments on the Second Inaugural Address), and pp. 558–60.

72 Barth, *Church Dogmatics*, III/4, pp. 156–58.

73 *Ibid.*, pp. 164–65.

74 A sharp difference from Maurice is to be noted here. For Barth, Christ is Lord first of every instant, person, and particular situation. The persisting patterns are not as real as the concrete events. Thus in marriage it is a particular decision of particular people that is the focus of attention. For Maurice, on the contrary, the two partners enter a state which exists prior to them; Christ is Lord of the Kingdom of relations within which persons live. See *Social Morality*, p. 44.

concrete decision of faith of the believer, of the concrete reality of Christ's Lordship over nature and the historical events in which we live. Barth quotes with approval some passages of Bonhoeffer's *Ethics*. "The commandment of God is the total and concrete claim laid to man by the merciful and holy God in Jesus Christ. . . . [It is] not a summary of all ethical propositions in the most general terms. It is not the universally valid and timeless in contrast to the historical and temporal. It is not principle, as distinct from the application of principle. It is not the abstract as opposed to the concrete, or the indefinite as opposed to the definite. . . . Both in its contents and in its form it is concrete speech to concrete man. God's commandment leaves man no room for application or interpretation. . . . it can only be heard in a local and temporal context. If [it] is not clear, definite and concrete to the last detail, then it is not God's commandment."[75] This does not imply some direct inspiration in each moment of life, nor does it imply that we grope in the dark because of the contentless character of God's command. Rather, it is given us concretely in history; it is manifest in Jesus Christ, and comes to us in the reality of life. For Bonhoeffer this means that it comes to us in the four mandates of Church, family, labor, and government. Barth rejects this "mandate" definition of the place, but agrees with the more basic principle.

Concreteness refers both to the definiteness of God's claim, and therefore to the definiteness of the place in which we witness to God's grace, on the one hand, and, on the other, to the content of the command of God, the reality of Jesus Christ.[76] The continual focus on specificity and concreteness, on the definiteness of the place of action, may tend to give the impression of moral chaos, of thousands of believers doing hundreds of different things in a situation, with no consensus among them. But this sheer solipsistic individuality of response is checked on two sides. God is not a capricious God, executing whims and fancies here and there. Rather, he and his commands are good, and his work is sovereign. He commands

[75] Bonhoeffer, *Ethics*, pp. 244–45; quoted in Barth, *Church Dogmatics*, III/4, p. 14. See also, Bonhoeffer, *ibid.*, 248, quoted in Barth, pp. 14–15. See also Søe, *Kristelig Etik*, pp. 113–121, "The Problem of the Concrete Decision."

[76] See Barth, *Church Dogmatics*, II/2, pp. 566–83 for Jesus Christ as "The Content of the Divine Claim" and pp. 661–708, 710 f., for elaboration of "The Definiteness of the Divine Decision." Jesus Christ as the content is discussed later in this chapter, and extensively in Chapter V.

nothing which is not proper to him. In the singularity of his decision
—which we freely obey—he loves the right, he is friendly, and he
wills and effects the wholesome. God is the sovereign decider and
actor in the right decisions of every man; thus there is no chaos. The
other check on moral chaos is God's will to create fellowship among
men. It is no less true that he speaks to all men in common than that
his address to each man is particular and diverse. Fellowship is the
inner connection among believers, and also among nonbelievers; it is
an "inner connection of all that God wills and requires yesterday,
today, and tomorrow, from this or that man, in this or that situation."[77]

But the double character of control does not imply that one
objectively applies some knowledge of God's will about which a com-
mittee has come to consensus! God's rule does not lend itself to this.
It is "not merely a general rule but also a specific prescription and
norm of each individual case. . . . The divine decision [i.e., our
election in Jesus Christ] in which the sovereign judgment of God is
expressed in our decisions, is a very definite decision. This means
that in the demand and judgment of His command God always
confronts us with a specific meaning and intention, with a will which
has foreseen everything and each thing in particular, which has not
left the smallest thing to chance or our caprice. . . ." We meet
God's decision in such a way that "absolutely nothing either outward
or inward . . . is left to chance or to ourselves. . . . Even in every
visible or invisible detail He wills us precisely the one thing and
nothing else."[78] We are to witness to Christ freely in obedience to
God, who wills and determines the precise, concrete detailed action
in the place to which we are called.

By now, one's moral common sense has perhaps been exasperated
by assurances of the divine permission to do the good, which is to do
what God determines us to do—freely—in a concrete place. There
must be some place to look for knowledge about what Christ wills;
indeed, since momentary intuition is rejected (though it is hard
always to tell what difference it makes to transfer the insight from
our intuition to the objective work of the Holy Spirit), something
must replace it. Barth is against intuitionism, legalism, formalism,

[77] *Ibid.*, p. 711.
[78] *Ibid.*, pp. 663–64.

biblicism. What replaces these? What serves the function these errors have for the misguided mass of men? What is the definite content? Various answers are given, some of which have been suggested, and others of which receive more extended discussion in subsequent chapters. Jesus Christ, in his call to discipleship, directs us. The law of God is the *form* of the gospel. The Bible becomes our teacher by analogy. The law is the instructor to life in faith. Life is to be conformed to its true spiritual constitution, or to reality. These suggestions take us back to things which Barth rules out if they are the starting point of ethics.[79]

Follow Jesus Christ[80]

What must I do? Be what you are! Witness to the reality, Jesus Christ. He sits at the right hand of God, over all rule and authority and power and dominion (Eph. 1:20–21). But does this "high" Christology give us more than what appears to be a vague admonition? What does it mean to witness to Christ? What is the content of this? One might suspect that with the exalted Lord as the center of ethics the lowly Jesus of Bethlehem, Nazareth, and Gethsemane is lost from sight.

But the contrary is the case. With genuine piety that would put many so-called liberal theologians and their fixation on the Jesus of history to shame, Barth and Bonhoeffer look to Jesus for content and pattern in the Christian life. Christ as the pattern or example and man as his follower are close to the center of the moral life of the Christian. What is required is not the medieval Jesus-piety of Thomas a Kempis or Brother Lawrence, nor the modern Jesus-piety of Charles Sheldon in which the businessman's first question is,

[79] The stress on concreteness of the act is not unique to the Christological theme of this chapter, though the overall framework in which the act is governed is unique. E.g., West has pointed out that both Barth and Reinhold Niebuhr in effect have an "empirical ethic" which takes guidance from the situation in which men live, i.e., is "realistic." *Communism and the Theologians*, pp. 207–8. Whereas Barth's concreteness is determined by Christ's election of man, and Niebuhr's more by the wariness of utopianisms born of pietism or liberal theology, and of the need to struggle for "rough justice," Gustaf Wingren's is determined by a dynamic view of God's law and creative action (See *Creation and Law*, pp. 57–69, and the section "The First Use of the Law," pp. 149–73).

[80] See Chapter V, "Jesus Christ, the Pattern." Here the treatment is brief, and only shows that this theme is used by those who stress the Redeemer-Creator.

"What would Jesus do?" To be sure, there are many possibilities of subtle and gross distortions of the theme of discipleship. But looking to Jesus stimulates a definite action: obedience to his gracious commands, belief in him, action in faith in him in concrete, unambiguous situations. Obedience to God means obedience to Jesus. All demands are to be judged by this criterion: Do they proclaim indirectly the life and rule and victory of Jesus?[81]

Christ the Redeemer-Creator Lord is Jesus, born in Bethlehem, man among men in Nazareth, teacher of disciples, obedient even in death. Thus the life that witnesses to Christ's cosmic Lordship witnesses to Jesus' own obedience, love, gracious action, humility and joy. If one rightly follows Jesus, one will rightly act.

LAW IS THE FORM OF THE GOSPEL

To obey the command of Christ is to obey God's law. The gospel has a structure—the law of God.

For Barth's understanding of the ethical implications of Christ's redemptive Lordship, much can be subsumed under the law as the *form* of the gospel. In 1936 he published a brief paper, *Evangelium und Gesetz*, which in its very title reverses the traditional order of the terms—gospel and law, not law and gospel. The key sentence is a simple one: "The law is nothing else than the necessary *form of the Gospel*, whose content is grace."[82] The world of Lutheran theology quaked and continues to quake from the revision of the order of the words. But the revision does not merely disrupt verbal habits; it has far-reaching theological and moral importance. Law is not God's rule of creative and governing work in distinction from his redeeming work. It is the form of his redeeming work. Gospel is not now freedom from the law. It takes the law under itself as its own form.[83]

---

[81] See Bonhoeffer, *The Cost of Discipleship* (New York, 1948); Barth, *Church Dogmatics*, II/2, pp. 556 ff.; IV/2, pp. 533–53; Søe, *Kristelig Etik*, pp. 88 ff. This theme is not of great importance to Maurice. I have found no evidence of its use.

[82] Barth, "Gospel and Law," in *Community, State, and Church*, p. 80.

[83] The discussion since 1935 is mostly in German and Swedish literature, and continues. Most major European Lutheran theologians have commented directly or indirectly on Barth's essay, largely incorporated into *Church Dogmatics* II/2; e.g., Ragnar Bring, Gustaf Wingren, Edmund Schlink, F. Gogarten, Paul Althaus, Helmut Gollwitzer (who is accused, with Ernst Wolf, of revising Luther in the image of Barth), and Helmut Thielicke.

We live by grace, but the law is a gift of grace. Thus we can, in God's grace, freely obey what, in God's grace, is given in the law. The *law* is the form or structure of the gospel. But it is (to use a very Barthian literary device of stressing words in sequence as a means of exposition, used also by Kierkegaard) the form of the *gospel*. The law is subsumed under the gospel. "Ruling grace is commanding grace. The Gospel itself has the form and fashion of the Law. The one Word of God is both Gospel *and* Law. . . . In its content, it is Gospel; in its form and fashion, it is Law. It is first Gospel and then Law."[84] Grace is prior, but the prior grace is ruling and commanding grace. Thus ethics is derived from theology, what man ought to do from what has been and is being done.

Since the command of God is always concrete, precise, and direct, the law must be interpreted within the context of those prior notions. The law does not provide universally valid rules. Rather, the commandments of the law are given as summaries of God's command. "As several beams of light are brought to a focus in a lens, or several threads in a cable, so many particular commands are united and expressed in these comprehensive demands addressed to the people in the Old Testament and the Church in the New."[85] How does one claim that the law is the form of the gospel, and still keep the moment-to-moment flexibility of immediate obedience and witness? The Ten Commandments "are to be interpreted as part of the direction given for the concrete shaping of the people's life. . . ." In a strict sense they "do not contain any direct commands, but only prohibitions or. rather delimitations." "They mark off the sphere within which" God's dealings with his people and their conduct "are to run their course." Key words here are "direction," "delimitations," "sphere within which" life runs its true "course."[86] God's commands are not simply repetitions and applications of the Decalogue.

The Sermon on the Mount must be seen in the same light with the addition of its own distinctive element. "Its imperatives, too, have primarily and decisively the character of indicating a position and laying a foundation."[87] Its newness lies in its revelation of the

---

[84] Barth, *Church Dogmatics*, II/2, p. 511. See also de Quervain, *Die Heiligung*, pp. 225–62.

[85] *Ibid.*, p. 681.

[86] See use of these words and phrases throughout the discussion of the Decalogue, *ibid.*, pp. 683-88.

[87] *Ibid.*, p. 688; see also p. 697.

new man. Its sayings show forth "an intensified indicative which has
the force of an intensified imperative." No more universal moral
principles are revealed there than in the Ten Commandments.
Rather, the witness of both the sayings of Jesus and the Decalogue
testify to "the basis and the sphere of the kingdom in which God
confronts man. . . ."[88]

Barth attacks "universal moral principles" in part because of their
generality and vagueness. In the hope for concreteness and specificity
of command, and in the framework of his own doctrine of election,
however, a different kind of vagueness appears. The law gives a basic
direction and sets limits, it indicates a position and lays a foundation.
But it does not relieve us of the burden of deciding what to do. The
notion of the law as the form of the gospel, which appeared to
promise much content, becomes another witness to the gospel, in the
imperative mood. But there is more importance to Scripture than is
so far disclosed. The issue of biblical authority in matters of human
conduct requires further definition.

BIBLE AS SOURCE OF ANALOGIES

We are to act as Abraham and Peter acted. The Bible offers
analogies for our action.

Barth makes a distinction between casuistic ethics and a "practical
casuistry," which is important in seeing what the function of the
Bible is in his ethics. Casuistic ethics fixes God's command in a text
of law, and claims a method and technique for using these texts to
guide the action of man. Good and evil are deduced from general
rules and texts. This is wrong and impossible, for the ethicist assumes
the throne of God, deciding and judging between good and evil.
Casuistic ethics, as we have earlier seen, makes God's command a
general rule, or the pure moral form of such rules, and it cripples
Christian freedom. All this is wrong.[89] But a kind of practical
casuistry is necessary in the process of moral reflection. Our faith
gives us primarily the right attitude, and openness to the newness
of truth rather than moral knowledge and insight into the consequences of our actions.[90] But in the process of reflection we need some

[88] *Ibid.*, p. 700. Cf. *Church Dogmatics*, IV/2, pp. 546–53. Søe, *op. cit.*,
pp. 64–68.
[89] Barth, *Church Dogmatics*, III/4, pp. 8–15.
[90] *Ibid.*, II/2, pp. 644–51.

basis of guidance. The Bible then becomes a source of insight in the processes of practical casuistry or moral reflection. It gives us analogies, but not examples, rules, or ethical universals.

The formula might be expressed in the following terms. As the act of Jesus in cleansing the temple was an obedient act witnessing to God's gracious power in that situation, so my act of obedience in a comparable modern situation might be similar. But it might not be! The key is not *what* was done, but the *obedience* in which it was done. Here Barth is clearer about what this use of the Bible does not mean than he is about what it does mean. It does not mean that the Bible is "a kind of supernatural register or arsenal containing all sorts of counsels, directions and commands" for men in varied circumstances. We cannot "consult it as a kind of box of magic cards."[91] We are rather set in an analogous position to the biblical relation between God and man. We are "invited to be contemporaneous and likeminded with the biblical men"; we are "to hear the command of God as they heard it." "And so the command given to them and heard by them becomes directly the command given to us and to be heard by us. Their task becomes our task." The divine command given to us "cannot either formally or materially differ from that which was given to them and heard by them." All the biblical laws and ordinances, all the specific directions given to individuals "concern us directly and not merely indirectly." In our own very different time "we should not only act *like* Abraham, Peter, the centurion of Capernaum, the Israelites or the Church at Corinth, but again act as those who then and there were addressed by God, allowing the command given to them to be again, in our very different time and situation, the command given here and now to us. . . ." Our task is a "renewal and confirmation of their task."[92] This does not imply that the Bible gives temporary expressions of the divine command from which an eternal truth is to be deduced. Rather, precisely its temporary or temporal expression gives it eternal and valid content. We should hear the divine command given concretely to Abraham or Peter just as concretely in our time and situation. Thus the Bible is freed from legal authority, but we read it as truth, and hear God's

91 *Ibid.*, p. 704.
92 *Ibid.*, p. 706.

command to us in our place as we see Abraham or Peter listening to it in their places.[93]

THE "THIRD USE" OF THE LAW

Not all who make Creation and Redemption in Christ a theological starting point for ethics agree with the subtle sophistication of Barth, who wants strong biblical authority for ethics, but not in such a way that the Bible gives precise moral counsel. The early decades of the Reformation were replete with discussions of the status of the law within the context of redemption. Luther clearly had two uses of the law—the "political use," or the governing of God through laws and state and men in order to preserve justice and order in a fallen world, and the "theological use" through which our inability to save ourselves by meeting the required perfection of the law is made clear to us, so that we are led to repentance and faith.[94] Melanchthon and Calvin added a third use (scholars debate whether it is implicit in Luther or not), that is the law as counsel in a life and a world redeemed in Christ.[95]

Thus we are implored by those who have a third use of the law: "What ought we do in Christ's world? Turn to the Scripture, obey its prescriptions and counsels." It is given not only to bring us to our knees, but also to guide us on our way. It is an expression of God's law of nature. Calvin called the third use the principal use of the law. Those "in whose hearts the Spirit of God already lives and reigns" have the law inscribed and engraven on their hearts, but nevertheless derive advantages from the written law. It instructs them; "they find it an excellent instrument to give them from day to day, a better and more certain understanding of the Divine will to which they aspire, and to confirm them in the knowledge of it." It exhorts the Christian; "by frequent meditation on it he will be excited to obedience,

[93] How much Barth can derive out of (or perhaps pour into) Scripture on various specific issues can be seen in *Church Dogmatics* III/4, which deals with "special ethics" under the command of God the Creator. Here he discusses not only marriage but the vocation to remain single, the problem of divorce, the general status of women in relation to men, and many other very specific issues under various general rubrics. It is amazing how much can be written under the admonitions of the general theological framework of his ethics, part of which is a critique of ethics itself.

[94] See Luther, *Commentary on Galatians* (London, 1953), pp. 151 ff.

[95] See Melanchthon "Loci praecipui theologici," in *Glaube und Handeln*, eds. Schrey and Thielicke (Bremen, n.d.), pp. 152–53; and Calvin, *Institutes*, II, 7, esp. 12 (Allen trans.), Vol. I, pp. 388–89.

he will be confirmed in it, and restrained from the slippery path of transgression." Even the spiritual man needs a whip and a spur; the law serves this function. It does not permit him to loiter.[96]

The "third use" has contemporary expounders. Alfred de Quervain, like Barth, stresses the priority of gospel over law. Law and the state are in the realm of the sanctified; they do not rest alongside the gospel. Christ's Lordship implies theocracy, as the people of Israel knew it.[97] The use of the law must be seen in this framework. Our task is to show "that Christ the Lord is over everything we have, and that we have it only in him."[98] Because the Christian belongs to Christ, and is made holy by him, he finds the commandment of God to be a comforting word. We are to obey God's commands in such a way that we glorify Christ's obedience.

In the framework of the kingly Lordship of Christ, then, we can understand the commandments given to Moses. For example, the command not to kill is grounded in the gracious will of God revealed in the life and death of Christ. It is not morally self-evident; it is no proposition of natural law. Murder is an act of unbelief. The murderer acts as if he, and not Christ, were Lord; he cuts off the life of his neighbor from the promise of God. The life of the neighbor is worth nothing in and of itself, but is worthy only because God in Christ has mercy on him. Thus the command not to kill becomes positively the command to love the neighbor for whom Christ lived and died.[99] For de Quervain, as for Barth, however, the prime fact to be witnessed to is Christ's Lordship.

CONFORM LIFE TO ITS SPIRITUAL CONSTITUTION, TO REALITY

Christ is Lord of every man, we are told. This is reality. The moral life, then, conforms the self, society, and history to its true foundations. Underlying the legal relationship of human life, Maurice said, is a spiritual law, a spiritual society. Man's moral responsibility is to bear witness in the realm of historical society to this spiritual

---

[96] *Institutes* II, 7, 12; see also II, 7, 13, and the whole of II, 7 and II, 8 which expounds the moral law within the full context of Calvin's theology of the law. Psalm 119 lends itself to those who seek a positive doctrine of law.

[97] *Die Heiligung*, pp. 275–77. Hillerdal, in *Gehorsam gegen Gott*, pp. 185–94, gives an exposition of the meaning of de Quervain's almost Christocratic ethic for the state.

[98] De Quervain, *op. cit.*, p. 279.

[99] *Ibid.*, pp. 402 ff. De Quervain deals with implications of this for suicide, the taking of life by the state, war, etc.

kingdom. Human life is out of its true relationships, which are given in creation and known in redemption. To restore life to the true life that exists underneath it, that is the moral task.

In order to bear witness to the true constitution of life we must have some understanding of what it is, unless we believe that a life of reaction to stimuli in and of itself mirrors what God created man to be. What can be said about the "spiritual constitution" that might incline us to act in one way and not another? Is it something like a democracy? Does it imply for us the support of socialism? Is it a pattern at all? Or is it a powerful process? Our attention is turned by these questions to Christ, and to the communal nature of our existence. Man has a social nature; we exist as sons and fathers, as brothers, as members of a nation. This is not only a "natural" state of life; as a part of our nature, human relationships are a means of our ascent to knowledge of the divine. Thus "every breach of a human relation, as it implies a violation of the higher law, so also is . . . the drawing of a veil between the spirit of man and his God."[100] Thus by implication, every honoring of the communal relationship in which we are created, and over which Christ is Head, unites us to God and actualizes in history his Kingdom. The human community is not merely among men; it is also communion with God, the Father, the Son, and the Holy Spirit. "All the intricate interrelations of love in the Godhead, of the Father's love of men and of Christ's, of the human and divine natures of the Son, of the Creating and Redeeming Word, of man's love of neighbor in God and of God in the neighbor, or family, nation, and church, have their place."[101] Christ's Kingdom does not set aside the human relationships of family and nation; rather, it justifies their existence, and reconciles them to itself. There is no rule of life about socialism or democracy forthcoming. Maurice was not a man of practical moral action. The Church best serves man by exercising its true function, which, as he wrote to the more practical Christian Socialist Kingsley, "is to proclaim to men their spiritual condition, the eternal foundation on which it rests, the manifestation which has been made of it by the birth, death, resurrection and ascension of the Son of God, and the

---

[100] *The Kingdom of Christ* (1958 ed.), Vol. I, pp. 242–43; see the whole of Vol. I, Part 2, Chs. 3 and 4, and *Social Morality* for elaboration of the spiritual constitution. Cf. H. Richard Niebuhr, *Christ and Culture* (New York, 1951), pp. 220 ff.

[101] Niebuhr, *Christ and Culture*, p. 221.

gift of the Spirit."[102] *The moral and religious tasks are one, i.e., becoming rightly related to Christ, the Head of the universal Kingdom.* The lived knowledge of Christ morally transforms human life. Man and his communities become what they really are. They become what man has been created and redeemed to be in Christ; man is to live in this light. This is the guidance that can be given.

Bonhoeffer also suggests that conformity to reality is the essential character of the ethical life. The strictures against various types of legalism, by now familiar, are made in order to show that conformity to reality is an immediately present requirement that takes particular form in each situation. Man does not need to overcome the resistance that reality offers to his preconceptions of the good or the right. Rather, "he sees in the given situation what is necessary and what is 'right' for him to grasp and to do." "His action is in the true sense 'in accordance with reality.' "[103] What does correspondence with reality mean? It is neither servility to the factual, nor a revolt against the factual in the name of a higher reality. Rather, it is action "in accordance with Christ." In Jesus Christ, the "real man," "all factual reality derives its ultimate foundation and its ultimate annulment, its justification and its ultimate contradiction, its ultimate affirmation and its ultimate negation." We live in reality, in a factual world which is given to us in and through Jesus Christ. One is reminded of various concepts of the "fitting" action in the way Bonhoeffer develops the more specific implications of this. Our action is to be *pertinent* to the concrete situation in which we are responsible. Our relation to things is pertinent when it "keeps steadily in view their original, essential and purposive relation to God and to men," when it conforms to the law of being that is inherent in each and every thing.[104] Thus correspondence to reality is acting in accord with Christ who is the source, goal, and ground of all facts, things, indeed, of reality. All things created and restored in Christ have their own inner law of being and purpose—in effect their true natures. We are to act in deputyship to Christ by acting pertinently in accord with this order of nature. Thus the circle is completed—from reality, to Christ, to facts, to the law of being in things, and back to reality. To act according to reality is to be pertinent in each concrete situation in the light of Christ as *the* Reality.

[102] *Life of F. D. Maurice*, Vol. II, p. 272.
[103] Bonhoeffer, *Ethics*, pp. 197, 198.
[104] *Ibid.*, pp. 205, 206–7.

None of the specifications, for examples, discipleship to Christ and law as the form of the gospel, of the ethics of those who view Christ as the Lord who is Redeemer and Creator become precise in their direction and counsel. The basic themes of a critique of prescriptive ethics and of the affirmation of the redeemed world in concrete action remain dominant. The theological foundation is the basis of action, not ethical ideas derived from it. "Believe in Christ, and do what you please" is too simple a summary of the ethics of this Christological theme, but it is more accurate than "Always act with a good will"; or "Always do what Jesus would do," or some other moral maxim. Christ, the Lord who is Redeemer and Creator, is the one to trust and to know; then act in accordance with the manifold implications of him.

SOME REFLECTIONS ON THE MORAL LIFE IN RELATION TO THE REDEEMER-CREATOR

Since the theme we are concerned with is so theological in the special sense of referring to the nature of God, one is forced to ask of the ethics forthcoming from it: "Is this a valid Christology?" Ethics, in this theme, is so clearly an implication of a dogma that some judgment about the dogma appears to be required. A tremendous task thus unfolds, which leads far afield from the basic course of our interest. The issues must be pointed out without being fully developed.

First it must be remembered that themes are being isolated from their contexts for analysis. What has been delineated as the Redeemer-Creator theme is not necessarily the exclusive meaning of Jesus Christ for the authors for whom it is the principal one. The use of Christ as example, or pattern, has been indicated; the notion of Christ as Justifier and Sanctifier has been alluded to. Thus the theological question can be narrowed: Is the Redeemer-Creator theme valid as *a* theme? More difficult to judge is: Is it the central, dominant theme?[105]

On what grounds does one answer these questions? Certainly on biblical grounds there are texts which stress Christ's Lordship in

[105] See Gunnar Hillerdal, *op. cit.*, pp. 241 ff., for a discussion of the adequacy of the biblical exegesis of not only Barth, Ellul, and de Quervain, but also Althaus, Elert, and Gogarten, as it relates to Christology and the ethics of the state.

Creation and Redemption. The frequent use of Johannine materials in Maurice and Barth, and of the Christology of Ephesians and Colossians, and certain Pauline texts in Bonhoeffer and Barth is significant. The Bible undeniably witnesses to Christ in and through whom all things are made, and who has subjected all principalities and powers to himself. But is this *the* biblical Christology? Is this the dominant theme, so that all others are to be interpreted in its light? At least until other themes have been explored, we cannot say that it is.

But there are other bases of judgment besides the biblical. Are other theological issues adequately answered by the dominant use of the theme of Christ as Redeemer-Creator? For example, is the problem of historical evil grasped in the fullness of its depths as a human, existential problem? Do the logical implications of this Christological theme point to only a "shadow" character of evil and sin? Is this adequate? The writers we have looked at take evil and sin seriously, but not as seriously as if evil existed in a powerful independence from the good. To make a judgment on the adequacy of this, one needs to bring to bear biblical, logical, and experiential criteria.

The whole series of questions discussed in theology under the rubrics of *nature* and *grace* and *law* and *gospel* are seen to be important for Christian ethics in the light of the perspective delineated here. Clearly there is a rejection of a radical duality between the work of God the Creator and his work as Redeemer, a duality that is stressed in the theology and ethics of Luther and many Lutherans, as well as in the writings of Emil Brunner. Are we to speak of a "graced nature," as seems to be suggested at points in the three writers whose work has dominated this chapter? Does nature have the proper autonomy (and thus does general ethics have the theological dignity) that it deserves, and can have with other formulations of the nature-grace problem? Are we considering in this chapter a "transformed" nature? If so, what does this suggest for the way in which the moral man proceeds in his reflection and action? These vast questions of dogma can be raised by pressing from the moral experience of men into the assumptions theologians make when they seek to describe in a normative way what the task of Christian ethics is.

Law and gospel, or gospel and law: the importance of this has previously been suggested in this chapter. The ordering of the words, and the explication of the order, again moves one quickly into the doctrine of God that is operative, and from this one sees ramifications for ethics. To come to a settlement of this question is most difficult, since there are such varied interpretations not only of the New Testament on this issue, but also basic theological affirmations. But clearly some decisions about these things are implicit in the theology from which the ethics discussed in this chapter are derived, and we have seen some of their consequences for understanding the moral life.

But our analysis must be bound by the issues stated in the first chapter, in spite of the fact that the prior issues in this theme are more distinctively dogmatic than ethical. Perhaps the approach we are obliged to make can be stated as follows: From the point of view of questions of ethics, what judgments can be made about both the dogma and its ethical implications? What are we to say about the ethical and thus the theological implications we have delineated? For example, about the antilegalism, the affirmative character of one's approach to life, etc.?

The question of ethics is almost one with the question of faith in Jesus Christ in this Christological-ethical theme,[106] and yet it is not an exclusivistic ethic. Christian ethics is not an objective moral truth from the Christian tradition or the Bible that can become a guide for social policy or for personal moral life to all who inquire of it. Christ is the object of the faith, obedience, and trust of Christians; his relevance to all others is not known or understood apart from faith in him. To try to convince a Muslim or an agnostic that his concrete affirmative action in the world is based on the fact that all things are in Christ is useless; but the *believer* might say, from his knowledge in faith, that the Muslim and the agnostic can be affirmative and concrete because of Christ. The Christian and the unbeliever both exist within the Kingship of Christ or the election of man in Christ; the difference between them is that the believer, in faith, knows this, and the Muslim and the agnostic do not.

If this is so, does the fact that we are Christians make any differ-

---

[106] See Barth, *Church Dogmatics*, II/2, p. 641: "But are we in faith? Or will we be found amongst those who have rejected the stone which was to become the chief cornerstone? This is the question which is the true theme of all ethical enquiry."

ence in what we do? We have shown some answers to this question; we must now make judgments about them. What kind of difference would we expect to find between the actions of believer and unbeliever? At what point does Christ's Lordship in creation and redemption have a decisive effect upon our action? Is it in our motive? Our "attitude"? Our decision about what field of moral responsibility we shall choose? Our general area of vocation? The "quality" of our act? The specific external action, as it can be empirically observed? Our moral insight? Our perception of good and evil? The goals of our action? The rules that guide us?[107] This Christological theme speaks more of the "ontological" basis of moral life than its psychological or pedagogical basis; this we have noted. What difference does it make in my action, then, to believe in this ground of life and not another, for example, that the world is a battlefield in which the two superpowers of good and evil are struggling for a victory?

Faith in Christ, the Redeemer and Creator, makes its greatest difference in *the basic attitude* or disposition of the moral man. For those who do not share this vigorous *faith,* many objections from human experience can be brought against this position. For those whose faith in Christ is expressed by a different delineation of who he is and what he does for man, these ethical implications of his Lordship may not be acceptable. Thus we meet a combination of *faith* and *Christ,* as he is particularly understood by this theme. One can construct an objective, unified, dogmatic system in which Christ's Lordship is the center and is drawn to its most extensive and rigorous conclusions. But unless one really *believes* and *trusts* in *this* Christ, and his Lordship over all things, the ethics forthcoming from this position defy experience and logic at many points. Or if one has faith in Christ, who forgives sins but is not the sovereign ruler of all things, the far-reaching ethical implications of the theme of this chapter do not make sense. It is the double fact of Christ so understood, and man's faith in him, that is at the root of the freedom from prescriptive and calculating ethics, of the openness to the world and its infinite possibility in an affirmative, positive outlook, of the permission-character of ethics, and of the concreteness of the moral life.

---

[107] See Troeltsch's essay, "Grundprobleme der Ethik" for a very suggestive discussion of these questions, in *Gesammelte Schriften,* Vol. II Tübingen, 1913), pp. 552–672.

Neither faith in Christ defined without the stress on this theme, nor Christ so defined without the firm conviction of his reality, would issue so clearly in the moral life of hope, moment-to-moment obedience, and freedom from bondage to literalistic interpretations of what right motives, right rules, or right actions are to be.

Should one fail to appreciate this theme and its ethics, he can be subjected to a double question by its adherents. Do you really *believe* that Christ is Lord? And do you really believe that *Christ* is Lord? If one does not *believe* that Christ is Lord, the ethics make little sense; they are not subjectively true. If one does not believe it, one is likely to take refuge for moral certainty in law and laws, in the cultivation of human virtues, in defensive tactics against moral and historical evil, in programs of political and social reform, in human definitions of the temporal and eternal good, indeed, in "ethics." If one believes in Christ defined in more limited or other terms, for example, as a moral ideal, or as the source of the personal forgiveness of sin, he is not likely to have the cosmic optimism that finally is the ground of life, the assurance that the war is already won, that the abyss of love is greater than the abyss of death; he is not likely to trust his own understanding, to love so freely, to be so emancipated from concern for calculation of the consequences of his actions.

While a basic attitude appears to be the human moral counterpart to Christ's Lordship, the theme prohibits much speculation or analysis regarding the nature of this disposition. To make a human outlook, even in faith, the subject matter of study is to give it an autonomy it ought not have in the eyes of Barth and others; it is to make man, not God, the subject of ethics. The Christian witnesses to the Light, he obeys his commander who permits him to do freely what is required of him. The Christian's love is a *witness* to God's love. But it is *Christ* to whom he witnesses; *Christ* whom he obeys. Christ is the prime power, prime reality, prime direction. Man is, to use a favorite metaphor of Calvin's, merely a mirror. He reflects a reality not his own—the reality of Christ, and the reality of the world in Christ, which in the end are one reality. There is a difference in the world not because we make it, but because Christ makes it. Christians are really changed; yet they remain in pride, sloth, and misery. What then is *really* changed? This is a point of some obscurity; their *relation* to God is changed, and thus their relation to man and the world. To speculate about the psychological consequences of this gives the self improper status, for, after all, the gospel is primarily about God, who he is and what he does. To be sure, it is about what he has done for man, but the focus of attention is God and his action.

Do the ethical implications of this theme make sense to moral experience and insight? Barth and Bonhoeffer would say that this is a mistaken question. Christ's Lordship is true because it is God's revelation and because it is biblical, not because it is a powerful myth that illumines human experience. Its ethical implications are true so long as they are grounded in the premise of Christ's Lordship. Whether they are in any sense "true" to moral experience is incidental to, and not constitutive of, their real truth.[108] Recognizing, then, that our question is not their question (though one might guess that an element of experiential verification is present, but for purposes of theological consistency not admitted), we can explore its answer as a part of our ethical quest. If the ethics makes sense, why does it make sense? *Only* on empirical grounds? If this is so, ethics is reduced to one of its elements, namely a description of moral experience. Accuracy of description becomes the test of moral truth—a statement which taken alone and literally defies the whole of the Western moral tradition and human conscience. What other elements enter in? Conviction in faith? A discussion of these issues provides the material for our tentative judgments about the ethics of the theme, Christ, the Lord who is Redeemer and Creator.

An exploration of the similarities between the actual empirical conduct in the concrete situation of one instructed by Barth and Bonhoeffer, and one instructed by existentialism or pragmatism, would be an interesting and probably fruitful venture. Important affinities can be detected between these Christian ethicists and the two secular groups in their common critique of formalism, legalism, and ontologism (i.e., goods as ideal essences, etc.) in ethics. All would stress the time- and place-bound situational character of the moral act, though with varying stresses on the passionate character of

---

[108] For F. D. Maurice this is not the case. We have indicated how the Bible and moral experience illumine and substantiate each other in his work, e.g., God's love is proclaimed in the Bible, but it is also reflected in, and known through, the love of others for a particular person. Their love is better understood in the light of the Bible; the Bible is better understood in the light of human love and forgiveness.

the decision. The pragmatists and Christians share an affirmative faith, though for pragmatists this faith is more a function of their unconfessed loyalties than their technical pragmatic philosophy. How are such similarities possible when the underlying assumptions of the points of view have almost nothing in common? It may be because certain elements are verified by the human moral experience of many (not all) men. Men find themselves acting pragmatically and concretely. The theological framework can be separated from the description of the *form* and to a lesser extent from the content of moral action in Barth and Bonhoeffer. The form or pattern of action they describe is in part a description of how many men do act, no matter what their faith is.

This is particularly the case as Barth and Bonhoeffer turn their carving knives to the carcasses of the rigidities of legalistic, rationalistic, formalistic ethics. Men who share the particular context of a moral decision often find universal rules or moral propositions to be of limited use. The nuances of personalities involved, the lack of clarity about the relative moral merits of alternative actions, the facts and figures that make the stuff of moral action, all stand as barriers to a simple application of a rule, or a maxim, or a realization of an essence of the good. Popular morality speaks of the shades of gray that confront the responsible man; there are no blacks and whites. Action always involves concrete decisions; at some point all ethicists who are concerned for a theory of action, and not merely for the ideas of ethics, must account for this.

The double character of permission and commandment has counterparts in experience, though none that precisely matches the dialectical character of the understanding of Christian theologians. The psychoanalytic ethics of Erich Fromm perhaps come closest to the conversion of external obligation to inner desire; but unlike the ethics of Barth and Bonhoeffer the demand element is swallowed up and lost in the overflowing superabundance of love.[109] Christians, according to all who affirm the power of Christ's Lordship, act out of what has been done for them. Their action reflects thankfulness, faith, and trust in the power and reality of God. Non-Christians can understand the visible stages of this Christian behavior; that is, they

[109] See Fromm, *Man for Himself* (New York, 1947), and "Conscience," in *Moral Principles of Action*, ed. R. Anshen (New York, 1952), pp. 176–98.

too do many things, not out of a sense of obligation to authority, but out of inner desire and overflowing compassion or enthusiasm. But the grounds for this are understood differently. Further, for Barth and Bonhoeffer, what is permitted is yet commanded; the One who enables us still rules over us.

When content becomes more specifically biblical, or Christian, the divergence begins to show. This is so as one moves in two directions from the act, with its empirical character; toward the reasons for action, and toward the norms of action. The latter is of interest partly because of its rather formal character; that is, those who stress Christ's Lordship are never quite specific about the authority of the biblical moral teachings for moral action, as we have seen. The relation to God, faith, or obedience, is the point of *specific* direction or obligation; not the precepts of the Decalogue or the Sermon on the Mount. When this "specific" normative content is set in the framework of the concreteness of God's command, it does not give a "Christian position" on a problem that believers can follow. The basis of decision becomes the same as that which an unbeliever has in the same situation, that is, the facts, the analysis of them, the judgment about them in seriousness. Ethics becomes pragmatic and existential.

When one moves from the empirical action to the reasons for acting, as we have noted, the focus does affect the general perspective and fundamental disposition. The affirmative character of the ethics is grounded in Christ; both the freedom to be pragmatic and the confidence one has in his moral judgments and actions are grounded in Christ. This has no small effect on conduct, though a precise analysis of its determinative character is not made by men who stress this theme. Barth comes close to it in *Church Dogmatics*, IV/2, but as we shall have occasion to note in the chapter "Jesus Christ, the Sanctifier," his objectivism prohibits his giving attention to the Christian man in such a way as to illumine this issue. The concepts and language of Scripture are actually insufficient and inappropriate to develop this issue unless they are supplemented by ideas from nontheological disciplines.

The moral actor faces exasperation and frustration if he turns to the ethics of Christ the Redeemer-Lord for some objective, authoritative answer to the question, "What ought I to do in my situation?" Certainly there will be little or nothing that others can necessarily identify as "Christian" in what he does. He might be for the development of atomic weapons or against them (most Barthians were against them).[110] He might be for population control or against it. He might drink whiskey, or he might not. He might be for an increase in steelworkers' wages; or he might believe that wage increases are the key to inflation, and that the control of inflation is the necessary direction of policy. What ought I to do? Witness to Christ, to the Light. But in Christ, the Lord who is Creator and Redeemer, the meaning, outlook, and attitude of the moral life is given. In the empirical situation with its ordinary human and historical content, it is Christ whom man obeys, Christ who frees him to act, Christ who redeems the consequences of the decision. It is Christ's Kingdom that is established and to which he bears witness. Christ makes him open, free, and responsible. This is everything, say some theologians. It is much, and it is important, but it may be too simple. Others would claim more significance for Christ both in what faith in him does to and for the self and for his teaching and example in determining the state of affairs that ought to be.

---

[110] See the journal *Junge Kirche* through the 1950's, for the certainty about an anti-American, anti-Adenauer policy that many of the Germans influenced by Barth had, for examples, Gollwitzer, Iwand, and Niemöller.

III ∫ JESUS CHRIST,

The Sanctifier

But you are not in the flesh, you are in the Spirit, if the Spirit of God really dwells in you. . . . But if Christ is in you, although your bodies are dead because of sin your spirits are alive because of righteousness.

ROMANS 8:9–10

You, therefore, must be perfect, as your heavenly Father is perfect.

MATTHEW 5:48

For by a single offering he has perfected for all time those who are sanctified.

HEBREWS 10:14

No one born of God commits sin; for God's nature abides in him, and he cannot sin because he is born of God.

I JOHN 3:9

. . . asking that you may be filled with the knowledge of his will in all spiritual wisdom and understanding, to lead a life worthy of the Lord, fully pleasing to him, bearing fruit in every good work and increasing in the knowledge of God. May you be strengthened with all power, according to his glorious might, for all endurance and patience with joy.

COLOSSIANS 1:9–11

Christians are saved in this world from all sin, from all unrighteousness; that they are now in such a sense perfect, as not to commit sin, and to be freed from evil thoughts and evil tempers.

JOHN WESLEY, *Standard Sermons,*
"Christian Perfection" (Sugden ed.), Vol. II, p. 173

For if we truly partake of his death, our old man is crucified by its power, and the body of sin expires, so that the corruption of our former nature loses all its vigour. If we are partakers of his resurrection, we are raised by it to a newness of life, which corresponds with the righteousness of God. . . . The children of God are liberated by regeneration from the servitude of sin; not that they have already obtained the full possession of liberty, and experience no more trouble from the flesh, but there remains in them a perpetual cause of contention to exercise them.

CALVIN, *Institutes*, III, 3, 9 and 10

And if we believe, then he gives us his Holy Spirit, which guides us and leads us to all good virtues and works. . . . Then the faith makes us partake of all Christ's righteousness, and gives us the same to own. . . . Therefore who rightly believes, he is righteous and pious before God through the righteousness of Christ. . . . He is therefore righteous before the world because of the love and its fruit that the Holy Spirit puts forth in his heart and realizes in him.

ANDREAS OSIANDER, quoted in Emanuel Hirsch,
Die Theologie des Andreas Osiander, p. 117

To be continuously and receptively open to the influence of Christ, and continuously active in will for His Kingdom, is the life process of the new man.

SCHLEIERMACHER, *The Christian Faith*, p. 519

So, as it appears to me, in the righteousness that is to be made perfect much progress in this life has been made by that man who knows by his progress how far he is from the perfection of righteousness.

AUGUSTINE, *The Spirit and the Letter*, 64 (36)

A thing is said to be perfect in so far as it attains its proper end, which is the ultimate perfection thereof. Now it is charity that unites us to God, Who is the last end of the human mind, since "he that abideth in charity abideth in God, and God in him" (I John 4:16). Therefore the perfection of the Christian life consists radically in charity.

THOMAS AQUINAS, *Summa Theologica*, II, Part 2, Question 184, Art. 1

T HE CHRISTIAN ASKS, "WHAT SHOULD I DO?" HE HEARS THE ANSWER, "Allow the renewing work of Christ in and through the presence of the Holy Spirit to take its full course in your life and in history. The One who has set you free from the curse of the law and the powers of sin and death works his way and will in your heart and through your action. Christ is a regenerating person and power; he acts in and through man, he sanctifies." This answer to the moral question of the personal "ought" claims that Christ changes the moral selfhood, the "moral psychology" of the Christian.

Upon further specification this answer may mean various things. First, it may mean that "God has made you righteous. You are morally righteous because of what he has done." Through faith and through experience of conversion one is made *de facto* as well as *de jure* a new creature; he has a new birth. The old man dies and the new man is alive in Christ. For some authors this implies a conversion of man's *will*, man's *intention*, man's *heart*, so that he is no longer able to sin. Or it may imply that through repentance and discipline with the aid of gracious life from Christ, one progressively overcomes the evil and sin that remains from the old man. This is the answer of many Christians in the revivalist and pietist traditions. Christ's work of sanctification creates in us a holiness which is moral as well as religious in character, and makes possible, if not actual, our religious and moral perfection.

The significance of the sanctifying work of Christ may also mean, "God offers the possibility of moral and religious growth through the fellowship of the Church." The spirit of Christ creates a fellowship with him out of which our God-consciousness grows, and in which is found power and strength to manifest the new life in relation to our neighbors. Sin continues, our God-consciousness is never perfect, as Jesus' was; but we know our sin is forgiven and that it need not be an impediment to our moral and religious progress. The Spirit works in and through our fellowship with Christ and with one another in the Church to regenerate us. This is the answer of "liberal" theologians, such as Schleiermacher and many influenced by him. Christ sanctifies us, regenerates us, though not wholly, through his influence in and through the Church. Regeneration is part of our moral and religious experience in this life.

Third, this answer may mean, "Through the Church, the sacraments, and the various works of the Holy Spirit, Christ has instituted ways in which new life is infused into us." The means of grace of which we partake are God's gifts to us, through which he empowers us to overcome sin, to grow toward perfection, and to develop in our lives the moral and theological virtues. Sanctification by God's grace through the means by which we partake of Christ himself gives a renewal of the mind and an energizing of the will. We are substantially renewed. Qualities of excellence are formed in us. This Catholic answer is developed variously by Augustine, St. Thomas Aquinas, and others. The character of the self, its lasting dispositions, are brought to accord with man's true nature by the sanctifying grace of Christ.

In addition to these answers are many others of importance, though for various reasons they do not claim as much behavioral transformation. This is partly because the biblical texts that announce a new creaturehood are very difficult to interpret, and there is no ready consensus of opinion on what they precisely mean. Barth, for example, says we are all *de jure* sanctified; there is an actual transformation, a conversion to God, a new determination; but only those awakened to faith have grasped and acknowledged sanctification *de facto*.[1] For those who confess Christ, the Holy Spirit "creates saints by giving them direction."[2] Seeds of new life are sown and developed, there is a new "ruling and determinative factor" in the being of believers. But sin remains; Christians are *disturbed* sinners. Sin is relativized, its existence radically threatened. Sanctified man has a different source of initiative, a different spontaneity in his action. There is willingness, readiness, courage, and joyfulness to be a new man. Yet he is *simul justus, simul peccator*, as Luther said; indeed he is totally the old man and totally the new man at once; he stands under two total determinations that are mutually exclusive, something which "is certainly hard to grasp."[3]

Simul justus et peccator becomes a symbol for various turns and twists on the theme of sanctification. If justification is taken to mean more than imputed righteousness alone, the atonement more than a

[1] Barth, *Church Dogmatics*, IV/2, pp. 499 ff. See esp. p. 511.
[2] *Ibid.*, p. 523.
[3] *Ibid.*, p. 572.

forensic transaction, and the Christian life more than the freedom to sin, the idea of being both sinner and justified refers also to a positive change in the human experience of the Christian. While distinctions are made in Christian thought between justification and regeneration, no theologian completely separates the two. Herein lies the problem: both moral experience and Scripture testify to a double character of the Christian life—regeneration and continuation of sin, the coexistence of the old man and the new. Or this double character is interpreted to mean that man stands under two objective powers—sin and God's righteousness—at the same time. In this chapter we are chiefly concerned with writers who claim much for the experience of regeneration, but others who are either more cautious or more dialectical must be noted, for, like Barth, they do not deny some effect upon this life from Christians' sharing in the new life of Christ.

The issue is much discussed in Luther interpretation.[4] Clearly for Luther, Christ alone is true sanctification; he alone can make men holy through the work of the Holy Spirit, with the Word and the sacraments as his means. Through faith alone, this sanctifying work has its effect. The Christian remains sinner and unbeliever, but his sin is forgiven; he is "graced." But through the Spirit we can grow in faith; sanctification is the "obliteration, washing away, and death" of sin.[5] We partake of God's righteousness; Christ comes to dwell in our hearts. In faith, the Holy Spirit works through our person, in our acts of love. We are not only declared righteous, not only freed from the reckoning of our sins against us, but also we begin the new life, and we grow in the struggle against sin and the flesh. By daily repentance and faith the old man daily dies; the new man is daily brought to live by the presence of Christ and to act in love. Watson indicates what a less intensive study of Luther seems also to show, namely, that sometimes Luther stresses the *justus*, as in the "Treatise on Christian Liberty," and at other times the *peccator*. But over all, it is clear that the sanctifying power and presence of Christ and the Spirit is not without fruits of love in a new life.

The arguments within the Reformation tradition about how to state precisely what sanctification is were bitter. On the Lutheran

---

[4] See, among others, A. Gyllenkrok, *Rechtfertigung und Heiligung* (Uppsala, 1952) and Philip Watson, "Luther och helgelsen," *Svensk Teologisk Kvartalskrift*, Vol. 33 (1957), pp. 24–36.

[5] *Weimar Edition*, Vol. 50, p. 624, quoted by Watson, *op. cit.*, p. 29. Many other citations are made by Watson.

side, Osiander, under various historical influences, claimed that man was *made* righteous. The problem was not only discussed with reference to the person of the Christian, but also to the place of the law in the life of faith. Thus Melanchthon's insistence upon the "third use of the law" as a normative guide for the Christian life became another point of controversy. The Formula of Concord only officially settled these and other questions, and there, of course, only for Lutherans. They remain as lively issues in some Protestant theology today.

Calvin, it is often noted, placed his discussion of the new life in Christ ahead of his doctrine of election, and his discussion of regeneration ahead of justification. We are not to consider Christ as standing apart from us but, rather, as dwelling within us. He "not only adheres to us by an indissoluble connection of fellowship, but by a certain wonderful communion coalesces daily more and more into one body with us, till he becomes altogether one with us."[6] Thus we come to live and be directed by Christ's spirit. We are in communion with Christ; we participate in his body. This means for us new life, the strength to struggle against sin. "No man will be so unhappy, but that he may every day make some progress, however small. Therefore, let us not cease to strive, that we may be incessantly advancing in the way of the Lord; nor let us despair on account of the smallness of our success."[7] Men will not achieve perfection until the coming reign of Christ, but they can and do grow in participation in Christ's body. Sin is not eradicated; indeed, men are justified, not by their progress in regeneration, but by the imputation of Christ's own righteousness. Thus we must live in faith and repentance, though growing in new life, and in the ability to obey God's law.

The dialectic of the theology of the Christian life in regeneration is governed not only by the complexity of the New Testament texts and the interpretation of sin and grace. It is also shaped by a reaction against other theologies, i.e., by those who in the interest of simple consistency or moralistic predilections, or one-sided reading of texts, tend to oversimplify the gospel. For example, the Reformers moved between and against the claims for sanctification made by Catholics and sectarians, on the one hand, and claims that would make the action of Christ totally ineffective, on the other. Earlier Augustine

[6] Calvin, *Institutes* III, 2, 24 (Allen trans.), Vol. I, pp. 625–26.
[7] *Ibid.*, III, 6, 5, p. 750.

had faced the too simple moral optimism of the Pelagians with an affirmation of both man's sin and his dependence upon God's grace. Against them he affirmed, "The human will is divinely assisted to do the right" in such a way that it is not only created with an ability to choose and be given instruction, but also man "receives the Holy Spirit, whereby there arises in his soul the delight in and the love of God, the supreme and changeless Good. This gift is here and now, while he walks by faith, not yet by sight."[8] The Holy Spirit fires the heart and kindles the mind; it leads us to covet the good. Grace restores the will, and the restored will fulfills the law.[9] Grace renews in us the image of God; it mends nature. We depend for our new life upon the powers of God.[10] Indeed, perfect righteousness of life has no examples among men, yet it is not impossible.[11] But man continues to live in sin and need God's grace, and the mark of our progress is growth in our awareness of our imperfection.

Barth, Calvin, Luther, and Augustine have all been popularly characterized as "pessimists." If this means they do not put much hope in the moral striving of natural man, it is correct. But if it means they have no hope and joy about the ultimate end of things, it is false, for all trust firmly in the powers of God's righteousness, and all show that in some measure it bears fruit in the life of faith as men receive and partake of Christ. In America, Reinhold Niebuhr represents a renewal of a stream of Christian interpretation that is "realistic" about man's sin, and takes a "biblical" view of man against those of classical thought, the enlightenment, and Christian perfectionism. But Niebuhr is not completely one-sided in viewing the significance of Christ. To be sure Christ is primarily the revealer of God's law of love and thus the one who leads us to knowledge of our sin, and the revealer of God's forgiveness and mercy and thus the one who leads us to freedom. Niebuhr is clearly more worried about assuming too much for the power of Christ or grace in human experience and history than in affirming too little for it. Typically he writes, "The sorry annals of Christian fanaticism, of unholy religious

---

[8] Augustine, "The Spirit and the Letter," 5 (3), *Later Works*, ed. Burnaby, p. 197.

[9] *Ibid.*, 15 (9), p. 205.

[10] This is not the place to go into problems in Augustine's distinctions between will and powers, and others which are necessary for a proper understanding of his whole point of view.

[11] Augustine, "The Spirit and the Letter," *op. cit.*, 63, p. 247.

hatreds, of sinful ambitions hiding behind the cloak of religious sanctity, of political power impulses compounded with pretensions of devotion to God, offer the most irrefutable proof of the error in every Christian doctrine and every interpretation of Christian experience which claim that grace can remove the final contradiction between man and God. The sad experiences of Christian history show how human pride and spiritual arrogance rise to new heights precisely at the point where claims of sanctity are made without due qualification."[12] Niebuhr finds in St. Paul a double movement, sometimes claiming more and sometimes less for the presence of Christ in us. For all the "realism," Niebuhr sees that life, individual or social, has a double possibility. "It becomes apparent that there are infinite possibilities of organizing life beyond the center of the self; and equally infinite possibilities of drawing the self back into the center of the organization. The former possibilities are always fruits of grace (though frequently it is the 'hidden Christ' and a grace which is not fully known which initiates the miracle)."[13] Grace is both power in and mercy toward man, but in the face of human existence in general and the perilous historical consequences of perfectionism it is wiser to live in the light of the reality of sin and its forgiveness than to assume a present historical effectiveness of divine regeneration.

As we shall see, men who have believed most in the moral effects of the power of redemption never lost completely from view the actuality of man's rebellion or resistance against God. The complications in the discussion of the sanctifying work of Christ, however, lie not only with the dialectic of sin and grace and the assessment of their fruits in the moral life. There are also significant differences among interpreters of the Christian life as to *what the means of* sanctification are and what the *state and effects* of sanctification are. The principal means for some is the experience of evangelical *conversion* complemented by a vigorous *discipline* of the moral and

[12] Reinhold Niebuhr, *Nature and Destiny of Man* Vol. II (New York, 1943), p. 122. Note here the use of human consequences of a religious conviction as the major test of its rightness. Cf. the whole chapter, "Wisdom, Grace and Power," pp. 102–30, and also Paul Lehmann's excellent analysis, "Reinhold Niebuhr's Christology," in Kegley and Bretall, eds., *Reinhold Niebuhr* (New York, 1956), pp. 252–80.

[13] *Nature and Destiny*, II, p. 123. See for one criticism among many D. D. Williams, *God's Grace and Man's Hope* (New York, 1949), pp. 27 ff. and elsewhere.

religious life. For others it is our *communion with Christ* as his Spirit exercises its influence in and through the fellowship of the Church. For others it is the *gift of grace* through the rightly ordered Church and ministry. For some the principal effect is a new *will*, rightly directed by Jesus Christ. For others the *disposition* is changed—or there is a new motivation or a new intention to seek the good of the neighbor. Extreme perfectionists would tend to include a new *mind* and more perfect *knowledge* as fruits of sanctification, though they are consequently plagued with the problem of how to interpret mistakes of fact and judgment. For those who think less in sub-stantive terms, i.e., the transformation and perfection of character or qualities and traits of the self, sanctification often means a new *relation* to God and man, a new standpoint that in turn affects one's total outlook and action. And one may find various combinations of these themes.[14]

The themes discussed in the main body of this chapter assume a significant if not perfect transformation of the self through the work of Christ's sanctification. The change in the self is viewed in some-what substantial terms—it is will, mind, habit, consciousness, and intention, that are affected. Such a focus upon Christian experience can be set in contrast to those views which focus upon a change in a man's *relation* to God and neighbor rather than a change in the self. But, as we shall further note, to speak of sanctification in terms of

---

[14] Sometimes the distinction between "perfection" and "sanctification" is not made clearly, sometimes they are sharply separated. Newton Flew, in *The Idea of Perfection* (London, 1934), indicates the confusion that ensues in the use of these terms in his introduction and in the variety of ideas he includes in a book on perfection. Primarily perfection is an "ideal" for Flew; it is not actual "sin-lessness" though that is an element in the ideal. Yet the word can be applied to "a certain degree of attainment in this world" (p. xiii). In this chapter I am not concerned with an *ideal* of perfection, but rather a *process* of life by which Christ's work becomes manifest in man's moral life and action. Precision of terminology on the questions of sanctification and perfection can lead to a false quantification by which "growth" or "progress" is measured. In the useful article, "Perfection, Christian" in the *Encyclopedia of Religion and Ethics*, Frederic Platt, writes that "Christian perfection is never identical with absolute perfec-tion." Rather, one can speak of a "perfect conversion," "perfect justification," "perfect obedience," etc. The question of "perfection" comes into this chapter because the issue of sanctification and the New Testament texts force it in, but the possibility of religious and moral perfection in some measurable terms is not my primary question. I am concerned to show how theologians understand Christ's relation to man as the one who transforms the personal moral life. Thus the effect of Christ upon the human moral character is the object of attention.

relationship does not give a simple answer to the intellectual quest for clarity on the question: How does Christ's sanctifying power affect my moral actions and outlook?

TRANSFORMATION BY CONVERSION TO CHRIST

The Christian asks, "What shall I do?" The answer is heard, "Moral regeneration and spiritual regeneration are one. You will act as a Christian not by striving to do so, but by being brought to repentance and faith. The power of Jesus Christ then converts you, not merely by giving freedom from bondage to the law, but by regenerating and sanctifying your whole being. Your moral righteousness and action are the disciplined outgrowth of Christ's inward sanctifying and perfecting work."

Such a theme is common, and it is easily oversimplified by those who do not believe it. There are few. thoughtful persons in the evangelical pietistic tradition who assume that all the contradictions between God and man in human experience are removed, and that repentance and humility are not daily required. Yet currently popular, oversimplified antagonism to the belief that conversion bears moral fruit often assumes this to be the case. Thus before engaging in a critique, the theme of moral transformation by a conversion of life to Christ must be spelled out with attention to its relation to the objective work of Christ, to justification by faith alone, and to the work of the Holy Spirit.

John Wesley, as a historical fountainhead of a great stream of Anglo-Saxon evangelical Christianity, is worthy of attention as an exponent of this theme. That he believed in a moral transformation of individuals and communities as the result of conversions, there can be no doubt. After a revival at Kingswood, for example, he wrote in his *Journal* (December 27, 1739), "The scene is already changed. Kingswood does not now, as a year ago, resound with cursing and blasphemy. It is no more filled with drunkenness and uncleanness, and the idle diversions that naturally lead thereto. It is no longer full of wars and fighting, of clamour and bitterness, of wrath and envyings. Peace and love are there."[15] Such social effects were the fruits of individual, converted lives. "The drunkard commenced sober and

---

[15] *John Wesley's Journal* (abridged ed.; London, n.d.; preface dated 1903), p. 91.

temperate; the whoremonger abstained from adultery and fornication; the unjust from oppression and wrong. He that had been accustomed to curse and swear for many years, now swore no more. The sluggard began to work with his hands, that he might eat his own bread. The miser learned to deal his bread to the hungry, and to cover the naked with a garment. Indeed, the whole form of their life was changed: They had 'left off doing evil, and learned to do well.' "[16]

The whole of life was changed. Behind the external, more observable change was an inner change, wrought by the work of Christ. While Wesley had, much like Luther, striven to master himself, as one can see in the resolution to better himself (*Journal*, February 28, 1737), he was changed, not by allegiance to manuals of discipline such as William Law wrote, but by the powerful work of the Spirit in the famous Aldersgate meeting. He could say that he had trusted in righteousness by works, but now he trusted in Christ and thus had power to ward off temptation and sin (*Journal*, May 24, 1738). This confessed dependence upon Christ and his power is immediately reflected in his sermons. Within a month he preached, "All the blessings which God hath bestowed upon man are of His mere grace, bounty, or favor; His free, undeserved favor." "Grace is the source, faith the condition, of salvation." The believer assents to "the whole gospel"; he is in "full reliance on the blood of Christ." God works in us our justification, which includes our "deliverance from the [whole body] of sin."[17]

Wesley felt compelled to break from his loyalty to William Law's disciplined self-mortification as a result of his conviction that the powerful foundation of our justification and sanctification was Jesus Christ. He could write, "The sole cause of our acceptance with God (or, that for the sake of which, on account of which, we are accepted) is the righteousness and death of Christ, who fulfilled God's law, and died in our stead."[18] In contrast to righteousness by law,

[16] "A Farther Appeal" (1745), *The Works of John Wesley*, Vol. VIII (3rd ed.; 1831), p. 203, quoted by Harold Lindström, *Wesley and Sanctification* (Stockholm, 1946), p. 114.

[17] "Salvation by Faith," preached June 11, 1738, *The Standard Sermons of John Wesley*, 2 vols., I, ed. E. H. Sugden (London, 1921), pp. 37–52, quotations from pp. 37, 38, 40, 45. See Lindström, *op, cit.*, "Atonement, Justification and Sanctification," pp. 55–104, for a comprehensive discussion of the evangelical theological convictions underlying Wesley's view of sanctification.

[18] *The Poetical Works of John and Charles Wesley* (London, 1868, 1872), Vol. I, p. xx; quoted by Lindström, *op. cit.*, p. 59.

he could speak of the righteousness of faith, which is "that condition
of justification (and, in consequence, of present and final salvation, if
we endure therein unto the end) which was given by God to *fallen
man*, through the merits and mediation of His only-begotten son."
This new covenant in Christ does not say, "Perform unseeming
obedience, and live."[19] It does not say, "You must first do this or
that, conquer sin, do good to all men, go to church, say more prayers,
and then you will be reconciled to God." No; it says, "First believe."
"Believe in the Lord Jesus Christ, the propitiation for thy sins. Let
this good foundation first be laid, and then thou shalt do all things
well."[20] "Indeed, strictly speaking, the covenant of *grace* doth not
require us to *do* anything at all, as absolutely and indispensably
necessary in order to obtain our justification; but only to *believe* in
Him who, for the sake of His Son, and the propitiation which He
hath made, 'justifieth the ungodly that worketh not,' and imputes his
faith to him for righteousness."[21] Thus Wesley's view of justification
and sanctification had an evangelical ground. He cannot be simply
accused of a works-righteousness, something more characteristic of his
unreformed allegiance to Law's pattern of the Christian life which
Wesley found deficient. But Wesley was clearly more interested in
spelling out the life of sanctification, the fruits of faith, than were
many who would share this evangelical note. In this sense he kept the
focus on man's life in faith, and laid out steps toward sin and
sanctification in such a way that they almost overshadow the objective ground of Christian life in Christ's work for man.

The experiential effect of Christ's work is given a rather elaborate
delineation even in the sermons preached shortly after the Aldersgate
experience. Wesley is, in the balance, more interested in the moral
consequences of Christ's work than in an explication of its theological foundations. He did, after all, live in the England of *Tom Jones*
and *Fanny Hill*. Thus he preached, "He that is, by faith, born of God
sinneth not (1) by any habitual sin; for all habitual sin is sin reigning: but sin cannot reign in any that believeth. Nor (2) by any
willful sin; for his will, while he abideth in faith, is utterly set against
all sin, and abhorreth it as deadly poison. Nor (3) by any sinful desire;

---

[19] John Wesley, Sermon, "The Righteousness of Faith," *Standard Sermons,*
Vol. I, p. 136.
[20] *Ibid.*, p. 144.
[21] *Ibid.*, p. 137.

for he continually desireth the holy and perfect will of God; and any tendency to an unholy desire, he by the grace of God, stifleth in the birth. Nor (4) doth he sin by infirmities, whether in act, word, or thought; for his infirmities have no concurrence of his will; and without this they are not properly sins."[22] This almost "scholastic" cataloguing continues to be characteristic of his work.

For Wesley, the Christian lives by the power of Christ and the presence of the Holy Spirit. This affects the habits, the desires, and the wills of men. What is not related to the will is by definition not moral; thus natural infirmities are not of significance in sanctification. Christians have a new birth, marked by faith, hope, and love. Faith is not merely assent to divine truth but "a disposition which God has wrought"; it is a trust and confidence bearing the fruits of power over sin, "over outward sin of every kind; over every word and work," and the fruit of peace, "serenity of soul." Hope is the testimony of the Spirit of God bearing witness that we are heirs of God, the children of God. Love is the fruit of God's love; it is love of neighbor. Love is "universal obedience to Him we love, and conformity to His will, obedience to all the commands of God, internal and external; obedience of the heart and of the life."[23] But Wesley is not satisfied to leave much mystery in the hyphen between faith-fruits, or presence of Christ—sanctified life. There are stages, steps, and disciplines on the way to perfection. While our justification is based on Christ's work for us, and our sanctification on the Spirit's work in us, we must also work, observe, and examine ourselves and strive for perfection. William Law's influence is not lost.[24] There is nothing automatic

[22] "Salvation by Faith," *op. cit.*, pp. 44–45. For other statements of the relation of God's work to man's sanctification, see also the sermon "Justification by Faith" in which Wesley distinguishes between justification—"what God does for us through His Son," and sanctification—"what he works for us by His Spirit," *ibid.*, p. 119. Works done before justification are not good works because they did not spring from faith in Jesus Christ. Faith is a "divine, supernatural conviction that God was in Christ" and that "Christ died for *my* sins." See also "The Righteousness of Faith," "The First Fruits of the Spirit," "The Spirit of Bondage and Adoption," "The Witness of the Spirit," the latter three being on texts from Rom. 8, a key biblical source for sanctification doctrines with an evangelical (in contrast to idealistic or moralistic) basis.

[23] Sermon, "The Marks of the New Birth," quotations from *op. cit.*, pp. 285, 293–94.

[24] See Chapter VIII, where Law's work is used to illustrate a theme of perfection in self-mortification in the imitation of Christ. For a very informative study, see M. Schmidt, *John Wesley* (London, 1962).

about man's growth in the Christian life for Wesley. Nor is the work
of the Spirit so formal, dialectical, or objective that its effects evade
measurement in empirical terms. On the contrary, the believer can
examine his own behavior, and others can examine it as well, to
measure the quantity and test the quality of his Christian life. A
preoccupation with man quickly sets in.

In 1746 Wesley preached a sermon in which he compared man in
three states, that of nature, that under the law, and that in grace.
Natural man neither fears nor loves God, man under the law fears
him, man under grace loves him. Natural man has no light in divine
things and walks in darkness, under the law man "sees the painful
light of hell," and in grace "the joyous light of heaven." Natural man
has false peace, awakened by law he has no peace, but the believer
has "true peace—the peace of God filling and ruling his heart." The
heathen has "a fancied liberty which is licentiousness," the Jew "a
grievous bondage," and the Christian "the true glorious liberty of the
sons of God." The unawakened sin willingly, those awakened by the
law sin unwillingly, the children of God do not sin. "To conclude:
the natural man neither conquers nor fights; the man under the law
fights with sin, but cannot conquer; the man under grace fights and
conquers, yea, is 'more than conqueror through Him that loveth
him.' "[25] The definition of states is made rather precisely here, and
Wesley appears to believe that these are three progressive and
mutually exclusive states.

Lindström, drawing on various sources in the Wesley material, lists
the stages of the Christian life in various ways.[26] Using primarily the
sermon "The Scripture Way of Salvation," he defines a pattern of six
stages. The first is prevenient grace working in man's nascent desire
for God, his first promptings of having sinned, his tendency to life.
The second is the work of "convincing grace," the first real step toward
salvation. One is convinced of sin and guilt, and in the light of God's
wrath is repentant. The fruits of this repentance before justification
are a desire to amend one's life, the forgiveness of others, and doing
good instead of evil. Penitence in repentance brings an outward
change in the whole form of life. The third stage ensues from this,
that is, justification. Both justification and new birth are bestowed on

[25] Sermon, "The Spirit of Bondage and Adoption," *op. cit.*, p. 194.
[26] Lindström, *op. cit.*, pp. 112–13.

man in a single instant, but are to be distinguished from each other. Justification is liberation from the *guilt* of sin, it is forgiveness of sin and acceptance by God. Man is no longer subject to God's wrath. Justification is the objective side of salvation. New birth, the fourth stage, as we have seen, is liberation from the *power* of sin, it is the subjective side of salvation, the work of God's spirit in man. From this comes the fifth, the gradual work of sanctification. Man experiences God's love; he possesses the fruits of the Spirit. Though sin is no longer supreme in the believer, it continues to be present, and thus a continual life of repentance and of God's forgiveness ensues. The awareness of sin in the new life brings, not fear in the face of God's wrath but, rather, consciousness of God's forgiveness. Repentance after faith brings works of piety (prayer, Bible study, receiving Holy Communion, fasting) and works of mercy and love for the neighbor. Through gradual sanctification in the penitence and faith of the new life in Christ, one moves toward the final stage, Christian perfection. The Christian is freed not only from the power of sin, but from the root of sin.[27]

Wesley's view of perfection needs special elaboration, for it makes very strong claims for the efficacy in man's moral and religious life of Christ's work and presence.[28] During his long life Wesley defined what he meant by Christian perfection in several different ways, though they are in general consistent with each other. The pre-Aldersgate concern he had was given a new context in the light of the evangelical experience, but it was never lost, as we have seen, even in the first sermons following his conversion. The sermon "Christian Perfection," from 1741, is not atypical of the combination of dependence upon the objective work of Christ and man's own potentialities to achieve full santification. Christians are not free from ignorance by virtue of God's grace, though they know God's revelation; nor are they free from making mistakes even in regard to the Bible. "All those inward or outward imperfections which are not of a moral

---

[27] *Ibid.*, pp. 113–20. Lindström's study at this and other points is clear, judicious in judgment, and thoroughly documented.

[28] Major sources are various sermons, but particularly "Christian Perfection," *Standard Sermons*, Vol, II, pp. 150–74, and *A Plain Account of Christian Perfection*, various editions. On the American scene the nineteenth-century revivalist-theologian C. G. Finney was the fountainhead of another stream of evangelical perfectionism.

nature"[29] remain; bodily infirmities, slowness of understanding, incoherence of thought, heaviness of imagination, and the like. Nor are Christians perfect in the sense of being free from temptation. Nor does any man attain such holiness that he still need not " 'grow in grace,' and daily to advance in the knowledge and love of God his Saviour."[30]

Some men are children and some are more mature in the Christian life, according to Wesley; even babes in Christ at least "are made free from outward sin." Much biblical evidence points to the sin of holy men, such as David and Moses, "But if you would hence infer, that all Christians do and must commit sin as long as they live, this consequence we utterly deny."[31] Since the gospel was given, "he that is born of God sinneth not." Even if Peter and Paul sinned, one cannot infer that all the early Christians sinned, or that any Christian *must* sin. "*A Christian is so far perfect as not to commit sin.*"[32] The strong in the Lord are "freed from evil thoughts and evil tempers." When Christ lives in a man his heart is no longer evil; he is purified from pride, from self-will, and from anger in its evil forms. "Christians are saved in this world from all sin, from all unrighteousness; that they are now in such a sense perfect, as not to commit sin, and to be freed from evil thoughts and evil tempers."[33]

But perfection is not only sinlessness and purity of intention; it is also love of God and neighbor. Near the end of "A Plain Account of Christian Perfection," Wesley specifies all three of these factors as aspects of our perfection in Christ. "In one view it is purity of intention, dedicating all the life to God. It is the giving God all of one's heart; it is one desire and design ruling all our tempers. It is the devoting not a part, but all our soul, body, and substance to God. In another view it is all the mind which was in Christ, enabling us to walk as Christ walked. It is the circumcision of the heart from all filthiness, all inward as well as outward pollution. It is a renewal of the heart in the whole image of God, the full likeness of Him that created it. In yet another, it is the loving God with all our hearts and our neighbors as ourselves."[34] Wesley time and time again stressed

29 John Wesley, *Standard Sermons*, Vol. II, p. 155.
30 *Ibid.*, p. 156.
31 *Ibid.*, p. 159.
32 *Ibid.*, p. 169.
33 *Ibid.*, p. 173.
34 John Wesley, *Christian Perfection*, ed. T. Kepler (Cleveland, 1954), p. 142.

the imitation of Christ and fulfillment of the law of love as disciplines toward perfection.[35] He also stressed that Christianity is a social religion that requires a living and conversing with men. Religion, while always rooted in the individual heart, branches out in the fulfillment of the law of love.[36] Christian perfection is expressed in perfect and holy love to God and to the neighbor.

Man on his way to perfect sanctification is still tempted, however, and while there is an element of assurance of salvation given in conversion, one may lapse back into sin. There is no subtle dialectic of *simul justus et peccator* in its Lutheran or its Barthian form in Wesley's interpretation of the Christian life. Characteristically he thinks of *states* and *stages*, and can define the steps in man's falling from a state of grace to a state of sin. Born-again people sin, as many examples show with painful clarity. "What has long been observed is this: so long as 'he that is born of God keepeth himself' (which he is able to do by the grace of God), 'the wicked one toucheth him not'; but if he keepeth not himself, if he abideth not in faith, he may commit sin even as another man."[37] Four steps are involved: (1) falling to "negative inward sin" by not praying enough and not cultivating the life of the soul; (2) falling into "positive inward sin" by giving way to evil desire; (3) losing one's faith, and love for God; and (4) becoming weak enough so as to commit "even outward sin." In the same sermon he develops the process from grace to sin in a more theological framework. (1) Man has the "divine seed" of loving faith by being born of God, and this remains, but (2) temptation comes. (3) The Son of God warns him that sin is near and bids him to pray, but (4) man gives way to temptation and its fruits grow more pleasing to him. (5) The Holy Spirit is grieved, and man's faith is weakened. (6) The Spirit reproves him sharply, but (7) he turns

[35] See, for example, the sermon "Self-Denial" (Luke 9:23), where this theme is given an evangelical, yet in some ways moralistic, interpretation. Characteristic of Wesley, self-denial is "the denying or refusing to follow our own will, from a conviction that the will of God is the only rule of action to us" (*Sermons*, Vol. II, p. 286). "It is, to deny ourselves any pleasure which does not spring from, and lead to, God . . ." (*ibid.*, p. 287). Cross-bearing is a voluntary suffering of what it is in our power to avoid. But all this is not *disciplining ourselves*, but the embracing of God's will even when it is contrary to our own.

[36] See, among other sources, Wesley's fifth sermon on the Sermon on the Mount (Matt. 5:17–20), *Standard Sermons*, Vol. I, pp. 398–422.

[37] John Wesley, Sermon, "The Great Privilege of those that are born of God," *Sermons*, Vol. I, p. 307.

from the painful voice of God to the pleasing voice of the tempter.
(8) Evil desire spreads in man's soul until faith and love vanish and
then he can commit outward sin. This analysis of steps is not foreign
to Catholic and Protestant piety and in fairness it must be noted that
"the loss of faith must precede the committing outward sin."[38] But
an evangelical center point quickly is reduced in its conspicuousness
by an analysis of the processes of religious growth and decline in the
life of man. Indeed, even the theological substance is shifted to the
human side of the man-God relationship—it is "faith" that is lost.
The Son of God and the Spirit warn and reprove, but appear powerless in the light of loss of faith and presence of evil desire.

Certainly Wesley, like the larger pietistic and evangelical movement he represents, does not hesitate to spell out in terms of human
experience the effects of Christ's work. In comparison with Barth's
position, for example, the theme of sanctification in the pietistic tradition becomes more empirical in its description of the transformation of man in Christ.

One can state the present theme in the following way. It is man
who acts in the world, and man who is related to Christ. Man is
constituted by will, desire, intention, heart. His moral actions, indeed
the whole of his life, are expressions of his will, desire, and intention,
of this central subjective substance of the self. When one makes a
moral judgment about a man or his action, one looks, not primarily at
the actual consequences of his action, but at his motives and to his
purposes or his goal. If these are worthy of approval, then man is
good and worthy of commendation. Likewise, evil actions are the
result of evil desire.

When man comes under the conviction of sin in the hearing of the
gospel, it is his substantive self that is judged, his sins of desire,
intention, and purpose, as well as their outward expressions. Thus to
be saved means to be saved from these things; to be set free by
Christ's atoning work is to be freed from the evils and sins of the self.
The work of the Holy Spirit as it sanctifies, then, accordingly must
bring under its power and discipline the roots of man's action. It
must purify man's intention and motives, it must abolish the ground
of inner and outer sin, it must turn the self from its own pursuits of
pleasure to love of God and neighbor. Those aspects of man that

[38] *Ibid.*, p. 309.

constitute his nature as a moral creature are the ones that Christ's work affects. Through conversion, prayer, self-examination, discipline and the sacraments, one receives, is sustained, and grows in new life.

The claims of Wesley and others have a measure of appeal to common sense. They take at face value the scriptural references both to the power of Christ to give new life, and the command of Christ to be perfect. The subtle dialectic of sophisticated interpretations of St. Paul, for example, is ignored. Indeed, St. Paul is rather over-simplified by Wesley. Wesley does not have to show what is "very hard to understand," and what is finally paradoxical, namely, that one stands at the same moment totally justified and redeemed, and totally sinful and condemned. Nor does he have to show, as Bishop Nygren does in his interpretation of Romans, that man lives in two different aeons at the same time, the new age and the old age. To be sure, Wesley, like Barth, Nygren and others, had to make sense not only of the Scripture, but of experience. Thus he has, as we have seen, his own way of dealing with the issue of being in grace and yet falling from it. He gives unconvincing expositions of the nature of the perfection man may have in Christ, in which words are used in such ways as to make them cohere on the one side with the Scripture and the claims of Christian experience, and on the other with the empirical moral and religious existence of converted men. The appeal to common sense lies in the fact that Wesley assumes something occurs in the Christian life which is observable to the man who is converted and to those around him. If one believes Christ to effect these human consequences, one can measure the extent to which one is a "Christian." At least, for Wesley, the experiential claims and the truth claims of Christian faith have behavioral reference points, and one can make judgments about their validity without recourse to paradox.

The Wesleyan and pietistic enterprise, with all its naïveté and its morbid preoccupation with the religious man, has one asset: it assumes an important issue to be legitimate and valid. That is, if Christ's work is effective in the world through men, one must define insofar as possible what happens to men in relation to Christ so that his work does occur.[39] What do "the presence of Christ," "God's

---

[39] Reinhold Niebuhr's discussion of this issue remains one of the most realistic in the sense of awareness of both the scriptural and the experiential and historical sides of the problem. See *Nature and Destiny of Man*, Vol. II, pp. 107–

work," "the power of the Holy Spirit," etc., mean in their experiential effects or coordinates? In terms of man's action and being in the new life? Further, the Wesleyan issue assumes correctly that one must think about the *being*, the person through whom Christ's work is effective. He is no mere "tube" through which *agape* flows, no mere mask behind which God acts. He is concrete man—motives, desires, mind, will, and purpose. What is the effect of Christ on personal existence? The question is perhaps unanswerable in clarity and detail, and the effort to answer it might belong more to the realm of the psychology of Christian morality than to ethics. But it cannot be ignored by ethics, and indeed it is not. As one sees in the discussion of Christ's work of justification, men commonly speak of an inner freedom through grace and forgiveness, and this is one answer. But those who emphasize sanctification spell out the meaning of "new life in Christ" in terms of wider aspects of human experience. This attempt is a necessary but perilous enterprise. Its perils, some say, are so great, its mystery so profound, that it is better left alone. For others sanctification is a problem of "object" not "subject"—of God and his reality, not man and his life. What, then, are the difficulties in the Wesleyan answer?

First, there is the question of whether Wesley interprets the Bible properly. For example, in the various sermons on Romans 8 in which life in Christ and in the Spirit are discussed, does Wesley do justice to the subtleties of Paul's reflections on the relations of the presence of the Spirit and the new life in Christ to life in the flesh and life under the law? To be sure, Wesley acknowledges that the texts are difficult and have several interpretations. But in the main he thinks in terms of stages and states of life, for example, the natural man, man under the law, and man in the Spirit. He imposes upon the Scripture and experience patterns that are too simple, too temporally

---

26. Many theologians bypass the issue involved. E.g., Gustaf Aulen, *The Faith of the Christian Church* (Philadelphia, 1948), p. 164, writes, "As far as the Christian faith is concerned, the possibility of salvation lies entirely in the divine will and not in any human quality. Therefore, from the viewpoint of faith, it is idle to attempt to explain by rational means how salvation occurs. For faith there is no other explanation than that which refers to God's spontaneously active, unfathomable, and loving will." This is partly right—salvation is God's work finally, but God's work has consequences for man; these man seeks to understand. If theologians do not address this issue from their basic commitments, they leave the field wide open to psychological explanations that have quite a different basic point of view.

progressive, for the Scripture and for human experience. The subtleties of the problem of *simul justus et peccator,* for example, are not the creations of theologians bent upon creating complexity and profundity where all is really very simple. The subtleties are in the Bible itself and in Christian experience. But our main concern is not with Wesley as interpreter of the Bible.

Wesley and the movements he represents, we have said, have the asset of at least dealing with the issue of man in the old life and the new life. Man is not just a front for the mysterious action of God. But this asset creates the principal problem in Wesley as an ethicist. He is not, of course, concerned about the place of man between Christ and the world as an *intellectual* problem set in a systematic theological context. Rather he is a preacher, and the whole of theology becomes focused upon human existence itself, and largely in individualistic, subjective terms. While he does not fall into a works-righteousness (for he always has in mind that man's perfection is the consequence of what Christ has done) he nevertheless is primarily concerned with what Christ does for *me,* enables *me* to become. *Man is turned inward to himself* more than is necessary and proper. Wesley's early rigorism never leaves him, and the inward pulse-taking, self-evaluation, self-judgment that Wesley represents is characteristic of the pietistic movement in general. The freedom gained in Christ's righteousness, in justification, is lost, and a new bondage to the self replaces bondage to the law. The Christian becomes preoccupied, not with the objective work of Christ, but with his own state. Am I falling from grace through lack of prayer? Am I seriously tempted? If I am I must pray more fervently. Are my motives pure, my desires wholesome? Does my outward action testify to growth in grace? Such inwardness tends to become the center of the Christian life. The basic question it implicitly answers is proper, i.e., what are the consequences of Christ's redeeming and sanctifying work for man's action and behavior? But the point of focus for both the preacher-theologian Wesley and the less sophisticated converts shifts from a legitimate question to a false preoccupation with human behavior.

In this preoccupation both sin and the work of grace tend to be defined in terms of human traits, characteristics, and qualities. Sin equals sins. Sin is a quality that attaches itself to man's thoughts, his desires, his will, his purposes, his general subjective disposition. Sin is not in the first place, for pietism, a distorted relation to God; it is not a matter of unfaith. It is, rather, doing something wrong; it is break‧ing a commandment or fulfilling a selfish desire. It is acting in a way harmful to others. Thus the moral life is the overcoming of defi‧ciencies and bad habits insofar as these are subject to the will. Sanctification brings good desires, obedience to commandments, and the overcoming of evil ways. The power for this comes from the Spirit, to be sure, but the Christian must attend carefully to the cultivation of his new life so that he will not fall back into his sinful ways.

Two further points can be drawn from this. First, the preoccupa‧tion with definitions of stages and states, whether in Wesley's time or our own, fixes by necessity upon a dated psychology, a culturally relative mode of speaking about the self. To be sure, the use of words like "desire," "habit," and "intention" continues, but one who is informed by Freud would spell out the sanctification process on its human side in terms different from those William James used in his study of conversion, or those Zinzendorf used in Germany. The Scholastics had a psychology that so distinguished aspects of the self from each other that they appear to be almost autonomous, e.g., appetite, will, and intellect. The peril of precision in defining the steps by which one falls into sin or grows in grace lies in the double fact that (1) man's processes of life are complex of themselves and even more difficult to define in relation to Christ's work, and thus (2) the language used to describe them is always only partially adequate.

The second, and most important implication for our study is that Christian ethics is distorted by fixing the lens on man too sharply. God as the Good, God as power and end, is blurred. The conse‧quences of man's action for the neighbor's good are blurred. As a result, what is most sharply defined is seen out of context, and thus also distorted. Christian ethics becomes the study of right desire, pure intention, honest purpose, and motivation by love. It becomes the moral study of man, excessively isolated from the wider field of his life—his relation to God and the world. Rather than point to what God does for the world in Christ, ethics points to what happens to a man's state of life when he believes in Christ. Rather than point to the good of the neighbor that is forthcoming from acts of love, ethics studies the motive of love in the self, and how it can come into being.

The self as almost a "substance" is isolated from its relations. Its relations, so far as they are drawn in the picture, exist for the sake of the substantive self. The relation to Christ purifies the self; the relation to others and the world is at worst a threat to holiness and at best a means of expressing a new inward state. Ethics becomes the analysis of dispositions, motives, intentions, purposes, and desires.

This is a problem not only for the pietistic view of sanctification, but for the modern liberal versions as well. Though the process and the effects are differently defined, some of the same critical issues remain. The crucial point for our next analysis is the relation of man's "God-consciousness" to Christ, and to his moral actions.

THE EFFECTS OF FELLOWSHIP WITH CHRIST

The answer to the Christian's quest for moral direction can come in terms of the growth of the influence of Jesus Christ in the Christian so that he increases in his ability to know and do the good. The means for this sanctifying growth are given in fellowship with Christ through the Church. Schleiermacher's theology is taken here as an example of this view both because of its historical importance and because of its thoroughgoing consistency. Differences between Schleiermacher and later writers, for examples, Ritschl and Herrmann, are important but will not be developed here.

Schleiermacher, more than many theologians important for ethics, has governed his writing by a set of fundamental principles that rule the whole system. Wesley has much in common with the Reformation, with pietism, and with the discipline and devotion both of high-church Anglicans such as Law and of the Roman Catholic manuals of discipline; as a consequence one can work through his theological preaching without finding a single dominant motif. Schleiermacher, in contrast, has a determinative point of view; he is genuinely a systematic theologian. Thus our venture to look at his view of sanctification and its ethical consequences is hazardous, for justice cannot be done to the whole system of which it is a part.[40]

[40] Schleiermacher wrote a great deal on ethics, but we are concerned here only with the ethical implications of *The Christian Faith* (Edinburgh, 1928), some of his sermons, and *Die Christliche Sitte* (Berlin, 1843). For material on philosophical ethics and on methodological problems see, among others, *Grundlinien einer Kritik der bisherigen Sittenlehre* (2nd ed.; Berlin, 1834). For secondary treatments of Schleiermacher as an ethical thinker, see R. R. Niebuhr, *Schleiermacher on Christ and Religion* (New York, 1964), esp. pp. 92–116;

Schleiermacher's system is an explication of the "religious self-consciousness" of man, and particularly that of Christians. Thus it has an experiential reference point at its center and not at its periphery. This approach requires by implication a more or less empirical analysis of life in grace and life in sin, life in the Church and life in the world. With religious consciousness not only at the heart of the understanding of the Christian life, but also in the center of Schleiermacher's interpretation of Jesus Christ, the somewhat empirical analytical approach continues into the realm of problems usually dealt with in traditional theological concepts. The explication of sanctification follows in due course from the explication of the consciousness of grace, which refers back to Christ and his God-consciousness, and forward to man's life and action. Christian ethics is not *per se* discussed in the great dogmatics, but its basis is there. Christian ethics, Schleiermacher suggests, ought simply "to give an all-around description of how men live within the Kingdom of God." This means that it "will answer much better to its true relation to Dogmatics, and so to its own immediate purpose, if it drops the imperative mood altogether."[41] In *Die Christliche Sitte,* he says that Christian ethics deals with man's fellowship with Christ the Redeemer insofar as this becomes the motive for all the actions of the Christian. Christian ethics is a description of the various forms of action which follow from the governing of the specifically Christian religious self-consciousness.[42] These forms of activity, which take place both in the inner sphere of the Church's life, and in the outer sphere of the world, Schleiermacher describes as purifying (*reinigende*) or restoring (*wiederherstellende*) activity, propagating or dispersing (*verbreitende*) activity, and manifesting (*darstellende*) activity.

Schleiermacher was not interested in using the good behavior of redeemed Christians as a proof of the efficacy of conversion in the way Wesley was. Nor were the marks of the new life delineated in such precise moral terms; one does not find lists of sins men have been known to overcome as a result of conversion. But he was

---

Robert Munro, *Schleiermacher* (Paisley, 1903), pp. 224–86; Poul Jørgensen, *Die Ethik Schleiermachers* (Munich, 1959); Anders Nygren, *Filosofisk och Kristen Etik* (Stockholm, 1923), esp. pp. 65–84; Gunnar Hillerdal, *Teologisk och Filosofisk Etik* (Stockholm, 1958), pp. 105–31; and John Wallhausser, *Schleiermacher's Early Ethics,* unpublished Ph.D. dissertation, Yale University, 1965.

[41] *The Christian Faith,* p. 524.

[42] *Die Christliche Sitte,* pp. 32–33.

obviously more interested than were Luther before him and Barth after him in designating the effects of regeneration in the language of human experience. The subtleties of being totally sinner and totally sanctified at once, which are explicated with such dialectical skill by Barth and with such passion by Luther, are bypassed in favor of language which stresses the *replacement* of old life by new life, and the *continuities* in fellowship between the human consciousness of Jesus Christ and his perfect God-consciousness. While Schleiermacher insists on repentance and conversion, it is never as instant or dramatic as Wesley suggests. Life in the Church is the location of the transmission of the influences which bring men on the way to sinlessness.

The proposition of paragraph 100 of *The Christian Faith* makes the basic general point; namely, "The Redeemer assumes believers into the power of his God-consciousness, and this is His redemptive activity."[43] This statement indicates that it is a mistake to assume that for Schleiermacher the human subject of his own will fixed himself upon an ideal of new life given in Christ. Christ's activity is the initiating activity. Our life has been one of "consciousness of sin and imperfection"; we can know fellowship with him "only in so far as we are not conscious of our own individual life; as impulses flow to us from Him, we find that in Him from which everything proceeds to be the source of our activity also. . . . "[44] Indeed, for Schleiermacher all the well-known passages in the Pauline Letters and in the Johannine materials which speak of Christ living in us, of being dead to sin, or putting off the old man and putting on the new, point to this reality of *impulses* or *influences flowing* from Christ to believers.[45] Christ directs his God-consciousness against sin by entering the corporate life of man, sharing sympathetically his conscious-

[43] Schleiermacher, *The Christian Faith*, p. 425.
[44] *Ibid.*
[45] Cf. Horace Bushnell's sermon "Regeneration" on John 3:3: "And this is exactly what is meant by being born of God. It is having God revealed in the soul, moving in it as the grand impulse of life, so that duty is easy and, as it were, natural. Then we are in the kingdom, as being naturalized in it, or native born. Our regeneration makes us free in good." "He is born into God, restored to the living connection with God that was lost by his sin, made to be a partaker of the divine nature," *Sermons for the New Life* (New York, 1861), pp. 112, 120. Bushnell makes a distinctly Augustinian move when he indicates how the change is to be conceived. It is a change in one's reigning love. The disorder from which we are redeemed is a false center of life, "a *false love*, a *wrong love*, a *downward*, selfish love." Man is not "re-created" as if a new man displaced the old, and he does not simply find a new purpose, but he is changed "so that his life shall be under another love, a right love, a heavenly, a divine love . . ." (pp. 118 ff).

ness of sin, but "as something He is to overcome." Although for some theologians the manner by which the gracious work of God effects some newness of life in man is left undiscussed, or veiled in mystery, Schleiermacher proceeds to suggest how it happens. The Redeemer's assumption of us into fellowship with him is "a creative production in us of the will to assume Him into ourselves, or rather— since it is only receptiveness for His activity as involved in the impartation—only our assent to the influence of His activity."[46] The words "impulse" and "influence" are very significant, for they indicate how the self of the believer changes from what it was in sin to what it becomes in regeneration, avoiding any "magical" explanations (which Schleiermacher deplored) and avoiding immediate use of the Holy Spirit as a mysterious way of accounting for an alteration of the self.

Indeed, Schleiermacher likens our relation to Christ to the "attractive power" of those "to whose educative intellectual influence we gladly submit ourselves." "The original activity of the Redeemer is best conceived as a pervasive influence, which is received by its object in virtue of the free movement with which he turns himself to its attraction. . . . His every activity may be regarded as a continuation of that person-forming divine influence upon human nature" which had established itself as the being of God in Jesus Christ. By receiving this pervasive influence "the personal consciousness too becomes altogether different." All of a man's activities "are differently determined through the working of Christ in him, and even all impressions are differently received."[47] Just as this process takes place in the person, so also it takes place in the world. The influence spreads from consciousness to consciousness; there is "a new vital principle" in the world. The process is continuous, it is a kind of organic growth; "the total effective influence of Christ is only a continuation of the creative divine activity out of which the Person of Christ arose."[48] Schleiermacher thus fulfills his preference for an "empirical view" of the redemptive work of Christ which stresses the importance of his teaching and example on men, and is based upon the "inner experience of the believer."[49]

[46] _The Christian Faith_, p. 426.
[47] _Ibid._, p. 427.
[48] _Ibid._
[49] _Ibid._, pp. 428–31.

He describes the effects of this regeneration not only as a "different personal self-consciousness" and a new determination of the self, but also as the attainment of "a religious personality" that the believer did not have before. "Life comes under a different formula, making it life that is new; hence the phrases 'a new man,' 'a new creature,' which bear the same sense as our phrase 'a new personality.' "[50] In the homiletical rhetoric of a sermon on "Love and Service" he exclaims, "What a change is made on . . . a person by love to the Saviour, as soon as it takes possession of his soul! It pervades his whole being, transforms everything in him, gives a new direction to everything that has been used in the service of vanity, and sets it free to be a living power for good; so that he stands forth a new creature; all the powers of his soul united in active obedience to the motive that inspires him, and obeying no other."[51] So great are the claims made. Human occupation about earthly affairs to which "Christians, as men," are called comes rightly to us if in every moment and every part of our lives we are inspired by the right kind of love to Christ.

Indeed, the new life of the Christian resembles "its type and ideal, the resurrection life of Christ . . . *in its whole nature, way and manner.*" Just as the resurrected life of Christ was the same man, Jesus, so we are the same person in the new life, "only that the fire of the higher life is kindled in us . . . and also . . . that the remembrance of our former state is present in us." It is not just a new life of feelings and emotions, it is a life of action nourished by Christ "as the meat and drink of eternal life," in which each man strives "to make his new life intelligible to others about him, and to influence them by it."[52]

Schleiermacher sometimes suggests that the process toward sanctification is "natural," simply being receptive to impulses and the pervasive influence of Jesus. But the matter is more complicated. There is ample evidence that Schleiermacher believed that the death of the "old man" is necessary, that there is a struggle against sin, that the process is slow and at best progressive, and that while perfection is a possibility it is rarely attained.

[50] *Ibid.*, p. 476.
[51] *Selected Sermons of Schleiermacher* (New York, n.d.), p. 203.
[52] *Ibid.*, from an Easter sermon on Rom. 6:4–8, "Christ's Resurrection an Image of our New Life," pp. 266–78, quotations from p. 270, and pp. 272–73. This sermon is an important one for understanding Schleiermacher's view of the new life.

Schleiermacher's treatment of conversion in *The Christian Faith* is, as to be expected in a tome on dogmatics, much less dramatic than it appears in some of the sermons where the biblical language is not so demythologized. In the dogmatics he asserts that repentance, a "combination of regret and change of heart," and faith are the beginning of the new life. Regret over one's past life of sin arises out of "the vision of the perfection of Christ" and leads to a "continual abjuration of the fellowship of the sinful life," and a "desire to receive the impulses that come from Christ." There is a change of heart in union with regret and faith (which is the appropriation of Christ's perfection and blessedness) that marks the perfect and effective divine grace at work in the believer. In being received into fellowship with Christ there is evoked a "spontaneous activity" which brings newness of life.[53] In a Trinity Sunday Sermon on John 3:1–8, published in 1814, Schleiermacher uses the biblical language of "new birth." No cultural elevation of life, or efforts at self-purification will produce the spiritual life. An entirely different and new life must be led, beginning with a "new birth." "Between the beginning of our existence and our present life and aims there lies a time in which lust was the prevailing power; in which it conceived and brought forth sin." In that time the law of the spirit of life which the reborn man now loves and obeys was "far off and strange." For the new life to begin, the old one had to cease. "The beginning of the new life is the new birth." "If any man be in Christ, he is a new creature; the old is passed away, behold all is become new."[54]

Clearly Schleiermacher meant to explicate a change in the course of one's life, a conversion, even if in the end this theme is subordinated to the language of gradual growth through the good impulses that come from Jesus.

He also was aware of the continuity of the old Adam with the new, in spite of passages which indicate vast claims for regeneration and sanctification. "Since even in sanctification growth does not take place without a preliminary struggle between the old man and the new, this struggle cannot at any point in its whole course be viewed as an even advance to increase in the power of one and decrease in the power of the other. By the influence of the sinful common life

[53] *The Christian Faith*, pp. 480–95.
[54] *Selected Sermons*, pp. 88–89.

around us our own sinfulness is constantly being stirred up again."[55] Yet, in spite of the fact that "sin cannot be perfectly blotted out," it "remains something in process of disappearance," it "can win no new ground." Indeed, in the language of a sermon, the remaining traces of the former life make us all the "more vividly conscious of the great change that the life-giving call of God has produced in us," and thus evokes "the most heartfelt gratitude" for our redemption.[56]

The gradual but progressive character of the change in the Christian self is reiterated over and over by Schleiermacher. While "in living fellowship with Christ the natural powers of the regenerate are put at His disposal, whereby there is produced a life akin to His perfection and blessedness,"[57] the transformation does not take place at once. It is preceded by the new birth, which in turn is the effect of "the offering that He presented." "They are perfected forever to this very end, that they may really be able to be sanctified in a new life, after the conscience [consciousness] of sin and guilt of sin are taken away from them, and they have become partakers in the liberty of the children of God; the only position in which there can be progress in what is truly good."[58] The progress is possible through man's partaking of Christ, but in this fellowship there is a gradual development. "Oh, how gradually it gains its faculties in us, grows and becomes strong, only bearing still more than the new life of the Lord the traces of earthly imperfection. . . . How intermittent at first are the manifestations of this new life, and how limited the sphere of its action! . . . But in proportion as it becomes stronger, this new life ought the less to give the impression of being a mere phantom life. . . ." We are not to be anxious about this growth in new life even though "we are by no means conscious of this new life as an entirely continuous state," and even though "each of us loses sight of it only too often" among friends and among the cares and occupations of the world. The effect will be ever widening within us, and the circle of those who recognize the effect will be ever widening in the world. The language of the preacher makes it very vivid, if not persuasive. "And as soon as even the slightest premonition of it arises in a man's

[55] *The Christian Faith*, pp. 507–8.
[56] *Selected Sermons*, p. 271.
[57] *The Christian Faith*, p. 505.
[58] From a Good Friday sermon, "The End of all Sacrifices," *Selected Sermons*, p. 264.

soul, as soon as he has come only so far as to be no longer pleased and satisfied with the perishing and evil things of the world, as soon as his soul absorbs even the first ray of heavenly light; then his eyes are opened, so that he recognises this life, and becomes aware what a different life it is to serve righteousness, from living in the service of sin."[59] More prosaically Schleiermacher makes the same point in *The Christian Faith*, ". . . the content of time-experience becomes from the turning point of regeneration ever further removed from what preceded that crisis, and ever approximates more to pure harmony with the impulse issuing from Christ, and therefore to indistinguishability from Christ Himself."[60] Sin, while it cannot be "blotted out," "remains always something in process of disappearance."[61] But the germ of new life grows and bears fruit in "all good works," which are "natural effects of faith, and as such are objects of divine good pleasure."[62] The "life-process" of the new man continues in his openness to the influence of Christ, and in his activity for the Kingdom.

There appears to be an underlying pattern of thought in Schleiermacher's view of the new life. In contrast to a mode of thinking that uses the imagery of God speaking and man hearing, God commanding and man obeying, and thus stresses the discontinuities between God and man, Schleiermacher uses the language of impulses and influences spreading from the perfect God-consciousness of Jesus to the personalities of those who are receptive to him. The metaphor of the germ bearing fruit which Scheiermacher uses also stresses growth, continuities, gradual change. Indeed, the account he gives is almost a social psychological one in the sense that he lifts to prominence the effects of persons on others, and of Jesus on Christians as they are open to each other. It is a historical account in the sense that there is a chain of cause and effect from Jesus to us in the present. The natural powers of man and the course of history are altered by the influences of the Redeemer.

Within this framework, with what Schleiermacher called its "empirical" orientation, the Church has a central function. It is the

[59] The sermon, "Christ's Resurrection an Image of our New Life," *ibid.*, quotations from pp. 272, 276, 275.
[60] Schleiermacher, *The Christian Faith*, p. 506.
[61] *Ibid.*, p. 507.
[62] *Ibid.*, p. 517.

human, historical community that mediates the influences that make for new life. More than for most Protestant theologians, the Church has a central role in the Christian moral life as the transmitter of "influences" and thus as the shaper of the "new personality," of life under a "new formula." In this respect Schleiermacher creates a perspective that has been influential in American Protestant life and thought through such Congregational pastor-theologians as Horace Bushnell and Newman Smyth.[63]

The delineation of Schleiermacher's view of growth in the new life gives clear hints about the way in which the Church functions. Schleiermacher uses the idea of "common spirit" in the community as his central point; he uses the idealistic notion of the "corporate personality" of human groups, a notion spelled out with various refinements and qualifications by Dilthey, Troeltsch, and Gierke in Germany, by Durkheim in France, and in England by a group of which Ernest Barker is a more recent member. Indeed for Schleiermacher, "the expression 'Holy Spirit' must be understood to mean the vital unity of the Christian fellowship as a moral personality; and this, since everything strictly legal has already been excluded, we might denote by the phrase, its *common spirit*."[64] There is a common inner spiritual life in the Christian community, a "personality" which becomes Schleiermacher's "empirical" way of denoting the Holy Spirit.

This community has an outer circle and an inner circle, both of which function in the formation of the new life. "The new life of each individual springs from that of the community, while the life of the community springs from no other individual life than that of the

[63] For recent explorations of this concern see Gustafson, *Treasure in Earthen Vessels: The Church as a Human Community* (New York, 1961); "The Church: a Community of Moral Discourse," *The Crane Review*, Vol. 7, pp. 75–85 (1964); and "The Voluntary Church: A Moral Appraisal," in D. B. Robertson, ed., *Voluntary Associations* (Essays in honor of James Luther Adams) (Richmond, 1966), pp. 299–322. See also the splendid unpublished dissertation by Professor James B. Nelson of the United Theological Seminary of the Twin Cities, *The Church as Context of the Moral Life* (Yale University, 1962). Paul Lehmann's *koinonia* ethics assumes the Church to be the matrix of the Christian conscience, but he does not spell it out with reference to the kind of "empirical" approach characterized by Schleiermacher and others. See *Ethics in a Christian Context* (New York, 1963), pp. 45–73.

[64] Schleiermacher, *The Christian Faith*, p. 535. "The Christian Church is one through this one Spirit in the same way that a nation is one through the national character common to and identical in all" (p. 563).

Redeemer."[65] The preparatory work of grace is at work in the outer fellowship. In baptism infants are received into this fellowship so that they are conditioned by the common spirit, by fellow citizenship with the saints. It brings them into the outer circle and maintains them there until faith is awakened.[66] The inner circle consists of all who are living in a state of sanctification, who "feel an inward impulse to become more and more one in their common co-operative activity and reciprocal influence, and are conscious of this as the common Spirit of the new corporate life founded by Christ."[67] They share a common life by sharing in a common spirit; indeed, they grow in their new life as an identifiable Christian life through their inter-action with each other, as Christ's redeeming influence is spread in the preaching of the Word and the administration of the sacraments.

Thus Schleiermacher offers a social psychological theory of the Church which gives it an important position in the development of the moral life. The Church is the organism of which Christian morality is part of its life process.[68] Christian ethics quite logically becomes a descriptive enterprise; it describes how men live in their fellowship with Christ, with one another in the Church and in the world. The Christians live out their common spirit and their personal regeneration in love, in purifying and restoring actions in the human community. At every point in Schleiermacher's view of the Christian life, the Church is assumed as the community whose common spirit finds natural expression in the actions of its members in the world.

Schleiermacher's account is appealing to one who is interested in making some human experiential reference in his interpretation and explication of theological themes, something the ethicist cannot avoid. There is certainly no recourse to mystery; an "empirical" interpretation is offered on every major question. Like Wesley, but in very different terms, Schleiermacher makes a case for the moral efficacy of the work of Christ made known in the religious experience of men.

A view of man is postulated by Schleiermacher, and its substance as well as his uses of it have been subjected to severe strictures in

[65] *Ibid.*, p. 525.
[66] *Ibid.*, pp. 626–38.
[67] *Ibid.*, p. 560.
[68] See Holger Samson, *Die Kirche als Grundbegriff der theologischen Ethik Schleiermachers* (Zollikon, 1958), pp. 15 ff. This book is a very useful and thorough analysis of the function of the Church in *Die Christliche Sitte.*

recent Protestant theology. He has been variously described as a nineteenth-century optimist who does not know the depths of human egocentricity, or as a theologian who does not take sin and evil seriously. Barth's concern to begin theology with God as its prime object, or more precisely Jesus Christ as the revelation of God, quite self-consciously countermands Schleiermacher's independent anthropology, which sets up the conditions for the human response to the revelation in such a way that God's freedom is compromised and the revelation is distorted. The rehearsal of these criticisms is not my concern. I am more interested in looking critically at the understanding of the moral selfhood of the Christian as this is seen in Schleiermacher's thought.

Among the perspectives from which the moral self can be viewed, two contrasting ones have very wide ramifications for interpreting how the sanctifying work of Christ affects moral life. One perspective is Schleiermacher's, which can be typified as follows: The self in its action *expresses the personal history that it has accumulated* through its past experiences and associations. The second perspective is Kant's, and I believe also Barth's and that of the existentialists, and can be typified as follows: The self in its action is a *free self undetermined by its phenomenal history*, facing an imperative or a command of God, an open present and future, and acting out of this freedom to determine the future.

To continue in an ideal-typical mode for the sake of clarifying what is at stake, in the first there is a stress upon the continuities between selves both across time and across space. I am conditioned by the social and cultural history brought to bear upon me by my parental family, my regional culture, my schools, and my "attractive teachers" (to refer to one of Schleiermacher's comments on how Jesus can be understood). I am conditioned by my colleagues and students, my wife and children. These all sustain me as "impulses" and "influences" from them come to me.[69] It is appropriate to think of the relation of the self to its community in organic terms. The seed that is planted grows, affected by its environmental conditions, into a

[69] George Herbert Mead's theory of the self in *Mind, Self, and Society* (Chicago, 1934), would come under this type. The concern is analysis of the origins of selfhood in Mead's case; if his case is granted it has implications for understanding the moral self. See my discussion of these issues in "Time and Community: A Discussion," the appendix to *Treasure in Earthen Vessels*, pp. 113–37.

plant that bears fruit. These are influences exerted upon the self, and "seeds" planted in it bear fruit; its actions are then the "natural effects" of a "life-process."

In this type, then, the significance of the work of Christ is absorbed into the "seeds," "influences," and "impulses" which have a person-forming power. This does not take place without the assent of the self to these influences, and certainly faith is a special form of this assent in which the Christian participates in Christ's God-consciousness. The community, the Church in the case of Christians, has then a social and personal function.

In the second type a distinction of some sort is made between the "noumenal" self, free and undetermined, and the "phenomenal" self that is in the cause-effect process (Kant); or between the "real" self and the self that psychology, neurology, and philosophy describe (Barth). The self in this type is seen not so much from its past to its present as the end-product of a historical life process, but as a being with radical freedom, with discontinuities between moments, events, and decisions. It is looked at, in effect, downward upon the present with choices and options in which its decisions are not predetermined by its history, or, perhaps, it is looked at from a forward or future position to the present, asking, "What will I become?" rather than "What have I been?" or "What am I?" Its degree of indeterminacy is stressed rather than its degree of determinedness. It creates the new rather than actualizes what comes from the past; it obeys commands rather than expresses itself.

In this type, the significance of the work of Christ cannot be one cause in a multicausal process, or even become the dominating cause, simply because the self is not thought of primarily in causal, conditioned terms. Faith cannot be assent to person-forming influences mediated historically through the Church. The Church has less a socializing, person-forming function than one of proclamation of the gospel to evoke a response of trust in God.

The understanding of the human effects of Christ's sanctifying work are necessarily different in each of the types. The first can account for a regeneration or transformation of "natural capacities"; either there is a new root motivation that pervades all things, or, as in Bushnell, there is a new and proper love which redirects all things. Wesley also claimed a change in intention and other aspects, though without the organic analogy used by nineteenth-century writers.

What is given in nature is altered by grace, as a new force, a new power in life.

In the second type the gulf between God and man, though overcome by Jesus Christ, remains, so that any of the Schleiermacherian language of influence is ruled out. For Barth, as for Schleiermacher, the Christian participates in Christ, has a communion with him, but this does not lead to the almost predictable consequences for moral selfhood that Wesley and Schleiermacher claim. In a lively paragraph, which I quote at length in order to give the flavor of Barth's words, he says the following:

> Let us be honest. If we relate to ourselves, to you and me, to this or that Christian (even the best), that which is said about conversion of man in the New Testament, and which we have to say with the New Testament, it will have the inevitable smack of hyperbole and even illusion—and the more so the more we try to introduce it, either by way of analysis or assertion, in the form of statements about the psychico-physical conditions or impulses or experiences of individual Christians or Christians generally, or in the form of general or specialised pictures of the Christian life. What are we with our little conversion, our little repentance and reviving, our little ending and new beginning, our changed lives, whether we experience them in the wilderness, or the cloister, or at the very least at Caux? [Caux is the location of the Moral Rearmament Center in Switzerland.] How feeble is the relationship, even in the best of cases, between the great categories in which the conversion of man is described in the New Testament, and the corresponding event in our own inner and outer life![70]

Whereas Wesley and Schleiermacher each take the New Testament claims with a kind of positive literalness, Barth finds no experiential evidence for taking them literally among Christians. The truth of these statements, then, has to be dealt with in other than impulse terms and experiential terms. This is the case partly because, for Barth, man is both sinner and justified at once—totally both and not partly each, partly because theological terms like sanctification refer directly to Jesus Christ (He is the sanctified man) and only indirectly to ourselves, and partly because of his view of the self in which God's grace and command are given and addressed to the "real man" in his freedom to hear and obey, and do not effect a change in "psychico-physical" condition. What we say about conversion and santification is "in-

[70] Barth, *Church Dogmatics*, IV/2, pp. 582–83.

directly" and "genuinely" referred to us, but, "We should have much less, indeed nothing at all, if we tried to demand and seize more."[71] What does the transformation mean in human terms for Barth?

Paradoxically, he makes great claims. A "new form of existence for man" is given in which he lives as the "loyal covenant-partner of God." Man reflects and witnesses to Christ's sanctification particularly by receiving a new "direction." This consists of an "indication to a particular and new situation" and of "instruction which he is thereby given to adopt a particular attitude." This direction "falls, as it were, vertically, into the lives of those to whom it is given," and as such is effective with divine power. Barth slips into the "seed" metaphor, though if he exploited it I believe he would have to alter many things, "It is the sowing and the developing seed of new life." Indeed, this new direction becomes "the ruling and determinative factor in the whole being of those to whom it is given." It sets a limit to "their being sinners" by radically relativizing sin and threatening its continuance. The direction gives instruction by lifting the eyes to Jesus, the living Lord. It gives "a willingness and readiness, a courage and joyfulness to be the new man."[72]

The question is how such great claims for the new life can be made by Barth while at the same time he says that the New Testament passages on the new life smack of hyperbole and illusion. One reason is the absence of a view of the self in a *continuous* relation between Christ and man that is naturally interpreted. That there is a relationship of communion is affirmed by Barth, but he avoids explicating it in terms that violate his fundamental view of God and man in dialogue, speaking and hearing. There is a new direction for those who hear and believe, and this is a radical new determination, but not a transformation of experiences and the life process. In Barth's discussion of the sanctification of man, as in other sections referred to in Chapter II, man witnesses to and reflects an objective sanctified one, by the new direction of his life. He does not live out the natural effects of a conversion of his intentions and actions through impulses coming from Jesus. There is a new determination, but it comes vertically from above, and not horizontally through one's personal history.

71 *Ibid.*, p. 583.
72 *Ibid.*, pp. 511–33.

Barth, by his view of the self and his concern to preserve the integrity of revelation, evades the task of stating in nontheological language precisely what the efficacy of Christian faith is on moral behavior. This assertion needs some qualification, since there is a new direction and attitude. But he is not interested in trying to explain the "hows" of that transformation. Schleiermacher, while the language he uses is not as acceptable in our time as it was in his, at least has the merit of showing how the human self is conditioned and altered by faith. That there is such a self, indeed that Barth himself is such a self, one can accept as being the case. The influences of the Christian family, the Church and its life, of assent or openness to the biblical message do affect the manner of life. Barth does not want to give this process the dignity of "faith," nor its explanation the dignity of "theology."

Schleiermacher does help us understand what can happen to a moral life in Christian faith, though his claims are exaggerated. His view of the self has its own deficiencies for understanding the Christian moral life. The subtleties of sin and grace found in St. Paul are dealt with in a linear manner, as if new life on a time span were replacing old life, or as if healthy corpuscles were inevitably winning in the struggle with unhealthy ones. Not only is the New Testament message simplified; Barth is correct in the lively long quotation previously made in expressing human experience. "What are we with our little conversion . . .?" Self-examination reveals the hyperbole of radical claims made by Schleiermacher as well as Wesley. Christian experience is not as clearly a continuous or full transformation as these writers claim; our natural actions are not as redemptive as Schleiermacher cites them to be.

Also, to view the Christian self in a genetic manner, from a point of implantation to fruit-bearing, does justice to only one aspect of moral experience. Conscientious men face decisions in which options are given, and thus make choices which require reliance on more than their accumulation of even graced experience. One's formed life may rightly give an attitude and direction, but the determination of the measure of freedom, or power of initiation and control that is given in the moment of action requires much more than reliance upon what one has become. Here Schleiermacher had Christ as pattern, a theme to which we shall subsequently turn, but other elements need to be included in the account. The imperative comes in, as well as the indicative; the oughtness to be and become, the responsibility for, and obedience to others is also part of experience. Jesus Christ is important to moral life in these respects as well.[73]

CHRIST AND THE RESTORATION OF HUMAN NATURE

When Christians ask what they ought to be and do in their moral lives, they can turn to the Roman Catholic tradition for an elaborate and detailed interpretation both of what Christ has done for them and of what they are to do as a result. The New Testament speaks of becoming a new man, but it is difficult to discern from it whether newness refers to a new outlook, to a new motive, to a new spirit, to new virtues, life under a new law, or something else, or to these and other things in combination. Schleiermacher deals with what is transformed in the various implications of a new consciousness and, as we have seen, gives his "empirical" interpretation of both what occurs and how it occurs. Wesley relies on more distinctly moral language—new intention, freedom from sins, etc.—and believes it occurs through conversion. Catholic thought builds on the New Testament, and on St. Augustine as an interpreter of St. Paul. One finds in St. Thomas' expositions of the work of grace dozens of references to Augustine, and particularly to *The Letter and the Spirit*. A basic text for the tradition can be taken from that treatise. "For it is the work of the Spirit of grace to renew in us the image of God, in which 'by nature' we were made . . . not that nature is the denial of grace, but that grace is the mending of nature."[74]

Thomas explicates this with all the distinctions he absorbs from Aristotle, but the basic text from the Bishop of Hippo is not significantly altered. Modern Catholics are, of course, heirs of the whole tradition. Here we will look at writings of two moral theologians, and one lay philosopher among the contemporaries. Gerard Gilleman, S.J. in *The Primacy of Charity in Moral Theology* works very consciously

---

[73] Paul Lehmann's account sets the indicative mood as the proper one for Christian ethics, and he gives the Church an important but not well-explained role in the transformation of conscience. Christians are believed to have "imaginative and behavioral sensitivity to what God is doing in the world . . ."; they are given "a clear understanding of the environment and direction" of what they are to do. Lehmann, *Ethics in a Christian Context*, pp. 117, 116. He speaks of a new "motivation," etc. But he, like Barth, is not interested in trying to interpret this in an "empirical" way. At least Schleiermacher would run that risk, whether the path he took is satisfactory or not.

[74] "The Letter and the Spirit" 47 (27), *Later Works*, ed. Burnaby, p. 230.

within the Thomistic framework to show that "Sanctifying grace is not a substance added to our substance, but a completion and deepening of our being which renders this substance capable of being divinized while remaining integrally itself."[75] Love becomes the form of all the virtues, commanding them as the will commands all the active powers in moral activity. Father Bernard Häring, in *The Law of Christ*, a less technically written, but widely influential text, combines the traditional Thomistic apparatus with Pauline accents on being in Christ. He shows how Christian morality "is life flowing from the victory of Christ." "Our life must above all be a life in Christ. The essential orientation of this moral theology . . . is toward 'the mysteries of the children of God.' It is mystical identification of our whole being in Christ through the sacraments, a manifestation of the divine life in us."[76] Dietrich von Hildebrand ends the introduction to his *Transformation in Christ*, with a quotation from II Cor. 3:18: "But we all, beholding the glory of the Lord with open face, are transformed into the same image from glory to glory, even as by the Spirit of the Lord." He begins it: "God has called upon us to become new men in Christ. In Holy Baptism, He communicates a new supernatural life to us; He allows us to participate in His holy life. This new life is not destined merely to repose as a secret in the hidden depths of our souls; rather it should work out in a transformation of our entire personality."[77]

What does the restored or mended human nature appear to be among Catholic writers? In expositing St. Thomas' writing, some description of his basic view of man must be made (though I shall keep it to the necessary minimum for the purposes of this chapter) before one can sense the importance of what he says about graced moral existence. Obviously, one has to have in view what man's nature is, if one is to know what its restoration is. Man's nature is to seek his true end, his good, his happiness. Sinful man needs grace for two reasons: to do the supernatural good and to do the natural good. In the innocence of our first parents, before their sin, man had a natural integrity: "man by his natural endowment could will and do the good proportioned to his nature"; he tended toward the end of a proper natural order and happiness of life. For this he needed the

---

[75] Westminster, Md., 1961, p. 155.
[76] Westminster, Md., 3 vols. 1963–66; quotations are from Vol. 1, p. vii.
[77] Garden City, N.Y., 1962, pp. 8, 7.

help of God, the Prime Mover, just as all creation is dependent upon God. But our first parents sinned: "to sin is nothing else than to fail in the good which belongs to any being according to its nature." In the consequent corrupted state, man falls short even of what he could do by nature, though he is able by his natural endowments to perform some particular good, "such as to build dwellings, plant vineyards, and the like." Thus corrupted man "needs a gratuitous strength superadded to natural strength" not only to will and do the supernatural good, to contemplate God in perfect blessedness (even Adam needed this), but also to be healed from the effects of his sin.[78]

By God's sanctifying grace the ungodly sinner is justified, and he is able to move toward his true supernatural end, that is, his eternal happiness. But our concern is primarily not with man's eternal blessedness; we wish to attend to the claims made for man's temporal moral life as a graced life. If man can begin in grace to do the natural good that prefallen Adam could do, what happens to him that enables him to seek his true temporal end? If there is an "enabling of the will" and a "transformation of the mind" as papal encyclicals and other writings claim, how does this occur and what are its effects? To get at these questions in the work of St. Thomas I shall look primarily at two areas. One is the relation of the new law of the gospel to the old law; the other is the effect of grace upon man's moral habits, on the virtues.

A new law is instilled in the heart by the grace of the Holy Spirit. Indeed, "the new law is chiefly the grace itself of the Holy Ghost, which is given to those who believe in Christ." Thomas quotes Rom. 8:2 (which, incidentally, is the text from which Bernard Häring derives his theme for *The Law of Christ*), "The law of the spirit of life, in Christ Jesus, hath delivered me from the law of sin and death." This is in the first place inscribed in the heart, and only secondarily a written law which the faithful need for instruction. It both indicates to a man what he should do, and helps him to accomplish it.[79] It helps a man to avoid sin (i.e., failing to do the

---

[78] Thomas Aquinas, *Summa Theologica*, Vol. II, Part I, Q. 109, Art. 2 in *Basic Writings of Thomas Aquinas*, 2 vols., ed. Anton Pegis (New York, 1945), Vol. II, pp. 982–83. I intentionally cite articles which function as summaries of much that is expounded at greater length elsewhere, and often repeatedly.

[79] *Ibid.*, Q. 106, Art. 1, pp. 949–51.

good that accords with his nature), "yet it does not so confirm man in good that he cannot sin; for this belongs to the state of glory."[80] In contrast to the law of the Old Testament, a law of fear, the spiritual grace instills in the heart the law of love. This law of love explains the true sense of the commandments of the Old Testament, and adds to it some counsels of perfection.[81]

The new law makes men children of the light, who are therefore to walk in the light. It consists, as we have noted, "chiefly in the grace of the Holy Ghost," and this "is shown forth by faith that worketh through love."[82] From the promptings of grace there ensue external acts. Those acts which are clearly in keeping with faith that works through love are prescribed; those that are clearly contrary to it are prohibited. But in addition to these, there are acts which "have been left by the Lawgiver, i.e., Christ, to the discretion of each individual." In this discretionary realm we see the marks of the gospel as the law of liberty; it prescribes only those things necessary to salvation and prohibits only what opposes salvation, but leaves other things to individual discretion; and it "makes us comply freely with these precepts and prohibitions, inasmuch as we do so through the promptings of grace."[83]

The Sermon on the Mount "contains the whole formation of the life of the Christian," for in it man's interior movements are ordered both toward man himself and toward the neighbor. Both "the volition of what has to be done, and the intention of the end" are affected. The order of the law instilled in the heart prescribes that men should refrain from external acts that are inherently evil, and also from internal acts which become the occasions of evil deeds. Man's intention is ordered by the teaching that in his good works he should not seek worldly acclaim. In regard to the neighbor, the Christian is ordered not to judge him rashly and unjustly.[84] In addition to the commandments which direct men to a conformity of inner and outer acts to the law of love, there are the evangelical counsels of

---

[80] *Ibid.*, Q. 106, Art. 2, p. 952.
[81] *Ibid.*, Q. 107, Art. 2, p. 961.
[82] *Ibid.*, Q. 108, Art. 1, p. 968. I am deliberately stressing sections in which there is a distinctively Christian ethic worked out by St. Thomas. These sections are often overlooked in discussions of Thomas' ethics, but ought to be emphasized not only for purposes of this section, but also for ecumenical conversation.
[83] *Ibid.*, pp. 967–69.
[84] *Ibid.*, Q. 108, Art. 3, p. 973.

perfection, which are not binding but lead to exemplary Christian perfection, such as the renunciation of riches, of carnal pleasures, and pride of life.[85]

Against the stereotype that Protestants have of Catholic ethics, namely, that it is a rigid legalism imposed upon believers by an authoritarian ecclesiastical institution, it is proper to lift out these themes. For the believer, the new law is grace, it is the law of love written on the heart. The phrase normally used as the capstone of Luther's ethics, "faith working through love," is not foreign to this; indeed, St. Thomas uses it. What grace enables in man's volition, and directs as the proper end of his intention, has a definite shape, an order to which it is to be conformed. That order is given in the teachings of Jesus, as well as the more generalized "law of the Spirit of life." Thus the work of grace prompts a new life of love, commands that that life of love be in conformity with the grace which prompts it, and counsels even further conformity to the pattern of the Savior. It is, as Augustine so often pointed out, a life of liberty in that what law commands is done freely and joyously, as well as in the fact that in large areas the expression of this love is left to the discretion of the individual. In this new life man is directed properly toward his natural good as an individual and in relation to others, toward a new life of love which exceeds the bare minimum of human requirements, and toward the salvation of his soul and eternal blessedness.

A parallel pattern is worked out by St. Thomas in regard to the virtues. For his basic interpretation of the virtues, St. Thomas is heavily indebted to Aristotle's *Nicomachean Ethics*. As before we shall keep exposition and analysis to the bare essentials for purposes of this section. Like Augustine, Thomas understood man as a creature with certain fundamental tendencies or, in Augustinian terms, loves. The goodness of a human act derives from its tendency toward, or love of, a suitable object. "The goodness of a thing depends on its end."[86] The intellect, the powers of reason, function to determine the proper ends of human activity, and the will moves all the powers of the soul toward that end. The will is subject to habit, that is, to a lasting disposition of the self that is caused by previous actions in

[85] *Ibid.*, Q. 108, Art. 4, p. 977.
[86] *Ibid.*; Q. 18 deals with goodness and evil in human acts; the quotation is from Art. 4, p. 322.

accord with human nature, or out of such accord. "A good habit is one which disposes to an act suitable to the agent's nature, while a bad habit is one which disposes to an act unsuitable to nature. Thus, acts of virtue are suitable to human nature, since they are according to reason, whereas acts of vice are opposed to human nature, since they are against reason."[87]

Human virtues, then, are dispositions in accord with human nature. An act of virtue is the good use of free choice, that choice of an end that is in accord with nature; virtue denotes a perfection of a power in accord with its end.[88] St. Thomas distinguishes three types of virtues, the intellectual and the moral virtues following Aristotle's distinction, and the theological virtues.

For purposes of discussing the moral life, the principal intellectual virtue is prudence. "Prudence" he says, "is a virtue most necessary for human life." This is the case because the good life consists in good deeds, and this leads to some important considerations: what a man does and how he does it. Good deeds are done from right choice, and not from impulse or passion; thus proper reflection on both means and ends is required. Prudence is the intellectual virtue operative in reason that enables man to govern his will and appetite, and to direct them toward morally appropriate ends.[89]

Man's appetitive powers are governed by the moral virtues, as the intellectual powers are governed by intellectual virtues. Here, as in Aristotle, the other three cardinal virtues come into the picture: justice, which is the perfection of the power of the will; temperance, which governs concupiscence; and fortitude, which governs man's irascible power.

Our concern is for what God's grace does to the moral self, what effects it has on the self. Put quite directly, does grace affect in any significant way the virtue of prudence, and the moral virtues? Does the infusion of the theological virtues of faith, hope, and love free the cardinal virtues from corruption? Or is this infusion efficacious only for man's supernatural end?

St. Augustine was clear on the conversion for the classical virtues. Virtue is, he said, "nothing else than perfect love of God." The four cardinal virtues are four forms of love: "temperance is love giving

[87] *Ibid.*, Q. 54, Art. 3, p. 410.
[88] *Ibid.*, Q. 55, Art. 1, p. 413.
[89] *Ibid.*, Q. 57, Art. 5, pp. 436–37.

itself entirely to that which is loved; fortitude is love readily bearing all things for the sake of the loved object; justice is love serving only the loved object, and therefore ruling rightly; prudence is love distinguishing with sagacity between what hinders it and what helps it." The Christian is rightly directed to the right end or object of love; namely, "God, the chief good, the highest wisdom, the perfect harmony." The cardinal virtues consequently are reoriented by being rightly related to God so that "temperance is love keeping itself entire and incorrupt for God; fortitude is love bearing everything readily for the sake of God; justice is love serving God only, and therefore ruling well all else, as subject to man; prudence is love making a right distinction between what helps it towards God and what might hinder it."[90] For Augustine, when man, by grace, is oriented on the right object of love, on God, the virtues work for the service of God, and rightly for the service of the neighbor and the self. Both man's true and final end, God, and man's temporal ends are served properly through the conversion of the virtues.

It is certainly clear that St. Thomas intends to show that the theological virtues of faith, hope, and charity (love) are infused in men for the end of their supernatural and eternal blessedness, that happiness which surpasses man's nature. Man's natural powers, both before corruption by sin and after it, do not suffice to direct man to this end. Thus God alone infuses faith, hope, and love in man so that they direct him rightly to God.[91] These virtues "are above man's nature, while the intellectual and moral virtues are proportioned to his nature"; their end is God himself, who surpasses the knowledge of our reason, while the other virtues are "comprehensible to human reason." The theological virtues direct both man's intellect and his will toward eternal blessedness: providing certain supernatural principles which are to be believed—faith; providing a "movement of intention" which tends to that end—hope; and providing "a certain spiritual union, whereby the will is, in a way, transformed into that end"—charity.[92] While faith precedes the other two in the order of generation, in the order of perfection charity is the prime virtue.

It is thus in the "spiritual union" that charity moves and perfects

[90] Augustine, *On the Morals of the Catholic Church*, Chapter 15, in *Basic Writings of St. Augustine*, Vol. I, ed. Whitney Oates (New York, 1948), pp. 331–32.

[91] Thomas Aquinas, *Summa Theologica*, Vol. II, Part I, Q. 62, Art. 1, pp. 475–76.

[92] *Ibid.*, Q. 62, Arts. 2 and 3, pp. 476–79.

the link between the theological and cardinal virtues. "Charity is the mother and the root of all the virtues, inasmuch as it is the form of them all."[93] Charity needs the moral virtues, and the moral virtues need charity. Father Gerard Gilleman, S.J., in *The Primacy of Charity in Moral Theology*, builds his argument on the penetration of the theological virtues, particularly love, into the cardinal virtues, on the penetration of the supernatural end into the natural. "Supernatural finality does not suppress natural finality, but rather deepens it and leads it into contact with God."[94] Charity as a theological virtue "will elevate and give finality to our will, while the virtues will orient the diversity of our active powers. . . . The specific ends of the virtues are thus all subordinated to the ultimate end of charity."[95] The Christian participates in charity-love, so that even when he is not explicitly conscious of this love he is exercising it through his good acts. "As soon as our being is put into contact with God by sanctifying grace, it is wholly elevated; its substance by grace, its will by charity, and its sensible powers by the virtues."[96] Indeed, Father Gilleman can write of a "divinization" of our natural tendency to love, and of our acquired virtues.

To understand St. Thomas' thinking on the relation of the theological to the moral virtues, one must turn to the treatise on the theological virtues. It is clear from his discussion that "Charity is the form of the virtues." I Cor. 13:3 is quoted to show that apart from charity all good works are of no profit. Charity directs man to his ultimate end, the enjoyment of God, and draws up into itself man's particular activities directed toward proximate ends. This is not to say that an act for a temporal end has no value apart from being governed by the theological virtue of love. Particular goods can be genuine without charity. Thus one can work for the preservation of the state, for example, as a temporal end, and in so doing be directed by a true virtue. "It will nevertheless be imperfect, if it is not brought into relation to the ultimate and perfect good. Absolutely true virtue, therefore, is impossible without charity."[97] One may be correct on many points with reference to his acts of justice, for example, but

[93] *Ibid.*, Q. 62, Art. 4, p. 480.
[94] Gilleman, *Primacy of Charity in Moral Theology*, p. 184.
[95] *Ibid.*, p. 167.
[96] *Ibid.*, p. 172.
[97] Thomas Aquinas, *Summa Theologica*, II, Part II, Q. 23, Art. 7; quotation is from *Aquinas on Nature and Grace*, ed. A. M. Fairweather (Philadelphia, 1964), p. 353.

there can be no "absolutely true justice" without being properly related to the true end of man, "which relation depends on charity." Charity as a virtue in the moral agent directs the action of all other virtues to the ultimate end; it "gives their form to the actions of all other virtues" as their efficient cause. "Charity is compared to a ground and a root because all other virtues are sustained and nourished by it"; it "is said to be the end of other virtues because all other virtues serve the end of charity"; it "is said to be the mother of the other virtues because it conceives the actions which it commands in them out of desire for the ultimate end, as a mother conceives in herself by another."[98]

There can be an ethic of temporal ends in Thomas' thought, based upon natural law and acquired moral dispositions; this, however, has not been the point of our attention. What happens to the natural and corrupted man when he is graced by God? That is our concern. Clearly he is directed toward his proper ultimate or supernatural end. But does the infusion of the grace of the new law and the theological virtues affect his temporal moral existence? From what we have expounded it is clear that it does. There is a new law written on the Christian's heart, and charity gives a form to all the activities and other virtues of men. Thomas makes no claims for widespread moral perfection, though the graced man is free from the most grievous mortal sins. But the sanctifying grace of God shapes the Christian life so that the activities of men are brought into conformity to the grace they receive, and so that the particular moral virtues and acts are governed and directed by this grace. The virtues participate in the grace of charity, and in turn are appropriately expressed in human moral acts in the temporal sphere.

St. Thomas' views of the Church and the sacraments have been omitted from the discussion thus far, though with equal technicality and refinement they are explicated in his theology. Certainly it is through the Church and its sacraments that grace is brought to the faithful. Some contemporary writers who deal with the "new life" provide less precise treatments of this than St. Thomas and other theologians, but in a sense their writings are religiously and biblically richer.

"Put off the old man who is corrupted . . . , and be renewed in

98 *Ibid.*, Q. 23, Art. 8, p. 355.

the spirit of your mind: and put on the new man, who according to God is created in justice and holiness of truth." This quotation from Eph. 4:22–24 indicates to the Catholic lay philosopher Dietrich von Hildebrand the gate through which all must pass to reach the goal God has set for man. It indicates that a deep readiness to change, a "glowing desire" to become a new man in Christ, a passionate desire to give oneself over to Christ, is at the root of the transformed life. One must have a revulsion from one's sins, and be truly penitent for them. In self-knowledge and self-examination, man must "endeavor to get rid of all illusions of complacency, and to detect his particular vices and weaknesses."[99] He must make an unreserved decision to imitate Christ, and with such, "a brand new consciousness will necessarily permeate our life."[100] This gives men a new intention, awakens them to moral maturity, to an inward simplicity or unity of life so that one sees the world with new eyes. Christians are given strength to combat the glorification of self, the abuse of their freedom, and all other forms of pride. In true humility they can respond to the glory of God, confront him as the infinite Person, and live in fellowship with him. There are aspects of man's life which enable him to fulfill his "supernatural vocation" to transformation in Christ. One of the essential factors leading to this transformation is "participation in the uttered glorification of the Father, and this glorification takes place especially in the Liturgy."[101] Indeed, the Christian life is an unfolding of the supernatural life received in baptism.

What are the moral fruits of this devoted Christian piety? In opening ourselves to assent to our transformation in Christ, we are also called upon to "concur with" it "by subjecting ourselves to its demands." Man's "central personality" is moved "to conform to God's will, and to display a response to value pleasing to God in our single *acts* according to given concrete situations," and to the rectification of his moral character as such. We are enabled to "consciously create space in ourselves for right affective responses," and grow in

[99] D. von Hildebrand, *Transformation in Christ*, p. 47.
[100] *Ibid.*, p. 49.
[101] Von Hildebrand, *Liturgy and Personality* (New York, 1943), p. 18. This book is a moving interpretation of the significance of the liturgy of the Church in the shaping of the Christian life, and weaves in such themes as "response to value" which are explicated in great detail in the author's more philosophical book, *Christian Ethics* (New York, 1953).

"habitual being," the virtues. In our incorporation into Christ, the world of created things becomes the arena of our positive mission to others, as well as the arena for ascetical self-mortification. As in St. Thomas, grace enables, and grace requires the "striving for perfection" which is the Christian's vocation. "Yet, the ultimate and all-important source of our transformation in Christ lies not in what *we* do or what we *can* do by our free will, but in what God accords to us in the Sacraments: above all, our participation in the Holy Sacrifice of the Mass and the reception of Holy Communion."[102]

Von Hildebrand is clearly setting the Christian life off in distinction from the moral life that is possible for "natural man" in his sinful state. The life of man in the Church, and the discipline of his inner spirit, assenting to the presence of Christ's transforming presence, brings a newness of life. Like von Hildebrand, Father Häring also builds his view of the Christian moral life on biblical foundations, particularly using Pauline and Johannine sources. The religious life is the sustaining source and direction of the moral life. In distinction from a view of ethics which has religious sanctions "superimposed from without," Häring delineates an ethics "which springs from religion which animates it essentially." "The pure type of religious ethic is of the nature of response, in which moral conduct is understood as response to the summons of a person who is holy, who is absolute."[103] Thus the religious life of fellowship with God, of "I-Thou communion between God and the soul" is the well-spring of the moral life. It is to God, with whom the Christian has fellowship, that he is responsible in obedience for fulfillment of the moral order of creation.

Christians are incorporated into Christ; they participate in him, as St. Paul has indicated. In this communion there is a vocation to imitate Christ in true discipleship, an active participation in the service of Christ. Commandments and law remain, but rather than being external they become in the life of faith "the living words of Christ addressed to us." Christian moral teaching, like personal life, is centered "in grace-endowed fellowship of man with God, in the dialogue of word and response, in 'responsibility.' "[104]

The life of fellowship with God is brought into being and nour-

---

[102] Von Hildebrand, *Transformation*, p. 202.
[103] Häring, *The Law of Christ*, Vol. I, p. 35.
[104] *Ibid.*, p. 52.

ished in the Church through the sacraments and through prayer. There is a genuine and continuous conversion of the self, a return to God in repentance, and an entry into his Kingdom. This is not something that occurs automatically, "nor is it something spontaneous, as the urge to grow in a plant." The grace that converts is an imperative addressed to the free will of man. Like St. Thomas, Häring affirms that the new law written on the heart is not an invitation to license but, rather, "that the new existence in Christ, the new life in Christ, is the law which has laid hold of him. The divine life (*zoē*) itself is now the actual norm of his life. He feels bound from within to live up 'to the mature measure of the fulness of Christ' (cf. Eph. 4:7, 13)." The inner law does not contradict what is prohibited by the external divine law, but moves one freely to obey it. And beyond the Decalogue, "the Sermon on the Mount determines the ideals and goals toward which we must strive."[105]

Not only is life under a new law of the heart, but also as with St. Thomas, the infusion of faith, hope, and love sanctifies "the very root and source of the acquired moral virtues." The foundation and source of Christian virtue "is the Holy Spirit with His transforming and renovating grace," the "end and goal are Christ and the Father, the imitation of the spirit of Christ through the force of His Spirit."[106]

Thus for Häring, the "Christian virtues" refer not only to the theological virtues, but to the moral virtues as well, for in the new life these are transformed by Christ.

Further discussion of Häring's treatment of the virtues would accent his dependence on St. Thomas, as well as his own particular stress upon a more biblical and personalistic exposition of man's relation both to God and to his neighbor as he lives out the life of love. The important new emphasis in Häring is the religious and biblical context in which he places much of traditional Catholic morality. Men are given new life in Christ; this new life is also a new law of life. By the imperative of grace addressed to men through the indicative of grace they are called to a life of faithful obedience to Christ. There is a shape to this life: the Decalogue, the Sermon on the Mount, and the natural moral law. But what has too often been required in an authoritarian manner is now freely and joyfully executed.

105 *Ibid.*, p. 403.
106 *Ibid.*, p. 491.

The Catholics, like Schleiermacher, have no hesitation in delineating a view of the human self independent from the biblical revelation or Christological assertions. It is, of course, a very different view of the self. The organic growth language of Schleiermacher must appear to be highly deterministic and naturalistic to Catholic eyes, and the focus on consciousness must appear to be far too simple. In the Catholics' concern to offer a view of man, however, they are subject to the same strictures that Barth makes against "neo-Protestants." The independent view of the self determines how grace is to be received and what its effects are. If man is, on philosophical grounds, defined as a creature with tendencies toward the realization of certain ends, then the work of God's grace will necessarily affect the ends men seek and the dispositions from which their actions come in the realization of those ends. If, on philosophical grounds, man is viewed in a tripartite way, having intellect, will, and appetites, any transformation that grace enables has to be explained in terms of these parts of the self.

Thus one sees, as in the discussion of Protestant thinkers, that one's view of the self is crucial for one's interpretation of sanctification. This is unavoidable, even for those who seek to avoid it. There are three aspects of the view of man found in the Catholic writers we have discussed which are of particular importance for our purposes. They are: man as directed toward ultimate and temporal ends, man as creature who acquires dispositions or habits, and man who can govern his will to become what God enables him to be both in creation and in redemption.

A crucial distinction in the Catholic view of man is between man as moving toward a natural end and toward a supernatural end. Extensive discussion of this distinction would take us far afield, but its importance for moral life cannot be overlooked. For Catholics, as for most Protestants, the Christian faith has primarily to do with salvation, with bringing men to faith in God, or bringing men to eternal blessedness. The work of God's saving and sanctifying grace works primarily to that end. The primary concern is not with the development of a morally proper or effective Christian existence. To be sure, for Catholics one's moral condition is a matter of serious concern for one's salvation, but even here the end, with reference to the work of grace, is the supernatural one. But to know one's proper end, and to be properly directed toward it is a work of grace, of the presence of the Spirit infusing faith (belief), hope, and love. With this end as known, and with life moving toward it, one's other ends can move toward perfection. The general point, regardless of agreement or disagreement with the way in which it is worked out, is of constructive importance; namely, the Christian's transformation is in part the awareness of his ultimate end, and to be directed toward that end affects both what he becomes and what he does. To be moved by grace toward the end of the glorification of God is to be altered in one's basic direction and purpose of life.[107]

The Catholics' serious treatment of human beings as having acquired dispositions in accord with their nature, a basic Aristotelian view, is also to be taken seriously by theological ethics in any Christian tradition. Whereas Schleiermacher assumes that consciousness exists, which is changed by grace, Catholics have included not only a new consciousness (von Hildebrand), but also a penetration of the "habitual character" of persons. The self is not a totally undetermined entity, standing vacant before God to be determined only by the vertical movement of the command of God, as Barth in some places suggests. Nor does the past accretion of experience have to be expunged for the new man to exist. What is affected by grace is the dispositions of men. Häring and Gilleman make much of this, the latter primarily within his interpretation of St. Thomas (and perhaps more than is warranted in the texts from Thomas), as we have seen. Grace not only directs dispositions toward their proper end, but love, as one of the gifts, has the power to form and reform the habits. Further, what grace as a gift of the Spirit gives must take a particular shape and form through the self and its acts to be morally effective in the world. Grace uses the *character* of the self, and not merely freedom, to achieve moral ends. The Catholic theory of virtues is one way to account for the undeniable structured agency of concrete human characters in the explication of what Christ's work means for moral life.

The seed metaphor is notably absent among these writers, and von Hildebrand explicitly rejects it. Why? Because it tends to assume a process of Christian growth that is too automatic and spontaneous.

---

[107] Whether man is so exclusively end-seeker as appears to be the case in Aristotle and Thomas, I shall not discuss here. See H. Richard Niebuhr, *The Responsible Self*, pp. 47 ff., for a discussion of types of views of the self: maker, citizen, and responder.

There is a passivity about it, even in Schleiermacher, that is a mistake from the Catholic perspective. The concurrence of the will with what grace enables is a major theme in the Catholic views analyzed here, and for most serious moralists is an indispensable assertion in any view of the self. Grace in its prevenient form enables in a general way; all creation is dependent on God (as Prime Mover, for Thomas). Grace enables the will to respond openly to grace, and in turn to shape life according to what is enabled. Thus the Christian life is no automatic growth; Christian morality is not just expressive or purifying activity coming up out of the life process of the Christian and the Church; Christian ethics is not just a descriptive enterprise, indicating how men live in the Kingdom of God. Grace is both indicative and imperative, as Barth also affirms. But, in distinction from Barth, the will has a more positive and clearly defined function in bringing man's "habitual character" and his particular acts into conformity to the new law written on the heart. Man's "sovereignty over himself," to use a phrase from Kierkegaard, is fundamental to any serious moral view of life; the Catholics interpret the relation of grace to human nature in such a way that this cardinal point of ethics receives maximum attention.

But is the fulness of Christian liberty, as expounded by Luther and others, accounted for? St. Thomas allows for it in two forms: (1) doing freely what the law requires, in accord with St. Augustine, and (2) giving a realm of individual discretion between what is clearly prohibited and what is clearly prescribed. Häring can say that the power to do good derives from man's participation in the divine freedom. Freedom is a gift of the Spirit, and in the Christian life this freedom is to be exercised. But for both St. Thomas and Häring the creative freedom to love in new and open ways is restricted by law. Just as God's freedom "is governed by the inviolable law of the sanctity of the divine essence," or is under "the sovereign law of divine love," so "human freedom . . . is not submission to coercive pressure of external force, but self-fulfillment through inner love of the good *in accordance with* the pattern of the divine holiness which is the eternal law (*lex aeterna*) reflected in man's own nature (*lex naturalis*)."[108] One can contrast this with a contemporary Protestant, Paul Lehmann, for whom freedom appears to be the primary

---

[108] Häring, *The Law of Christ*, Vol. I, p. 103. Italics added.

attribute of God, governed by his "humanizing aims" and the primary gift of God's grace to man. Lehmann writes, "The *theonomous* conscience is governed and directed by the freedom of God alone."[109] Man in his graced freedom perceives what God in his freedom is doing to make and keep human life human. Lehmann, the radical Protestant, does not spell out the *order* of humanization, for the *order* of God's law is under the dynamics of his free activity, and is ever-changing. Christian liberty is maximized in living out the Christian life, inwardly and outwardly. The contrast is important, though the explication of its significance is reserved for the next chapter. For Catholics, Christian liberty is liberty to fulfill the order of life inherent in man and the world. The radical liberty that many read in Galatians, in some of Luther's writings, and in the Gospel accounts themselves, is missing.

REFLECTIONS ON THE ETHICS OF SANCTIFICATION

What ought I to do? For the theme of sanctification, as for the theme of Chapter II, this is not the first question, either in order of importance or in order of generation. "What is God in Jesus Christ doing to and for you in his work of grace?" is the first question. "For *you*" in the writers we have examined in this chapter is not to be interpreted forensically. What does grace do to the self, the personal existence of the Christian?[110]

We have noted the answers—it frees man from various forms of sin; it gives him a new intention; it motivates his will to do the good; it brings his life under a new law of love; it gives him a new con-

[109] Lehmann, *Ethics in a Christian Context*, pp. 358–59.

[110] I have, readers may be happy to know, considered the need for some economy of use of materials, and consequently omitted a discussion of "Christ as the inner light," a theme found in George Fox, William Penn, and explicated theologically by Robert Barclay. The "Quaker text" is John 1:9: "The true light that enlightens every man was coming into the world." Fox preached, for example, in 1649 about "the truth and the light which let them see all that ever they had done, and of their teacher within them, and how the Lord was come to teach them himself, and the Seed of Christ in them; how they were to mind that, and the promise that was the Seed of God within them, which is Christ" (*The Journal of George Fox*, rev. ed. by J. L. Nickalls, Cambridge, 1952), p. 48. Penn works out implications of this ethos in 1669, in "No Cross, No Crown," and in other writings. For a summary of the theme in Barclay, see Leif Eeg-Olofsson, *The Conception of the Inner Light in Robert Barclay's Theology* (Lund, 1954). Certainly this great theme deserves more than this footnote, especially in the light of the moral activity of Quakers!

sciousness by exerting impulses and influences on him; it directs him toward his proper eternal end; it writes the law of love on his heart so that he can will to follow it; in the form of love it becomes the form of all the virtues, etc.

What is claimed by all these writers, each of whom believes he is doing justice to Pauline, Johannine, and Petrine texts, can be seen in contrast to a recent statement of the significance of Christ for moral life; namely, that of H. Richard Niebuhr. Niebuhr states that Jesus Christ functions as a "symbolic form" in morality. "With the use of the symbolic form of Jesus Christ, the Christian—consciously or unconsciously—apprehends, interprets, and evaluates his fellow man," himself and the "Determiner of Destiny" or final end.[111] Niebuhr suggests that the function of Christ is largely that of giving a different *understanding* and *interpretation* of man, the world, and God, which in turn gives direction to human activity. In my judgment all the writers discussed in this chapter in one way or another include this element. Life is seen from a different perspective, which alters both its meaning and the believer's deeds. One's eternal end is known and kept in view, altering one's understanding of his temporal ends. One has a different consciousness. One knows the new law of his life. But whereas Niebuhr avoids spelling this out in terms of what God's grace does to will, disposition, intention, and limitation of sin, other writers, both Catholic and Protestant, make claims for these, as does the New Testament. In all of them, grace "replaces" or at least transforms the sin of self-centered will, the inertia of sloth, the more-than-cognitive dispositions of the human self. In all of them the possibility of moving toward perfection is affirmed.

Why do contemporary theologians, like Niebuhr and Barth, object to this? Partly because the self is not viewed in such "substantialist" terms; that is, it is viewed primarily in active, relational, open terms. H. R. Niebuhr suggests that the changes may affect one's "unconscious" as well as conscious response, and this opens the door for further exploration of the work of grace on the basic orientation, if not character, of the self, but he is reluctant to make assertions that would propose a necessary connection between being graced by God in Jesus Christ and one's deeds and actions.

They object also to the understanding of sin that seems to be involved in these "sanctificationist" writers. For each of them, in one

---

[111] H. Richard Niebuhr, *The Responsible Self*, p. 155; see pp. 154–59.

way or another, sin is virtually "something" that exists in the self, and thus can be chipped away or removed by displacing it with "something" else. But if sin is man's lack of confidence in God, his disloyalty to God, his unfaith—i.e., a relation and not a thing—it is not as easily displaced or chipped away. To be sure, a relationship can be restored; Barth certainly would claim this as part of what Christ has done for man and the world. But men's rejection or acceptance of the new or restored relation is a matter, not of infused disposition or growing seeds, not a once-for-all conversion; it is problematic in each day and each moment. One can fall from the subjective apprehension of newness of life at any time; and this is the case. One's deeds in relation to others can be corrupted from the core. Such a sense of sin has led some theologians to eschew serious claims for transformation of the human subject, and to see the importance of Christ's work to be a new freedom more than a new power, to stress justification by Christ more than sanctification. To some of them we turn in the next chapter.

The New Testament is indubitably the ground of claims discussed in this chapter. The ethic of Paul, while recognizing that the old man lives on, is an expressive ethic, giving shape in word and deed to what God in his grace has done for man in Jesus Christ. The great love ethic of the Johannine writings has human love to the neighbor impelled and compelled by the love of God in Christ. If the New Testament affirmations are hyperbole, many Catholic and Protestant writers have missed the point, for they have taken them at face value. But the New Testament never oversimplifies the efficacy of grace. Imperative is present, as well as indicative. For the New Testament and for the writers cited here, Christian ethics deals not only with maturity, but also with the requirements of the new life.[112] Both Christ as pattern and as teacher are part of the grace made known in Christ; for this reason a full treatment of the topic of the book must deal also with these themes.

[112] Cf. Lehmann. *Ethics in a Christian Context,* p. 54: "*Christian ethics aims, not at morality but at maturity.* The *mature* life is the fruit of Christian faith. Morality is a by-product of maturity." If Lehmann said that Christian *faith* aims not at morality as its first concern, he would be saying nothing unusual, but to say that Christian ethics does not is to use the word "ethics" in a very unspecified and unusual way. Morality as a "by-product" would appear to place Lehmann among those who make very great claims for the effects of grace—and I believe he belongs among them. The absence of the imperative mood in his ethics lends support to this. We return to Lehmann in the last chapter.

IV 〉 JESUS CHRIST,

The Justifier

The sabbath was made for man, not man for the sabbath.

MARK 2:27

Jesus then said to the Jews who had believed in him, "If you continue in my word, you are truly my disciples, and you will know the truth, and the truth will make you free."

JOHN 8:31–32

But now the righteousness of God has been manifested apart from law, although the law and the prophets bear witness to it, the righteousness of God through faith in Jesus Christ for all who believe. For there is no distinction; since all have sinned and fall short of the glory of God, they are justified by his grace as a gift, through the redemption which is in Christ Jesus, whom God put forward as an expiation by his blood, to be received by faith.

ROMANS 3:21–25

Now the Lord is the Spirit, and where the Spirit of the Lord is, there is freedom.

II CORINTHIANS 3:17

"All things are lawful," but not all things are helpful. "All things are lawful," but not all things build up.

I CORINTHIANS 10:23

For freedom Christ has set us free; stand fast therefore, and do not submit again to the yoke of slavery.

GALATIANS 5:1

116

I mean, brethren, the appointed time has grown very short; from now on, let those who have wives live as though they had none, and those who mourn as though they were not mourning, and those who rejoice as though they were not rejoicing, and those who buy as though they had no goods, and those who deal with the world as though they had no dealings with it.

I Corinthians 7:29–31

Owe no one anything, except to love one another; for he who loves his neighbor has fulfilled the law.

Romans 13:8

Lo, this is a truly Christian life, here faith is truly effectual through love; that is, it issues in works of the freest service cheerfully and lovingly done, with which a man willingly serves another without hope of reward, and for himself is satisfied with the fullness and wealth of his faith.

Martin Luther, "A Treatise on Christian Liberty,"
in *Three Treatises*, p. 276

Christ is the end of the law in that he gives man the freedom to live on a future basis and to live for the future, released from his past and from himself.

Rudolf Bultmann, *"Christ the End of the Law,"*
in *Essays*, p. 64

To understand that the Christ in us is not a possession but a hope, that perfection is not a reality but an intention; that such peace as we know in this life is never purely the peace of achievement but the serenity of being "completely known and all forgiven"; all this does not destroy moral ardour or responsibility. On the contrary it is the only way of preventing premature completions of life, or arresting the new and more terrible pride which may find its roots in the soil of humility, and of saving the Christian life from the intolerable pretension of saints who have forgotten that they are sinners.

Reinhold Niebuhr, *The Nature and Destiny of Man,*
Vol. 2, pp. 125–26

Significantly the same suffering love, the same *Agape* of Christ which reveals the divine mercy is also the norm of a new life.

Reinhold Niebuhr, *Faith and History*, p. 144

WHAT OUGHT I TO DO? THE CHRISTIAN IS ADMONISHED BY A GREAT
stream of Protestant ethics, "Be freed from legalism." "Be free
to love freely; be free to face moral issues in their own terms; be free
for the future; be free to be pragmatic." How is this freedom to be
gained? Certainly not by striving for it. It has already been gained for
man in Jesus Christ's crucifixion and resurrection. In Christ is the
certainty that man's sins are forgiven; man is to live freely in the
knowledge of the depths of God's mercy. In Christ, man is given
freedom from concern about saving himself; he is freed from earning
moral and religious merits. The moral question is again answered by
looking at the selfhood, the "moral psychology" of the Christian.

The concern for most theologians who think in these terms is
basically a religious one and secondarily an ethical one, as is true for
the writers discussed in other chapters. The great question that began
the Reformation stream was not, "How can I do morally good
deeds?" or even, "How can I live out the Christian life?" It was,
"How can I be saved?" The answer that is given is a Pauline one:
God has acted to save man in giving his Son to die on the cross. No
matter how hard man strives, he cannot achieve his salvation. It has
taken the grace of God to save man, and in grace salvation is a gift
given to all men. What is required is not works, but faith: a passive
trust in Jesus Christ through whom and in whom God has saved the
world. What is required is not belief in right doctrine (for some
theologians), or proper ascetical exercises, but confidence in the
gospel, the good news proclaimed by the Church.

While the writings cited in Chapter III press from the freedom
given in faith in God's grace to the formation of the life that is thus
graced, in this chapter we will look at writings that accent the
freedom of man given in faith. They say less rather than more about
the shape of sinlessness, about the growth into new consciousness,
about the effects of infusion of virtue. They are not as concerned
about the movement toward holiness in a moral sense but, rather,
stress the perilous state of man even in faith to fall back into unfaith
and sin. They are not as concerned to spell out empirical moral
consequences of faith, and if they suggest them, they tend to inter-

pret them as immediate gifts of grace rather than the outcome of a *causal process* that is initiated by God's grace and then worked out through consciousness or dispositions or intentions. This is not to say that freedom is absent as an accent in the theologies that stress sanctification; it is often there, but is sometimes limited to freedom to obey the law, not out of coercion, but out of love.

Here we shall be concerned with three themes that interpret the significance of justifying work as it pertains to a Christian's moral life. One is the freedom to love, to meet joyfully and spontaneously the needs of the neighbor. In faith man is open to the saving love of God, which flows through him to serve the neighbor in love. The Christian is not compelled to follow Christ or to obey his teachings as a new form of extraneous law imposed upon him; he can go beyond doing freely what the law requires in personal relations to genuinely new and healing acts of love. "Faith active in love" is the theme of Luther's ethics of Christians (though there are also ethics of law which the Christian, like all men, has to uphold).

The second stress is a contemporary one. It is the freedom to be open to the future, to obey freely as the demands of the occasion seem to require. In Christian existentialist ethics the openness to the world, to the future, is the dominant theme. There is little or no interpretation of the order of that world, determined by divine sovereignty, pressing upon the Christian and requiring his conformity to it. There is little or no guidance to be sought from the moral tradition, since to seek it tempts one to revert to legalism, works-righteousness, and the denial of the freedom God has enabled. There is no turning to the past for the authoritative models of conduct. To be a Christian is to be free for the present and the future. We shall discuss Rudolf Bultmann's ethics as an example of this theme.

Whereas Luther can affirm that man is *simul justus et peccator*, and sometimes put the weight of emphasis on the side of our justification rather than sin (though no one needs to be reminded how aware he was of lurking sin and the need for daily repentance), others are more impressed with the power and continuity of sin in the Christian life. They remind us that in human social life we find sin and evil to be main facts of life, and that the moral life of the Christian is always a struggle against them. *Simul peccator et justus,* with accent on the sin, does not vitiate the significance of Christian freedom; one can live with and fight against sin and evil in the

pragmatic way that they require with the assurance that God forgives,
and that his Kingdom shall come at the end of history. Reinhold
Niebuhr's Christian ethics will provide an occasion to explore this
theme.[1]

Certainly neither Luther nor Niebuhr believed that the gift of
freedom was the only gift of grace through Christ.[2] We have noted
in Chapter III how a new life of love is one of the major fruits of
justification and sanctification in Luther, and we shall discuss that
theme more fully here. We also noted how Niebuhr wrote about the
"infinite possibilities of organizing life beyond the center of the self"
that are "always the fruits of grace." Indeed freedom is never an end
in itself in the Christian life as it is discussed in Christian theology; it
is freedom to love, freedom to be open, freedom to be an active
participant in the struggles of life.

FREEDOM TO LOVE

The gospel frees man from bondage to the law. It gives him an
inner freedom from domination by the powers of this world. By his
trust in God he becomes inwardly free. He is free to obey the civil
law without external coercion, for he knows it and its administrators
to be servants of God through the rule of the earthly order. But he is
also free to love the neighbor, to be Christ to the neighbor, meeting
his deepest needs freely in Christian love. This, in part, is the
message of Luther to the Christian man: You have been given

---

[1] One could use eschatology as a concept for differentiating patterns of Christian ethical thought. In this and the preceding two chapters there are different
accents on that theme. The writers we discuss here tend to stress the futuristic
conception of the Kingdom of God, though not denying its present significance.
The Kingdom will come at the end of history, says Reinhold Niebuhr, and the
life in history remains a struggle between good and evil. Similar stresses can be
found in Bultmann and some who are deeply indebted to him. In the second
chapter we found the present reign or Lordship of Christ emphasized; to be sure,
history is not completely under God's rule, but the assertion that in the resurrected Christ he does rule is a major theme. In Chapter III, we have a less clear
consensus of eschatological thought, though particularly Schleiermacher and the
Catholics share a stress on the efficacy of Christ's Kingdom in personal and
historical experience.

[2] To avoid the typing of ethics under the headings of our chapters, it is
important to indicate that the theme under discussion is to be found in writings
that are discussed in other chapters. We have noted the claims for freedom in
some Catholic thought, and also in Barth. Calvin's section on Christian liberty is
not to be forgotten. Thus, the reader is again asked to recall that we are studying
themes, and not typologizing authors.

freedom in your faith in God's grace made known in Jesus Christ; shed abroad, then, the love you have received.

Any venture into the tangled currents of Luther interpretation is done with trepidation on the part of those for whom Luther research is not a large part of their vocations. One finds characterization of an existentialist Luther in Gogarten, a conservative Luther in Elert and Künneth, a "Barthian" Luther in Helmut Gollwitzer, and yet another Luther in Wingren and other Swedish scholars, already to oversimplify the complexity.[3] One finds charges and countercharges of warping the texts: the discreditation of men like Troeltsch, and the charge of psychologizing against Bainton, not to mention Erik Erikson. But, nonetheless, one finds a fairly clear picture of at least portions of Luther's ethic by looking at two themes, law and gospel, and man as sinner and justified, both of which lead to the affirmation of the Christian's freedom, and his consequent power to love.

Luther's treatment of law and gospel is of basic importance for understanding his view of the Christian life. The law, for Luther, is God's means for accomplishing two things for man,[4] neither of which can justify man or make him right and acceptable before God. The law is powerless to save man, to redeem him, but it does act as a restraint of sin, "to bridle the wicked." This is its first, or civil, use. The second use is "theological," or "spiritual," which is "to increase transgressions," "that is to say, to reveal unto a man his sin, his blindness, his misery, his impiety, ignorance, hatred and contempt of God, death, hell, the judgment and deserved wrath of God."[5] The law accuses man of his sins, and through it God prompts men to turn in confession and repentance to him. But "it justifieth not," for justification is the gift of God's grace given to man. To be noted here

---

[3] Friedrich Gogarten, *Der Mensch Zwischen Gott und Welt* (Heidelberg, 1952), Werner Elert; *The Christian Ethos* (Philadelphia, 1957); Walter Künneth, *Politik Zwischen Daemon und Gott* (Berlin, 1954); Helmut Gollwitzer, "Zur Einheit von Gesetz und Evangelium," *Antwort* (Zollikon-Zurich, 1956), pp. 287–309; Gustaf Wingren, "Evangelium und Gesetz," *ibid.*, pp. 310–22, and *Luther on Vocation* (Philadelphia, 1957). These are obviously but a small sample of the materials that pertain directly to Luther's ethics.

[4] We need not get involved in the debate about a third use in Luther, i.e., counsel to Christians in the new life, though it is important for ethics.

[5] Luther, *Commentary on the Epistle to the Galatians* (1535 [London, 1953]), p. 298. This commentary and the treatise "Against Latomus" (1521), *Luther's Works* (Philadelphia, 1958), Vol. 32, pp. 137–260, are major sources of Luther's discussion of law and gospel.

is Luther's concern for man's salvation; he is not primarily concerned for what Christian morality is to be, though obviously law in its civil use has a moral function for mankind as a whole under the rule of God.

The gospel, then, proclaims man's freedom from the law—of sin, of wrath, of death. What is given man in faith in the gospel? In the sermon, "Two Kinds of Righteousness" (1519), Luther differentiates "alien righteousness" from "proper righteousness," both of which are given by God. Alien righteousness is "instilled in us without our works by grace alone," and sets itself against the power of original sin. Through it, "Christ daily drives out the old Adam more and more in accordance with the extent to which faith and knowledge of Christ grow." It "makes progress, and is finally perfected at the end through death."[6] The second kind of righteousness is the product of the first, "actually its fruit and consequence," the "fruit of the Spirit" as this is enumerated by St. Paul in terms of love, joy, peace, patience, and self-control. It is "that manner of life spent profitably in good works," which Luther here spells out as "slaying the flesh and crucifying the desires with respect to the self," as "love to one's neighbor," and as "meekness and fear toward God." It "follows the example of Christ and is transformed into his likeness" as it hates the self and works through love to seek the good of another.[7]

In "Against Latomus" (1521), he states the theological ground for this righteousness in more technical terms. The gospel, he says, "teaches and preaches" two things, the righteousness of God and the grace of God. The gift of righteousness heals the corruption of nature, and is set against original sin; grace is the companion of righteousness and is the mercy and good favor that God bestows in faith, against his wrath. By God's *grace* everything is forgiven, and sin is dead, though not everything is healed through the gift of *righteousness*. God, by grace, treats sin as "non-existent and as expelled"; yet in human nature sin continues, which the gift of righteousness works to purge away and overcome.[8]

Neither righteousness nor grace is the work of a gospel that man possesses. Both are God's, both exist as objective to the self. Right-

[6] *Martin Luther, Selections* . . . , ed. J. Dillenberger (Garden City, N.Y., 1961), p. 88.
[7] *Ibid.*, p. 89, p. 88.
[8] *Luther's Works*, Vol. 32, pp. 226–29.

eousness is not infused, nor is it an "impulse" that extends its influence. It is always God's righteousness and not man's, and such overcoming of sin as occurs by it is God's work, not nature's or man's. The grace that regards sin as dead is God's grace; it is God's treatment of sin through his love and mercy, and not man's qualities of life that free him from the wrath of God.

Luther, like Calvin and others, uses the time-honored but ambiguous language of "participation" to explain man's relation to Christ and his righteousness. We *participate in* God's righteousness granted in Christ. It exists as independent of us, it has its reality objectively. But by baptism and faith we partake of it; we are in communion with it. This is to be conceived, then, as an internal rather than external relation to it. By being in communion with it or partaking of it, God's righteousness affects our lives. By his grace we are freed from his wrath, by his righteousness we are enabled to do works of love.

As we have noted, man is not made sinless, and although Luther can speak of "progress" in our proper righteousness, it is not to be conceived in terms such as we have seen in Schleiermacher or in Roman Catholics. One cannot conceive, in Luther's pattern of thought, of something called sin being replaced in terms of consciousness or a new form of the habits by something called righteousness. Writing about the sacrament of baptism, he says, "Sin in us after baptism is truly sin, but only according to substance, and not in its quantity, quality or action, for it is wholly passive. The motion of anger and of evil desire is exactly the same in the godly and the godless, the same before grace and after grace; but in grace it can do nothing, while outside of grace it gets the upper hand." Romans 8:2 is quoted by Luther to support this, just as it is quoted by Thomas Aquinas, Häring, and others to support their interpretations of the new life or new law of life. Sin loses its "tyrannic power, it can do nothing"; death impends, but since it has lost its sting it can neither harm nor terrify.[9]

The man of faith is totally sinner in that he continues to deserve the wrath of God, though God in his grace (mercy) does not count man's sin against him. But he is also totally justified because God treats him in His grace as though his sin were dead.

[9] *Ibid.*, p. 207.

Insofar as his "alien" righteousness (the gift of righteousness) is accompanied by "proper" righteousness (the fruits of the Spirit), man is overcoming sin as he is transformed into Christ's likeness. Thus he is also partly a just man, and partly a sinner. To summarize the distinction, one can say that with reference to God, man is objectively totally sinner and totally justified at once; with reference to his own subjectivity, his own spiritual, fleshly, and moral life, the Christian is partly sinner and partly justified.[10]

Though man is *simul justus et peccator*, "our righteousness is much more plentiful than our sin, because the holiness and righteousness of Christ our mediator doth far exceed the sin of the whole world, and the forgiveness of sins which we have through him is great, so large, and so infinite, that it easily swalloweth up all sins, if so be that we walk according to the Spirit."[11] The point of central reliance is made clear: the plentitude of God's work in Christ, of his righteousness and grace, is so great that man can walk in freedom. The liberty of the Christian is not like the liberty the emperor grants the Pope in providing certain immunities and privileges; nor is it the antinomian liberty to teach and do what one pleases, nor is it "civil" liberty. It is freedom from the wrath of God, freedom from bondage to the law, from sin, death, and "the power of the devil." The law loses its power to drive men to desperation; sin, though real, is not counted against man; death has lost its terror, "for Christ has made me free."[12] Thus the freedom of the Christian is an inward freedom by which he "is a perfectly free lord of all, subject to none" and "a perfectly dutiful servant of all, subject to all"[13] at one and the same

---

[10] This is a tricky notion in Luther. Under one aspect man is totally two different things which common sense seems to exclude from each other, under another aspect he is partly each. The difficulty is confounded, since Luther uses the pattern in different contexts with different shades of meaning; e.g., "Therefore in respect of the flesh we are sinners; but in respect of the Spirit, we are righteous: and so we are partly sinners and partly righteous" (*Commentary on Galatians*, p. 499). I am indebted to the unpublished dissertation, *Simul Justus et Peccator: A Study in the Theologies of Martin Luther and Reinhold Niebuhr* (Yale University, 1962), by Georg Hermann Dellbrügge, for the clearest analysis of this theme that I have encountered. Cf. Barth's treatment in *Church Dogmatics*, IV/2 pp. 57 ff., where he stresses the *"total-total"* character of the life of the Christian.

[11] *Commentary on Galatians*, pp. 499–500.

[12] *Ibid.*, pp. 441–44.

[13] From "A Treatise on Christian Liberty," Luther, *Three Treatises* (Philadelphia, 1943), p. 251.

time. The inward man is made free by his faith in the saving Word of God, by his union with Christ.

How is this freedom expressed? What difference does Christian freedom make to the deeds of men in the world? Two answers to these questions are of concern here. First, he is inwardly disposed to do what the law in its civil use and his vocation in society require him to do in a different spirit from what was once the case. Second, he acts out his faith in love to the neighbor in a spirit and manner that exceed the requirements of law and order. Basic to both is a new disposition, a new motivation, a new heart. Thus the ethic of Christians, for Luther, is basically a *Gesinnungsethik,* an ethic of disposition; it is not first of all a new external law of life (though in Chapter V we see how Christ is the pattern of the Christian life.) "Putting on Christ according to the Gospel, consisteth not in imitation, but in a new birth and a new creation. . . . Now Christ is no law, no lawgiver, no work; but a divine and an inestimable gift."[14]

The Christian man, like others, however, is placed by the ordering of God within certain social institutions in which he holds an "office" that is the place of his earthly vocation. The responsibilities given to man by his vocation constitute what Brunner calls the "sphere" of his obedience to God. He functions as a mask of God, as an agent of God's ruling work through God's law. Thus every man, Muslim or Christian, Catholic or Lutheran, has a morally significant function in the divine economy for the preservation of the world. Institutions like the state and the family, and what some contemporary sociologists call "roles" and "statuses" in those institutions, such as legislator and father, serve the sovereign God in his ordering activity. The dignity of these institutions and of human functions in them is not limited to a range of sociological necessity, nor even to a range of moral necessity. Social and moral necessities have a theological dignity and function; it is God whom man serves in his proper fulfillment of his duties and labors.

What might differentiate the Christian from the unbeliever in his office? Gustaf Wingren states it in these terms: "In the matter of vocation God's work is primarily ethical. He changes the character of it when the person who occupies the office, from having been 'flesh,'

---

[14] *Commentary on Galatians,* p. 340. Cf. Calvin's work, where the gift and the new law of life are more clearly unified, so that there is a third use of the law, *Institutes,* Book II, Ch. 7, esp. section 12.

has become 'spirit.' "[15] The outward act may not be altered; it is under the realm of God's law. But faith is active in the Christian's obedience. "Faith is concealed under obedience to commandment, but it is active and effects obedience."[16] For one thing the Christian knows that it is God who calls him to obedience in his work, and it is ultimately God whom he serves and obeys. This knowledge of the mercy of God enables man to do freely what God's law requires.

But partaking of the righteousness of God introduces another element. This "variable element is love, which can freely go its way, since it is God. The love of the new man, which shapes his 'use' of his office, is a form of God's new creation in the world."[17] In his treatise on Temporal Authority (1523), Luther describes what this might mean to the Christian prince.

He must give consideration and attention to his subjects, and really devote himself to it. This he does when he directs his every thought to making himself useful and beneficial to them; when, instead of thinking, "The land and people belong to me, I will do what best pleases me," he thinks rather, "I belong to the land and the people, I shall do what is useful and good for them. My concern will be not how to lord it over them and dominate them, but how to maintain them in peace and plenty." He should picture Christ to himself, and say, "Behold, Christ, the supreme ruler, came to serve me; he did not seek to gain power, estate, and honor from me, but considered only my need, and directed all things to the end that I should gain power, estate, and honor from him and through him. I will do likewise, seeking from my subjects not my own advantage but theirs. I will use my office to serve and protect them, listen to their problems and defend them, and govern to the sole end that they, not I, may benefit and profit from my rule." In such manner should a prince in his heart empty himself of his power and authority, and take unto himself the needs of his subjects, dealing with them as though they were his own needs. For this is what Christ did to us (Phil. 2:7); and these are the proper works of Christian love.[18]

---

[15] Wingren, *Luther on Vocation*, p. 67.

[16] *Ibid.*, p. 74. I believe Wingren's interpretation of Luther on these matters is very perceptive.

[17] *Ibid.*, p. 150. Cf. "Christian Liberty," in *Three Treatises*, p. 271: "These two sayings, therefore are true: 'Good works do not make a good man, but a good man does good works; evil works do not make a wicked man, but a wicked man does evil works;' so that it is always necessary that the 'substance' or person itself be good before there can be any good works, and that good works follow and proceed from the good person."

[18] "Temporal Authority: To What Extent It Should Be Obeyed," in *Luther's Works*, Vol. 45 (Philadelphia, 1962), p. 120.

Christian love, the inner new birth of the Christian, thus changes the prince's use of his office. What God provides as an "office" in his creation, is altered in its purposes by the work of the Christian who uses it with a new intention as a result of God's redemption. The justice meted out by the Christian prince may be no different from that meted out by the pagan, but it is inwardly moved by Christian love. What happens to mighty princes happens to lowly parents and soldiers as well. The new man in Christ serves God and the neighbor through his duties.

While much of the new life is expressed in and through the orders of the natural social world, love also "breaks through law, it is a spontaneous action, done in the freedom of faith, effected in pure gladness toward one's neighbor." The new man in Christ is "spontaneous, free and outgoing." "His freedom is God's own freedom from rules. His love is Christ working through him. His joy is the Holy Spirit dwelling in his heart."[19] The new man, always also the old, loves freely. "Therefore, in all his works he should . . . look to this one thing alone, that he may serve and benefit others in all that he does, having regard to nothing except the need and the advantage of his neighbor."[20] There is a specific time and place of service, a specific condition of the neighbor, a specific need. This cannot be anticipated, nor built into one's normal duties under the law. Christian love meets that need. The Christian will acquire funds to aid those in need; the stronger will serve the weaker; each will care for the other, bearing one another's burdens. "Lo, this is a truly Christian life, here faith is truly effectual through love; that is, it issues in works of the freest service cheerfully and lovingly done, with which a man willingly serves another without hope of reward, and for himself is satisfied with the fullness and wealth of his faith."[21]

A study of Luther's ethics impresses one in several ways. First, while the inner freedom given in faith, the freedom that comes with the knowledge of a merciful God, has ringing tones of spontaneity and joy, it is clearly not freedom without direction. In some respects it is not so different from Augustine and later Catholics as one might have been led to expect. In Christ man is made free to do what the law requires him to do in any case; he fulfills his duties in a place God has given him, but now as an expression of God's righteousness

---

[19] Wingren, *op. cit.*, p. 204.
[20] "Christian Liberty," in *Three Treatises*, pp. 275–76.
[21] *Ibid.*, p. 276.

given to him. There is an external order of obligations given in the world that is normally not violated or broken down in Christian freedom. To be sure, the interpretation of the grace and righteousness of God, and the way in which man partakes of them, is very different, but in terms of the liberty to conform to what creation and law require for human preservation or for man's temporal ends, the similarities are impressive. In Luther's writing, somehow through the vitality of his rhetoric one gets a more vivid sense of that freedom; this is abetted by his distinction between the "inner" and "outer" man, a distinction not found in St. Thomas and other Catholics. The elaboration of the nature of man one finds in St. Thomas is not present; thus the explication of the way God's work issues finally in and through human acts is neither as refined nor as precise in Luther. But even for Luther it is freedom to obey God as he requires man to act in accord with the needs of society.

For Luther, liberty issues in works of love; God's love brings freedom into being, and is freely shed abroad in the deeds of the Christian. In the Catholic writers we reviewed previously, love is also the expression of the new life. Romans 8:2, as we noted, finds its way as a crucial text in both Catholics and Luther. Catholic writers, to be sure, make love a new law; a law written on the heart as well as in Scripture; this love generally avoids saying, "Love freely." But nonetheless love, God's love in and through man in faith, gives the end and the shape of Christian moral behavior. Luther did not use the Aristotelian pattern of virtues to program the ways in which love is formed in the self or is the means of its embodiment. The good man does good deeds; the "substance" of the person must be renewed. But the delineation of that substance is neither as refined nor as clear in Luther. There is less definition of the sieve through which love is to be directed, and this certainly makes for a greater sense of spontaneity and freedom. Whether this is finally due to lack of interest on Luther's part, to the perception of a theological fault in portraying the self in such intricate terms, or to the overwhelming sense of new life Luther had, is not for us to decide.

Luther is not completely freed from the Catholic view of two ends of man, the supernatural and the temporal; at least he too works with a pattern of double possibilities and requirements, God's gospel and his law. God's law in its broad civil use must be kept, indeed it will be kept under his sovereignty. Whether the man who fulfills it participates in Christ's righteousness or not makes no necessary difference to the actual deeds required, though, as we have seen, the believer's intention is altered and as a consequence his deed may be changed. Is this very different from the Catholic view in which grace moves men to meet the requirements of natural life, though it does not radically alter that life? The similarities are worth emphasizing. There is a penetration of righteousness, or sanctifying grace, into the moral intentions and ends of man for which some claims are made about its moral effects. For the Catholics this leads to a growth in merit, which abounds to the achievement of the end of eternal blessedness; for Luther, obviously, faith alone is sufficient for salvation.

But the moral life of Christians rings with liberty and love in Luther. This is an ethic of ends only in the sense that the end of the neighbor's need is to be met; it is not tied to the fulfillment of man's own natural end. It is primarily an ethic of intention, of disposition; the Christian is disposed to love as God's love is given to him and flows through him. Christ is a pattern for the Christian life, to be sure, and the teachings of Jesus give a guidance to new life in faith, but the new birth is the primary fact of the Christian life. This ethic of inner intention (to love) in subsequent Lutheran ethics rarely is violated as the ethic for Christians. The Christian life above all things ought not to fall into legalism.[22] Thus, though Christians are dutifully to fulfill their vocational and civil obligations, they are not to use the revelation of God in Christ as a scheme for moral formation of the self or for social ethics.[23] What God has done for man in Christ is to enable man to love the neighbor freely. This makes the ethic of Christians in the personal sphere (that is, in person-to-person relations) highly "situational" or "contextual," to use modern terms. Both casuistry and careful analysis of the neighbor's situation and its causes are, or can be, omitted.[24]

[22] I heard an eminent biblical scholar open a lecture criticizing the state-folk Lutheran Church of Sweden with the apt comment, "The most successful thing the Swedish Church has done in the past fifty years is to convince the Swedish people that they ought not to be Pharisees."

[23] The most recent Lutheran essay I have seen that does seek to move from the gospel (not the law) to social ethics is Gunnar Hillerdal, *Kyrka och Social-etik* (Lund, 1960), but this is an unusual effort.

[24] Brunner's important book, *The Divine Imperative* (Philadelphia, 1947), is, in my opinion, basically in the Lutheran tradition in its structure. On the one side we have the orders of creation, the work of God the Creator; on the other side the gift and command of love. The spheres or orders provide the structure

But certainly for Luther, love was a power that had intention and direction; freedom issued in this love. Christ is example as well as gift. In contrast to this, modern Lutheran existentialist ethics, such as one finds in Bultmann or Knud Løgstrup opts for the freedom to be open to the present and future in a differently accented way.

FREEDOM FOR THE PRESENT AND THE FUTURE

What should the Christian do? Be free for the future and the present. Not merely: "Do what the law requires freely," but "Be as free as you have been made by faith." One must obey, but obedience is made radical in the concrete situation of the present; it is doing what the moment or the occasion requires. Is there a Christian ethic, in the sense of a specific pattern of life to be actualized in Christians? No. Jesus, even in the command to love, did not intend to establish "for love a particular program of ethics."[25]

A sentence from Rudolf Bultmann provides a text for this theme of Protestant ethics. "Christ is the end of the law in that he gives man the freedom to live on a future basis and to live for the future, released from his past and from himself."[26] In the context of discussing, not moral life, but the concern of his church for "pure doctrine," Bultmann makes another statement about this freedom, "The only person who remains true to the past is one who preserves a freedom

---

within which the interpersonal love can take place. E.g., "As Creator, God requires us to recognize and adjust ourselves to the orders He has created, as our first duty; as Redeemer, as our second duty, He bids us ignore the existing orders, and inaugurate a new line of action in view of the coming Kingdom of God" (p. 208). This new line is finally I-Thou relations of love, in my judgment of Brunner. A discussion of the implications of the doctrine of God, the "two hands" of Creator and Redeemer, I omit here, but suggest that the gulf between the two Reformers, Calvin and Luther, is still with us in the distinctions between the ethics of Barth for whom God is Redeemer-Creator, and Brunner and the Lutherans for whom creation and redemption appear to be virtually discretely different acts, both in time and in space.

[25] Bultmann, *Jesus and the Word* (New York, 1934), p. 110. See also in Knud Løgstrup, *Den Etiske Fordring* (Copenhagen, 1958), Ch. V, "Gives der en kristelig etik?" pp. 122–32, in which he also answers "No." There is a radical demand which Jesus knows, but the point of it is that God demands obedience and this demand comes not through a special Christian ethic, but through man's life in the world. Løgstrup acknowledges indebtedness to Gogarten and Bultmann. The contemporary emphasis on *secularity* has Gogarten and Bultmann as two of its major sources.

[26] From "Christ the End of the Law," in R. Bultmann, *Essays* (New York, 1955), p. 64.

for the future, i.e., who remains open to the freedom of God. . . ."[27]
In a way comparable to Luther, the freedom of the Christian is to be
active in love but, in some contrast to Luther, the moral content of
love is spelled out in absolutely situational terms. "The man of faith
is free for love, which opens his eyes to what God requires of him in
the moment."[28]

The significance of the work of Christ for the moral life in this
perspective is clearly located in the new disposition, the new stance or
position toward the world, that is made real in faith. It is the posture
of freedom, of "having and not having," and of love. It is, in Troeltsch's distinction, a *Gesinnungsethik,* an ethic of disposition, rather
than as *Objektivethik,* an ethic which provides norms or patterns of
moral behavior.[29] It makes ethics refer to the state of the moral
subject, the moral person, rather than to the ends of action that are
to be sought, the clarification of goals and appropriate means toward
their achievement. It eschews all formation of specific or detailed
imperative assertions on various grounds: they appear to be foreign to
the saving Word of Scripture; they become a new law, which enslaves
man to the past; they violate both freedom and love. Faith makes
man free and able to love. Evidence for this interpretation of
Bultmann is not difficult to compile.

What man is to do is not revealed to him by an ideal, but by the
command to *love his neighbor.* But the command to love is not, let us
say, an ethical principle from which rules can be derived; I myself at any
given time perceive what it demands at any given time. The demand of
the good is not made clear to me in a system, or an ideal representation,
but confronts me concretely in my encounter with my "neighbor." Who
my neighbor is and what I have to do for him I must perceive for myself
at any given time, and it is in love that I am able to do so. With a keen
and sure eye, love discovers what there is to be done. Love is not so blind
that it would have to weigh up conscientiously all the possibilities and
consequences of an action in a given situation. But that which in view of
these possibilities and consequences is demanded to be done at any given

[27] "On Behalf of Christian Freedom," in Bultmann, *Existence and Faith:
Shorter Writings of R. Bultmann,* ed. Schubert Ogden (New York, 1960), p.
245.

[28] *Ibid.,* "Faith in God the Creator." p. 182.

[29] "Grundprobleme der Ethik," in *Gesammelte Schriften,* Vol. 2 (Tübingen,
1913), pp. 621 ff., and elsewhere.

time cannot be imparted by any theory. On the contrary, it is love that
reveals it. And so man stands unsafeguarded in his decisions.[30]

This quotation clearly dismisses those efforts to formulate ideals, or
principles or theories, or even a conscientious weighing of possibilities
and consequences which might give rational guidance to human
action. All the considerations that men concerned with the objective
effects and ends of activity weigh so heavily are collapsed, and faith,
which is open to the future, expresses itself through love, which in an
unexplained way needs no assistance from "objective ethics." In vain
one looks for even the simple use that Luther makes of Christ as our
example, giving a shape and form to man's response to the neighbor's
need. God's gift in Christ is one of radical freedom which requires an
obedience, but faith and love are sufficient to determine the actions.
"The man of faith understands his now as one who comes out of a
sinful past and therefore stands under God's judgment, but also as
one who is freed from this past, by the grace that encounters him in
the word." Faith "is the momentary act in which he lays hold of
himself in his God-given freedom."[31] In this freedom one can serve
Christ in love, but "naturally, for one who stands in love, an 'ethic' is
no longer necessary, however much brotherly admonition, such as
Paul himself practices, can point out to another his responsibility and
show him what he has to do."[32] "The man of faith is free for love,
which opens his eyes to what God requires of him in the moment."[33]
He lives in the world "as though not" in it. Schubert Ogden rightly
points to the extensive use Bultmann makes of I Cor. 7:29–31.[34]
God grants in faith "a freedom that has the right to dispose of
everything in the world, but for which everything worldly has lost its

[30] From "The Understanding of Man and the World in the New Testament
and Greek World," in *Essays Philosophical and Theological* (New York, 1955),
pp. 79–80. This kind of confidence in freedom and love is reflected in J. A. T.
Robinson's chapter "The New Morality," in *Honest to God* (Philadelphia,
1963); p. 115, for example, "Love alone, because, as it were, it has a built-in
moral compass, enabling it to 'home' intuitively upon the deepest need of the
other, can allow itself to be directed completely by *the situation*. It alone can
afford to be utterly open to the situation. . . ." Italics added.
[31] From "The Concept of Revelation in the New Testament," *Existence and
Faith*, p. 87.
[32] From "Paul," *ibid.*, p. 145.
[33] From "Faith in God the Creator," *ibid.*, p. 182.
[34] "Introduction," *ibid.*, pp. 19–20.

power of motivation. . . . The only motive of action is love, which as complete surrender presupposes freedom from the world."[35]

Bultmann's ethics are "dispositional" in a particular way. In Chapter III we saw how "disposition" is used by Roman Catholics to describe those persistent tendencies of character that come into being as the self conforms itself to its true end. The virtues are dispositions; the words "moral habits" may almost be used interchangeably with "moral dispositions." But clearly Bultmann rejects any such possibility. Freedom and love are certainly not moral habits or qualities of moral life for him. Indeed the effects of Christ's work are explicitly described as not being moral qualities of the self. The prime significance, it appears, is forgiveness of sin, and not new life in the sense of "new consciousness," Christian virtues, or freedom from sins. "Christian existence takes place *not in 'works,' but in 'faith.'* "[36] There is no Christian morality, as there is no Christian virtue. The Christian message is that "God has revealed himself in the *cross of Christ* as the God of forgiving grace; Christ is the Word of forgiving grace. . . . Where this Word is heard and man responds to it, he is completely pure, and freed from his sin—completely 'just' or *justified.*" This means what, in moral terms? It "means not improved in moral quality, or a bit further advanced in his development on the way to the ideal, but that he has already reached his goal. He has not acquired a certificate of moral maturity, nor is this maturity even in some mysterious way made his own."[37] This appears to rule out even what Luther claims for the effects of man's participation in God's gift of righteousness; the work of Christ here instead is confined to the gift of grace, of forgiveness of sins. It rules out Paul Lehmann's assertion that "the point and goal of the Christian life are 'mature manhood.' " "The *mature* life is the fruit of Christian faith."[38]

Lehmann's case for openness to the future assumes that faith brings human maturity that can be expressed in man's conformity to what God is doing. Bultmann would find this claim to be excessive, partly because the gospel message is so centrally the message of the *cross* of Christ, not his present and actual kingly, priestly, and prophetic rule,

[35] From "Man between the Times according to the New Testament," *ibid.,* pp. 260–61.
[36] From "Humanism and Christianity," *Essays,* p. 156.
[37] *Ibid.,* p. 160.
[38] *Ethics in a Christian Context.* pp. 53–54.

as is the case for Lehmann. And, clearly, Bultmann's views rule out
any consideration of "love as the form of the virtues," as a new moral
habituation such as is central to Roman Catholic Christian ethics.
Justification "is not a moral quality," nor does it confer any on the
man of faith.[39] The signs of the new life are ambiguous. "This
Christian life itself is not a fact that lies before one's eyes, to which
he can appeal and with which he can reassure himself."[40] Christian
moral activity is never the extension of a change in character, consciousness, or ends of action wrought by grace. It is, rather, a life of
hope and a life in obedience to the imperative to love in the situation. The latter point we have already dealt with; it remains to
explicate more about this hope. "But how is this present life that is
given only to faith effective in the believer's concrete existence? It is
effective in hope! That hope is a power that determines the believer's
existence. . . ." It is expressed in Rom. 5:25. The text contains these
memorable phrases: "We rejoice in our hope of sharing the glory of
God." "We rejoice in our sufferings, knowing that suffering produces
endurance, and endurance produces character, and character produces hope." Bultmann comments, "Out of hope comes hope" and
"Hope is a vitality that, by bearing up in affliction and endurance,
becomes conscious of itself and, as it were, comes to itself and discovers its *existentiell* meaning."[41] Christians belong to the new aeon,
but this is to live in a life given only in hope. It is to act in obedience
to God's demand out of love and out of hope.

Certainly Bultmann's eschatology is determinative of his view of
the Christian moral life, and both are in turn functions of his focus
on the Christian message primarily as the forgiveness of sins through
the obedience unto death of Christ on the cross. One cannot have an
ethic of attestation or conformity to the reality of the good that is
present in the ruling, living Christ, nor can one have the life of
conformity to the pattern of the life of Jesus Christ. Bultmann's
Paulinism, and his interpretation of Paul, direct what he says about
the Christian moral life.

But his view of man is also a determinative factor. It appears that
Bultmann's conception of the self shares widely in the Kantian

[39] From "Grace and Freedom," in *Essays*, p. 170.
[40] From "The Concept of Revelation in the New Testament," in *Existence
and Faith*, p. 73.
[41] From "Man between the Times," in *ibid.*, p. 263.

heritage, with its distinction between two aspects of the self, the noumenal, undetermined self, which is the seat of moral decisions, and the conditioned, phenomenal self, which is the accrual of cause-and-effect processes. Any effort to speak of moral qualities of life coming into being from faith in Jesus Christ assumes that the moral self is susceptible to qualification in its persisting, phenomenal characteristics. This is clearly the case with the Catholic view of dispositions or habits that can be brought into conformity with man's true end, and with the Augustinian view that grace can reorient virtues by moving them in accord with the right end. Schleiermacher's conception of influence on consciousness and affections which in turn express themselves in moral activity also stresses the continuities of selfhood that are susceptible to a kind of formation process. While both Catholics and Schleiermacher retain a place for the free act of will, this act has a consistency with the graced natural self, and it is never as radically occasionalistic as is Bultmann's understanding. Bultmann's situational ethics is itself consistent not only with his stress on the work of Christ for man's forgiveness (to the omission of a more positive view of sanctification), but it is also consistent with a view of the self in which the essence of moral action is the free determination of the self in each new act. This free self is not under the obligation to obey reason's formulation of the moral law as in Kant, but it is under the radical obligation to obey God's address through the command of love. But this is a highly formal view of love; it is not "in-principled love," to use Paul Ramsey's phrase. Bultmann views the self as "unstructured," as existing in discontinuous moments of obedience, rather than as a character with qualities of life that, while subject to alteration, is nonetheless persisting and continuous from moment to moment. Grace or mercy frees and commands this "noumenal" self; it does not affect habits or consciousness.

This does not mean that the world in which a person obeys is without any pattern. Actions do not create something out of nothing. "This concrete moment is determined, however, by what are usually spoken of . . . as 'ordinances of creation.' " By this Bultmann does not refer to eternal laws or to predestined configurations of human community. He means "simply the conditions that make my world and my situation a concrete one and keep me from understanding myself and my neighbor as men in general, i.e., from supposing that we have to regard one another solely with respect to the eternal nature of the human spirit."⁴² The orders of creation cannot become the basis for categorical or hypothetical moral imperatives that in turn function as general rules of conduct. They locate man concretely in a place of obedience. Løgstrup shares this same approach and with greater subtlety and literary richness analyzes the actual conditions in which the moral life is lived in terms of trust and confidence in each other, in which there are the unarticulated demands upon us by virtue of our natural human relationships.⁴³ But these do not become the grounds for general imperatives; the imperative is, following Gogarten, the concrete imperative of the occasions through which God calls man to radical obedience.

One hesitates to speculate on the relationship between an author's intellectual system and his biography, and certainly one dares not make much out of such speculations as are evoked. But in his "Autobiographical Reflections" Bultmann avers "I have never directly and actively participated in political affairs."⁴⁴ In a powerful essay of 1933, "The Task of Theology in the Present Situation," which clearly has the political events of Germany in view, he wrote, commenting on his favorite I Cor. 7:29–31, "This does not mean that faith has a negative relation to the world, but rather that the positive relation that it has to it and to its ordinances is a *critical* one." "Therefore all of the ordinances in which we find ourselves are *ambiguous*. They are *God's* ordinances but only insofar as they call us to service in our concrete tasks. In their mere givenness, they are ordinances of sin."⁴⁵ For Bultmann the critical power of the faith was exercised according to the criterion of love. "The criterion for each one of us is whether, in his struggle, he is really sustained by love, i.e., by the love that not only looks to the future in which it hopes to realize its ideal, but also sees the concrete neighbor to whom we are now bound in the present by all the commonplace ties of life."⁴⁶ This, for Bultmann, meant a particular response, so that he forcefully asserts, "as a Christian, I

⁴² From "The Meaning of the Christian Faith in Creation," in *ibid.*, pp. 222–23; see also pp. 159 ff. See Thomas Oden's chapter in *Radical Obedience, the Ethics of Rudolf Bultmann*, "The Existential Analysis of Human Obligation," pp. 46–76.
⁴³ Løgstrup, *Den Etiske Fordring*, pp. 17–39.
⁴⁴ Bultmann, *Existence and Faith*, p. 286.
⁴⁵ *Ibid.*, p. 160.
⁴⁶ *Ibid.*, p. 163.

must deplore the injustice that is also being done precisely to German Jews. . . ."[47] Such ethics give a critical posture, but one may ask whether an ethics built on Christ's justifying work, an ethics of occasionalism, can ever provide an even tentatively prescriptive social ethics. Is it intrinsically "non-political," or does it leave the political in a Lutheran fashion to God's law? Its only positive function is to be critical, to express criticism out of freedom and love. But it is not a social ethics, and cannot be such on its own theological and philosophical grounds. The Christian message is primarily forgiveness (not an actual new ordering of the world—this is a hope); love is not a prescriptive ethic out of which principles for governing the community are shaped; the Christian life is the freedom of having and not having; love is expressed, not in long-range political considerations, but in the narrow time-and-space field of the moment. Christ is gift of mercy, but not example to the ruler, as he is for Luther.

Thus the significance of the work of Christ for moral life is not to give a pattern to moral activity, not to be the source of a moral teaching applicable to social or personal relations, but to provide the freedom and openness to obey the command of God in the present. In a sense this is an ethics of no-ethics; love knows what to do. It is an ethics of hope and faith; with confidence in forgiveness, in having and not having, man lives his faith. He is free for the future, but he is sinner and lives in the hope of the Kingdom to come. There is no guarantee of moral righteousness in the Christian life, yet Christians are free to be guided by the situation. "Christ is the end of the law in that he gives man the freedom to live on a future basis and to live for the future, released from the past and from himself."

FREEDOM TO BE REALISTIC AND PRAGMATIC

What should the Christian do? He is free to pursue the cause of justice, informed and judged by love, in the human moral struggle. He is free to be guided by the Christian norm of love in determining his conduct, and in influencing the conduct of institutions. His freedom and confidence should be tempered by a recollection of his natural finitude and of his sinful drag toward pride, but nonetheless he can trust in the merciful forgiveness of God, and have confidence

47 *Ibid.*, p. 165.

in the Kingdom which is to come. Thus he is free to be calculative, prudent, courageous, and pragmatic.

This theme is seen by interpreting Reinhold Niebuhr's ethics. One distinctive note sounded of Niebuhr, in contrast to Bultmann and Luther, is the more positive role that the moral teachings of Jesus and the self-sacrificial love made known on the cross have in giving guidance to Christian freedom and Christian hope in moral activity. We shall explore some reasons why Niebuhr is able to have "objective ethics" and not merely an ethic of intention within the Christological framework of Christ's justifying work. But surely the most significant reason must be stated at the outset. Niebuhr is concerned primarily with moral questions, with a formulation of Christian ethics that gives guidance to activity of men and institutions in history. It is important to note that Niebuhr moves toward positive or constructive ethics, and particularly social ethics, from the work and significance of Christ, in contrast to Bultmann and Luther who rely more heavily on the ordinances of creation to provide content and direction for social ethics. In this respect, Niebuhr is an heir to the great American social gospel tradition. His focus of attention is not concentrated as exclusively upon the saving work of Christ, or upon the salvation of man from sin and bondage. In a sense he assumes and explicates the fact that God has made known his redemption of man in Jesus Christ only to get on with the task of delineating the meaning of Christians' moral responsibility in society. Niebuhr is primarily an *ethical* thinker.

Three facets of the significance of Christ's work for the Christian's moral experience can be isolated in order to interpret the way in which one moves toward a more positive ethic than one finds in Løgstrup and Bultmann, and even Luther. These are the work of grace as mercy and forgiveness or, in Niebuhr's words, "the power of God over man"; the work of grace as "an accession of resources, which man does not have of himself, enabling him to become what he truly ought to be," or the "power of God in man;" and the revelation of a *norm,* of the law of love which is the law of life, to be approximated in the life of community.[48] It is the very positive

---

[48] The quotations are from *The Nature and Destiny of Man,* Vol. II p. 99, in the important chapter "Wisdom, Grace and Power." See Paul Lehmann's study of Reinhold Niebuhr's Christology, in Kegley and Bretall, eds., *Reinhold Niebuhr* (New York, 1956), pp. 252–80.

affirmation of the norm, and in the exercise of it in complex moral situations that Niebuhr moves beyond the simple proclamation of freedom, or the restricted, undeveloped affirmation of love.

What does Niebuhr claim and not claim for "an accession of resources" in Christian faith? When one recalls how Wesley virtually programed the steps and stages of regeneration, and Schleiermacher almost quantified the expansion of God-consciousness, Niebuhr's claims are modest and restricted. Two grounds for this modesty and restriction are of particular importance.

First, he uses a model of the self which does not lend itself to the organic metaphor of Schleiermacher or to the moral psychology of Wesley. The stress on man's capacity for self-transcendence locates man's moral nature not in habits, desire, and consciousness, but in freedom. Indeed, Niebuhr is not interested in formulating the question of man's moral nature in terms that lend themselves to the imagery of growth from a planted seed, or dispositions that can be formed and moved toward their proper end by love. The emphasis on man's self-transcendence notes not the ways in which behavior is determined by previous experiences, nor the cumulative effects of grace and love through the continuities of human life. Rather, it notes the indeterminacies, the discontinuities in human life, or in Niebuhr's language, the life of the human spirit that is not bound by the body or even the mind.

This is a characteristically Reformation note, and in this respect what Niebuhr says does not have a radically different effect on understanding moral life from what Bultmann says. Since man has the capacity for self-transcendence, since man is radically free, one dares not make predictions about how grace will alter persistent patterns of life. To make claims such as we have seen in some other authors assumes that men are determined by certain virtually psycho-physical processes, which in turn make the effects of grace almost predictable and measurable. Thus Niebuhr's claims are restricted.

In contrast to Bultmann, who could assert that in faith the "only motive" of the Christian is love, Niebuhr refuses to make that kind of claim. Bultmann has radical freedom, and yet makes a radical claim for a transformation of motive. Niebuhr's second ground for a limited claim to the effects of "accession of resources" becomes clear at this point: there is no evidence in the moral deeds of Christians or in the effects of the Church in history to warrant great claims for regeneration, even in terms of a new motive. Certainly Bultmann would agree that sin abounds, that man is *simul justus et peccator,* but what is distinctive about Niebuhr is his appeal to historical and behavioral evidences. The contradiction between man and God for him is an internal one; it is located in the conscious willing of man.[49] Man's sin ultimately lies in his unfaith for Niebuhr, to be sure, but its evidences are present in the Christian life in the inability to will the good that one knows. "The question is whether in the development of the new life some contradiction between human self-will and the divine purpose remains. . . . That question would seem to find one answer in logic and another in experience." Niebuhr says that the logic of regeneration would imply the overcoming of this contradiction through the *awareness* of the character of self-love and its incompatibility with the divine will. "This logic," he says, "is at least partially validated by experience. Repentance does initiate a new life. But the experience of the Christian ages refutes those who follow this logic and without qualification."[50] Experience, not just biblical exegesis, is appealed to as evidence for the judgment that the effects of regeneration are restricted; experience dictates modesty in the claims of the Christian.

If the effects of grace are circumscribed and not precisely predictable, what does Niebuhr say that they are? What comes from the "accession of resources," from the "power of God in man"? "Repentance does initiate a new life," he wrote. Clearly, as we shall see, he has more to say about the power of God "over" man than "in" man; he has more to say about forgiveness and hope than he has to say about realization of new life in experience and in history. But there are hints of what Christ in us might mean for moral life. When

---

[49] Rom. 7:13 ff. is interpreted in various ways, and a history of the views of the claims made for regeneration could be written on the ways this text is cited. Thus Niebuhr: "The plight of the self is that it cannot do the good that it intends," on Rom. 7:18 (*Nature and Destiny of Man*, Vol. II, p. 108). Compare Bultmann: "This non-Pauline anthropology—I will refer to it in brief as the subjectivistic anthropology—presupposes that the 'willing' of which Paul speaks is the willing that is actualized in the individual acts of will on the subject who is lord of his subjectivity; in short, it presupposes that the willing is *conscious*. This presupposition is false. For man is not primarily viewed by Paul as a conscious subject; the propensities of man's willing and doing which give him his character are not at all the strivings of his subjectivity" (*Existence and Faith*, p. 150). It is clear that the two theologians disagree on the right use of the passage.

[50] Niebuhr, *Nature and Destiny of Man*, Vol. II, pp. 121–22.

Niebuhr criticizes theologies that "have sought to do justice to the fact that saints nevertheless remain sinners," he accuses them of obscuring "the indeterminate possibilities of realizations of good in both individual and collective life."[51] This suggests that God's gracious love in us might make us sensitive to such possibilities. At another point he says that an examination of individual life and history make it "apparent that there are infinite possibilities of organizing life from beyond the centre of life." These "possibilities are always the fruits of grace (though frequently it is the 'hidden Christ' and a grace which is not fully known which initiates the miracle)." Yet with each such positive affirmation, in the same breath Niebuhr reminds the reader of the infinite possibilities of self-love, of new evil. "Yet the possibilities of new evil cannot be avoided by grace. . . ."[52]

Grace, then, even in the most positive claims made for it, offers or makes known new "possibilities"; it does not permit the observer of life to say, "Lo, here" or "Lo, there" is grace actualized. We are "to understand that the Christ in us is not a possession but a hope, that perfection is not a reality but an intention; that such peace as we know in this life is never purely the peace of achievement but the serenity of being 'completely known and all forgiven.' "[53]

To be "completely known and all forgiven," to have Christ as a hope, is of great significance for the moral life. "The power of God over man" is clearly the basis of forgiveness and hope, and gives Christians a freedom from fear, an assurance of mercy, and a capacity to deal with contingencies in their own morally ambiguous terms. There is an assurance of the meaningfulness of human existence even in the events that shake human confidence. In the suffering love of the cross there is a revelation that can be discerned by faith. "This love is the revelation of a divine mercy which overcomes the contradictions of human life."[54] "It is recognized by the eyes of faith as the point where the heavens are opened and the divine mystery is disclosed and the love of God toward man shines down upon him; and man is no longer afraid, even though he knows himself to be involved in the crucifixion."[55] The significance of Christian faith in

[51] *Ibid.*, p. 125.
[52] *Ibid.*, p. 123
[53] *Ibid.*, p. 125.
[54] Reinhold Niebuhr, *Faith and History*, p. 135.
[55] *Ibid.*, p. 144.

the resurrection points toward a life of hope, for "it is persuaded that a divine power and love have been disclosed in Christ, which will complete what man can not complete; and which will overcome the evil introduced into human life and history by man's abortive effort to complete his life by his own wisdom and power."[56]

These quotations point to a central theme in Niebuhr's theological ethics. Moral ambiguities remain in history in spite of grace; individuals do not overcome the ultimate contradiction between God's will and self-love. But God's love revealed on the cross provides the grounds of assurance that the ultimate power is love, is good; that this love is patient, merciful, and forgiving; that in the end the evils of human life will be overcome by the love of God in his Kingdom. This belief in, or this revealed understanding of, God's love provides the inner freedom to deal with contingencies precisely as such, and not assume that they can be overcome with some absolute eternal earthly good. It provides the clear eyes by which Christians can see historical evils without illusions, and can use the appropriate means to restrain or overcome them. It provides a liberation from self-justification, from the desire to be perfect in the eyes of self or of others. The revelation of God's grace, his love, gives a *knowledge* which in turn has its effects upon the inward man's stance or basic disposition toward the world; he can be realistic and hopeful at once; he can be pragmatic without illusions about fulfilling the ultimate good in his relative and temporal efforts. Grace does provide a *disposition* toward the world out of which men's moral actions come.

There is yet another significance of the revelation of God's love which Niebuhr reiterates over and over again. "Significantly the same suffering love, the same *Agape* of Christ which reveals the divine mercy is also the *norm of a new life*."[57] This is the point where his ethics goes beyond Luther's, Løgstrup's, and Bultmann's. Bultmann has love—but it is assumed to be a disposition more than a norm, an almost self-sufficient insight-giving power that works through faith from within the self toward the neighbor. To Løgstrup's question, "Is there a Christian ethic?" in the sense of an objective, normative ethic, Niebuhr answers "Yes," not "No." A norm is revealed, a law of

---

[56] *Ibid.*, p. 150.

[57] *Ibid.*, p. 144. Italics added. Many more citations of this point could be made.

love which is the law of life.[58] Luther finds that the command to love calls us to repentance, as does Niebuhr, and that Christ is example as well as gift. But Niebuhr makes more careful and skillful use of the normative character of Christian love than does the Reformer. It becomes for him the basis for social ethics as well as for interpersonal relations.

Reinhold Niebuhr's ethics have been the subject of so many intensive examinations and expositions that another treatment of them at length is not necessary here. The point that needs to be reiterated and illustrated here is that the work of Christ is not confined to providing an inward state, a disposition and intention in the self, nor to the provision of a standard in the light of which men know their shortcomings and are repentant, nor to an example for personal conduct. Grace, rather, provides knowledge of what persons and the human community are to be; it gives a goal toward which life is to move, a norm that the consequences of actions are to approximate, a universal principle in the light of which more proximate moral principles are to be judged and informed. Christian ethics for Niebuhr is objective ethics; Christian faith has to do with morality as well as salvation; revelation gives a moral knowledge as well as a restoration of faith; sin is not only man's lack of trust in God, but his isolation from the law of life, the right order of love within the human community.

These generalizations about Niebuhr's work can be seen in his willingness to "translate" theological terms like "nature" and "grace" into "socio-moral" terms. "Grace," he writes, "would correspond to the ideal possibility of perfect love, in which all inner contradictions within the self, and all conflicts between the self and the other are overcome by the complete obedience of all wills to the will of God." " 'Nature,' " he writes, "in this case represents the historical possibilities of justice."[59] Thus nature refers to sinful nature, and grace to an emancipation from sin: the noteworthy stress is that in this translation, nature, grace, and sin have primarily moral connotations. There is an "ideal possibility of perfect love," the substance of which is a

[58] On the point of love as the law of life, see George Lindbeck, "Revelation, Natural Law and the Thought of Reinhold Niebuhr," *Natural Law Forum*, Vol. 4 (1959), pp. 146–51, and Paul Ramsey, "Love and Law," in Kegley and Bretall, eds., *op. cit.*, pp. 80–123. Both authors believe that there is greater affinity between Niebuhr and "natural law" thinkers than he is willing to admit.

[59] *Nature and Destiny of Man*, Vol. II, p. 246.

state of harmony within and between selves. It would be achieved by "obedience" of all "wills" to the "will of God." This achievement is limited in history by the moral ambiguities of life; the historical possibilities enable only justice to be achieved. Love, or harmony, becomes a norm which is one pole of the dialectic, the other being the historical possibilities of justice.[60]

The possibilities of this Niebuhrian perspective for ethics, particularly for social ethics, have been remarkably fruitful and well-executed by Niebuhr himself. The process of moral decision-making becomes an objective one, indeed a highly self-conscious and intellectual one. The Christian, or any other man, is not left with freedom and a disposition to love as the basis of action; he is not left to assume that love alone will bear in on the moral target with accuracy. He does not assume that somehow his consciousness is made new, and that this newness somehow affects his moral choices. On the contrary, the revelation that gives freedom from fear, and some awareness of new possibilities, provides the norm in the light of which calculation can be made in any moral issue. The dialectical process is, no doubt, an independent one; that is, it is a way of reasoning which is itself not part of the revelation, and it is thus subject to its own philosophical scrutiny and criticism. But it does provide a rational procedure to determine what men ought to do. The information to be used is manifold: social analysis, ideas like justice, facts and figures about what the state of affairs is, and most authoritatively self-sacrificial love.

The norm is in some respects specifically Christian in character, though it refers to a universal law of life. It is a norm made clearly known in the crucifixion of Jesus Christ, but is universally applicable in a moral sense because of the conviction that it is the law of life. Niebuhr does not suggest an independent ethics of the orders of creation or of natural law as the basis of social ethical decisions. The work of Christ is not confined to the soteriological realm, as is the case with many European Protestants; for Niebuhr it has significance for our salvation but it is also a revelation of an "ought" of what life is meant to be. Like the social gospel theologians, Niebuhr grounds

[60] Niebuhr's most concentrated development of this dialectic is in the chapter, "The Kingdom of God and the Struggle for Justice," in *ibid.*, Vol. II, pp. 244–86. For a good secondary treatment, see Gordon Harland, *The Thought of Reinhold Niebuhr* (New York, 1960), Part One.

the understanding of the ought in Jesus Christ, but not in a general *logos* theology, as Barth does. The Christocentric ought arises, not from the assertion that "all things are created in and through Him"; indeed, this favorite Barthian text is hardly referred to. The ought is grounded in the absolute commands of Jesus (in *An Interpretation of Christian Ethics*, 1935) and in the crucifixion of Jesus. The reference is historical, not speculatively metaphysical or dogmatically creedal. There, in the crucifixion of Jesus and its meaning, is the specific, contentful norm of life.

But it is also the law of life. Niebuhr seems to want to ground the authority of the norm not only in a historical revelation, but also in life itself. How he would explicate this assertion is unclear and undeveloped. He fulminates against Catholic versions of natural law in several places, generally because he interprets them as ways men seek a "vantage point of the unconditioned in history" and as "untenable faith in the purity of reason."[61] He would probably have to reject the notion of love as a fundamental tendency in the self moving toward the realization of its own true end, since this would seem to be out of place with his view of the self transcending itself. "Law" in this sense of a tendency of a being, or tendencies of beings in relation to each other, would rely more upon continuities and development than upon the decisive acts of men in their freedom. Yet harmony seems to be what love would achieve—within the self, between selves, and between communities. If Niebuhr were willing to explicate such a view, what is revealed in Christ would make clear what men in their created natures move toward.

Not only the requirements of a more elaborate view of tendencies in the self prohibit Niebuhr from detailed explication of this; also the situation of man in sin is so severe that natural tendencies are not morally trustworthy. Thus the stress is on the obligatory norm of self-sacrificial love, rather than an enlightening and enlivening of what man tends to be. Man not only has to have the law of love made known, but he has to will to obey it. While Catholic theologians also stress the will to be what by nature we tend to be, both the natural tendency and the will are affected by grace. Niebuhr trusts neither man's rational ability to know his true end unaided by revelation, nor his directionality or tendency of the self; thus grace does not operate

[61] *Nature and Destiny of Man*, Vol. II, p. 253.

through reorientation of tendencies of the self, but by giving a new revealed norm for the self.

Why do some other Protestant writers eschew such proposals as Niebuhr's that God's love is revealed as a norm? There are many reasons, exegetical and theological. We have seen in the discussion of Bultmann's ethics how on exegetical grounds he persistently refuses to make love a law in the sense of an external obligatory norm, an imperative "ought." More significant is the theological concern that prohibits this kind of move. Most simply, there is a fear that the revelation of God's love taken as an "ought" will become a new form of legalism, a ground for self-righteousness, a denial of the freedom of God's grace. It is a fear that ethics will replace faith at the heart of the Christian gospel. Thus once again in this book we face the question of the relation of faith to morality in life, of theology to ethics in thought.

Is Christianity a "revealed morality"? Or is Christianity the revelation of a salvation for man? There are those, like Luther and Bultmann, who would say the latter, but who would go on to say that the new life is worked out through love in deeds to others. Deeds of love would be the performative consequences of faith. Insofar as there is a norm, as in Luther, it is the example of the one through whom faith comes. Niebuhr is not completely out of step with this: love as law is revealed in the self-sacrificial love of Jesus Christ on the cross. But he goes beyond this to affirm that this *agape* is the objective norm of life, and can function in a logic of judgment-making to bring morally better consequences than would occur without it. One basis for this is the conviction that the revelation in Christ is not confined to mercy, new life, and hope, but is a revelation of the moral law of human existence. Another is that Niebuhr is first of all a theological moralist. He is profoundly concerned with man's temporal good, with the quality and possibilities of existence within historical human communities, and between them. The Christian message is for him not first of all one about salvation and then about morality. It is through and through a message about both salvation and morality at one and the same time.

REFLECTIONS ON THE ETHICS OF JUSTIFICATION

The writers we have discussed in this chapter continue the debate about what claims can and cannot be made for the moral life of Christians, for the life that they have in God's grace. We have noted that they claim less, or at least different things, than do writers discussed in the previous chapter. None of them delineates a theory of the virtues, or of consciousness that becomes the framework for interpreting the significance of a Christian "transformation." None of them differentiates grades and types of sins, and seeks to state how Christian faith alters "habitual sins," and other sets of sins. Yet none of the writers is prepared to say that the grace of God, received in faith by the Christian, makes no difference at all in moral life. Indeed, the claims of Bultmann are as radical in character as the claims of Schleiermacher. Bultmann can write about the new freedom and love with a zestful affirmation of its reality; it is so overwhelming that the Christian does not need "ethics" in the traditional sense of that word. Luther surely proclaims a newness of life for the believer; a new freedom and a new love, as well as a new example in the one who gives the newness of life. But he maintains, as we have seen, the subtle dialectic between justification and sin, between two kinds of righteousness, between the inner and outer man that avoids the language of "replacement" of sin by newness of life, of wrongly formed habits by habits formed by love. Reinhold Niebuhr writes gingerly about the hidden graces, though he probably assumes much about their reality and power. And certainly the knowledge of God's mercy provides a newness of life, as well as a newness of norm for the life of the human community.

On what bases do these differences exist? Where would the issues lie between theologians who claim different effects on moral life for the work of Jesus Christ? We have seen in the critical expositions of previous chapters what some of the issues are. Here, as in previous discussions, one of the issues is Scripture, and how various texts are interpreted when the moral life is in view. One is immediately drawn also into the theological inferences that various writers draw from their biblical interpretation.

If there is a set of texts that seem to be formative for what holds together the writers we have discussed in this chapter, perhaps it is the "having, and yet not having" texts, and the texts that proclaim Christian liberty. In the traditional distinction between "Christ for me" and "Christ in me," the accent is perceptibly on the former. The New Testament is read so that Christ is more a hope than a possession, and perfection is not a reality in man's experience but, rather, is a reality in Christ's own righteousness. Yet the one thing that is a reality in human experience is freedom; to some degree love

can be added to that. Those who have wives are free to live as though
they had none; there is freedom from bondage to the law, freedom to
love, freedom to be realistic and pragmatic.

The "logos" texts that we found so central in the theological ethics
of Barth and Maurice have no such position in Bultmann, Løgstrup,
and Reinhold Niebuhr, nor in the aspects of Luther's thought that
we have dealt with here. If all things are created in and through
Christ, this does not become the ground for a moral life that bears
witness to the universal reality of this redeemed creation. If all things
have been put under his feet, this does not become the ground for a
moral life of attestation to the lordly reign of Christ over all things,
to the reality of Christ in which all things are already redeemed.

Texts that Wesley, Schleiermacher, and Bushnell used to preach
on the possibilities of a transformation of will, consciousness, and
love receive at the hands of men like Luther and Bultmann a more
dialectical treatment. One can say that for the former authors the
benefits of Christ's righteousness become man's righteousness,
though man is always dependent upon God's grace. For Luther, as
we have seen, though man participates in Christ's righteousness, it
does not become something man virtually possesses. What for
Wesley and others becomes a reality in the moral experience of the
Christian, for Bultmann is yet a hope; Bultmann's interpretation of
Paul's doctrine of man prohibits him from making the claims for
Romans 6–8 that one finds in Wesley and others. It is not only in the
interpretation of Paul's view of man that the issues lie, but also in the
interpretation of Pauline eschatology.

Another set of issues pertains to the understanding of the nature of
the moral self, not just in Pauline terms, but in more general
philosophical and ethical terms. Some of the points of contention
have been suggested in the previous chapter, but need to be indicated
once again here. None of these writers has a view of the self that
stresses the continuities between the self and the community, as in
Schleiermacher's view of the self in the Church. None has a view
that stresses the view of habits that becomes the ground for Catholic
interpretations of one of the effects of God's grace. The attention is
centered instead upon the self's capacity to transcend itself, on its
unpredictability and its freedom. In the absence of such a view of the
self as lends itself to specification in terms of consciousness and
habits, grace necessarily has its impact upon the freedom, the self-

transcendence of the self. Yet more is claimed; the self in Christ is able to love. The capacity to love is limited by the continuing rebelliousness and sin of man, and thus for Reinhold Niebuhr it is necessary to have the norm of love present. But for Bultmann particularly, there is a radical claim made for the knowing power of love, for its capacity to do what is right in the situation without disciplined reflection, without casuistry. What this love is—whether a new intention, or a disposition, or an end toward which life moves—is not very clear in Bultmann. It appears to be basically a disposition, but his confidence in it would seem to suggest that it moves the mind to judge properly what the neighbor's need is, as well as moves the will toward the fulfillment of that need.

Freedom and love can be seen as part of the Christian's basic disposition toward the world and the neighbor. He is not enslaved to the world; he has the capacity to seek the good of the other. But such a disposition as the moral counterpart to the knowledge that God has acted to save men is not necessarily a sufficient basis for ethics in the Christian life. We have noted how Luther has Christ as both gift and example, but how Bultmann seems to assume that the gift is sufficient for ethics. We have noted how for Reinhold Niebuhr the event through which forgiveness and newness of life are known also becomes the norm by which actions are to be governed. Niebuhr, with his primary concern for ethics, with his willingness to see the needs of moral man as data for his theological ethics, takes the important step of moving to the possibility of "objective ethics" coming from the work of Christ. In this he was by no means an innovator, for the tradition begins with the New Testament itself: teachings of Jesus are in some sense normative for Christians.

V ∫ JESUS CHRIST,

The Pattern

As Jesus passed on from there, he saw a man called Matthew sitting at the tax office; and he said to him "Follow me." And he rose and followed him.

MATTHEW 9:9

He who does not take his cross and follow me is not worthy of me.

MATTHEW 10:38

Whoever would be great among you must be your servant, and whoever would be first among you must be your slave; even as the Son of man came not to be served but to serve, and give his life as a ransom for many.

MATTHEW 20:26–28

For I have given you an example, that you also should do as I have done to you.

JOHN 13:15

Have this mind among yourselves, which you have in Christ Jesus.

PHILIPPIANS 2:5

And walk in love, as Christ loved us and gave himself up for us.

EPHESIANS 5:2

Be imitators of me, as I am of Christ.

I CORINTHIANS 11:1

For to this you have been called, because Christ also suffered for you, leaving you an example, that you should follow in his steps. He committed no sin; no guile was found on his lips. When he was reviled, he did not revile in return; when he suffered, he did not threaten; but he trusted to him who judges justly.

I PETER 2:21–23

And let us run with perseverance the race that is set before us, looking to Jesus the pioneer and perfecter of our faith, who for the joy that was set before him endured the cross. . . .

HEBREWS 12:1–2

To meditate on the life of Jesus should therefore be our chief study.
THOMAS A KEMPIS, *The Imitation of Christ*, Book I, Ch. I

The moralist is the man with an ideal. . . . The Ideal is given to men in the Person of Christ, who was the real example of it, and the influence of whose Spirit is a creative power of it in the lives of other men. . . . We discover a clear and radiant reflection of a wonderful moral personality in the gospels.
NEWMAN SMYTH, *Christian Ethics*, pp. 49, 52, 53

But it becomes a pious mind to rise still higher, even to that to which Christ calls his disciples; that every one should "take up his cross." . . . It is the destination of all the children of God "to be conformed to him."
JOHN CALVIN, *Institutes*, III, 8, 1

Why this lowliness and humiliation? It was because He who in truth is to be "the pattern" and is concerned only with followers must in one sense be located *behind* men, to drive them on, whereas in another sense He stands *before* them beckoning them on.
SØREN KIERKEGAARD, *Training in Christianity*, p. 232

Jesus summons men to follow Him not as a teacher or a pattern of the good life, but as Christ, the Son of God. . . . Discipleship means allegiance to the suffering Christ. . . .
DIETRICH BONHOEFFER, *The Call to Discipleship*,
(1948 ed.), pp. 50, 75

The Christian life is here understood as a re-enactment from below on the part of men of the shape of the revelatory drama of God's holy will in Jesus Christ. . . . Suffering, death, burial, resurrection, a new life— these are actualities which plot out the arc of God's self-giving deed in Christ's descent and death and ascension; and precisely *this same shape of grace*, in its recapitulation within the life of the believer and the faithful community, is the nuclear matrix which grounds and unfolds as the Christian life.
JOSEPH SITTLER, *The Structure of Christian Ethics*, p. 36

WHAT OUGHT I, A MORTAL, MORALLY SERIOUS MAN, TO DO? "BE A disciple of Jesus; be conformed to Jesus Christ; follow Jesus Christ." This I am invited to do in two ways: by following his teaching (the subject of the next chapter), and by being conformed to his person. "Follow him—the man who was friend to harlots and fishermen; who healed mind and body; who loved even when his wrath was kindled against evil; who was despised and rejected of men; who suffered agony, loneliness, and doubt and yet was obedient to God; who, indeed, was crucified. Follow Him, Jesus Christ, the one depicted in the Gospels. He is the pattern, the example, the ideal, the form of the Christian life." The answer to the personal moral question refers to objective criteria and norms.

"Be conformed to Jesus Christ." Who is Jesus Christ to whom one can be conformed? What meaning does he have, to what form is one to be conformed? Some will answer in one way and some in another.

Be conformed to Jesus. The pattern is the carpenter of Nazareth, the man who had no place to lay his head, the friend of the despised tax-collectors and the "people of the land" who had no significant status in the eyes of men. Be conformed to Jesus, whose actions were loving; who was forgiving, healing, restoring; who had a vision of the Kingdom of God among men and who lived as if that rule now existed. Do what Jesus would do in your situation. Realize the ideal of man and society expressed in his life. He is not the pattern only because he represents a high moral ideal, though some would make this the crucial point. He is the example because he is true man, God's revelation. As Schleiermacher said, he can be the example (*Vorbild*) only because he is the true image of man (*Urbild*).

Be conformed to Jesus Christ. He is the pattern because he was the obedient one. Conform to the pattern of true obedience. This means, some would say, not that you follow what he *did* in terms of the specific deeds; this makes an idol, a deadly principle, out of a living reality. Rather, conform to him, who is obedient love, whose obedience led to humility, to suffering, to death. Be obedient in your situation as Christ was in his; not to copy the particularities of Jesus' empirically observable action, but to embody the particularity of his relation to God and man is what one is called to do. Be as pertinent to your situation as Jesus was to his in each instance of his life, be as concrete and decisive as he was, as humble and loving as he was. The pattern is not his action, but who he was, his relation to God and man.

Conform to Jesus Christ. This, for some, is more mystical than moral, more a way of cultivation of merits against the judgment day than a witness to others. Thus Catholic and Protestant piety often invoke Christ as the image. Who is this Christ, then? He is one who mastered the desires of the flesh, who was earnest and serious and did not participate in foolish levity, whose thoughts were fixed on higher things and who was unprovoked by the things of this world. He is the crucified one—the one whose mortification of the flesh is the model for our own daily crucifixion of the flesh so that our souls may be at peace and our armor strong against temptation. Love him. Conform to him, and receive his aid in striving against evil thought and desire.

Be conformed to Jesus Christ. Conform to the "shape of the engendering deed," God's deed, God's action in Christ. Conform to the reality in which you participate. Christ became man for our sakes, he died and was resurrected. Our old self is dead in Christ, our new self is alive in him. To conform to the action of God in Christ is to do for others and to be for others, in a sense, what Christ has done and been to us and for us. Conform to Christ; this is to re-enact God's action, the whole of the event Jesus Christ.

In the exhortation to be conformed to Christ, then, there are several emphases that can be distinguished. In each, as has been the case in the previous chapters, the definition of Christ and his significance is isolated from the fuller Christology in which it is set. Just as Christ the moral ideal can be set in a wider context of Christ, the *logos*, so Christ the pattern of true obedience can be set in the context of his Lordship and Justification. The relationship to Christ both as pattern and as teacher is discipleship. It includes both imitation and "following after" (*Nachfolge*). Discipleship in this chapter is seen in relation to the man Jesus Christ, his actions and his life; in the next it is seen in relation to the teachings of Jesus.

Christ, as pattern, has been distinguished in four ways. He is the moral example and ideal, whose way of life is the object of imitation or application in contemporary life. He is the form of obedience, suffering, and humility; the inward Christ and his relation to the

Father are the example for us. He is the revelation of the action of God, in God's becoming man, dying, being resurrected, and ascending. We are to recapitulate this and express its implications in the Christian moral life. Finally, and ethically of least significance, we are exhorted to imitate his passion, his mortification; we are to crucify our desires and flesh. This imitation-of-Christ mysticism is erotic (in the technical theological sense); it deals with a way to save our souls and find a way to God and personal blessedness. Each of these emphases will be taken up in turn.

CHRIST, THE MORAL IDEAL

The morally serious Christian has a moral ideal of life, set before him in Jesus Christ. In him there is an example to be followed, to be duplicated. In him there is a model to be imitated. In him there is a way of life that is morally attractive and is valid for all men in all times and places. Christ shows us what life is intended to be.

As moral ideal, Christ is the basis of many inferences. He is a pattern of the life of self-denial and self-sacrifice; we act as Christians insofar as we take up our cross and follow him. He is a pattern of nonresistance to evil; he meekly followed the way of the cross, though in all respects the case against him was unjust. He reveals the highest ideal of the full life, a life of love and service to others, a life of inner unity and consistency, a life of sinlessness. He shows what life can be if it be absolutely honest, pure, and loving. There is a consistency between what he taught and what he lived, and the moral idealism of the two can never be separated. The fact, however, that a *life* manifested the ideal, that deeds showed forth the validity of the teaching, stands as an inspiration to every generation. We are not confronted with a series of moral imperatives, or a bloodless, lifeless picture; rather, we are confronted with a living person, from whose life emanates a spirit that kindles our spirits to follow him. He stands, making us humble for our failure to be shaped by his image, yet beckoning us onward to a realization of life as he embodies it in his person and actions.

Theological ethics in the past forty years, however, has heard no theme more consistently than "Jesus expresses no conception of a human ideal . . ."[1] in its various ramifications. The conception of

---

[1] Bultmann, *Jesus and the Word* (New York, 1934), p. 53.

Jesus as a moral ideal has been thoroughly attacked from various bases. New Testament exegetes have shown his similarities to other men and their teaching, and have questioned the reliability of the records which point to certain aspects of his uniqueness as a person. Theologians have set his life in the context of its revelatory power and meaning; Jesus would not be the Son of God, and thus the one remembered, had he not been crucified and resurrected from the dead. What was *done for us* in and through Christ is the center of the New Testament message. Ethicists have noted that the notion of Christ as the Ideal is too simple for most moral situations. But for popular piety the moral image of Christ in part remains; and even for those who, like the Reformers, do not attend primarily to the ideal, something of its usage persists. The New Testament evidence exists; but the manner of its interpretation differs from time to time and place to place.

No significant theologians have reduced Jesus Christ to only a moral ideal, or to a goal to be sought. The liberal tradition, in its sophisticated representatives, was always concerned with the relation of the moral ideal as goal to the moral ideal as idea or form of reality, and with Christ as one who empowers the Christian life. Certainly in Schleiermacher, the significance of the Redeemer as a means for establishing fellowship with God is greater than the significance of Christ as pattern. Indeed, "the relation of teacher and pupil, like that of pattern and imitation, must always remain an external one," whereas our consciousness as Christians "can only be made plain by reference to 'Christ in us.'"[2] Indeed, Christ's exemplary function rests in ideality; that is, Christ manifests the *idea* of man,[3] but is distinguished from man by "the constant potency of his God-consciousness." Following Schleiermacher, the liberal tradition was more concerned with Christ as the means of forgiveness and new life and power than it was with Christ as moral example. The notion of discipleship to the Master is, in proportion to other Christological themes, by no means dominant. This is the case in Ritschl's thought, as well as Wilhelm Herrmann's *The Christian's Communion with Christ,* and his *Ethik.* Jesus' life and teachings are primarily a means of *life* and *power* for Herrmann; for Ritschl, Christ makes possible our dominion over the world.

[2] F. Schleiermacher, *The Christian Faith,* p. 438.
[3] *Ibid.,* p. 384.

The image of a moral ideal is found in its clearest and most oversimplified form in the popular moral piety. Perhaps the all-time classic of this is *In His Steps*, a book in which a Congregational pastor from Topeka, Kansas, Charles Sheldon, caught the enthusiasm and imagination of readers of at least twenty-two languages. This book is a passionate witness to the transformation of life that would occur if men would fix their thoughts on Jesus, and ask in every decision what Jesus would do; and it fed the moral idealism of its time. But Sheldon never pretended to be a theologian.

In the *Christian Ethics* of Sheldon's older contemporary, Newman Smyth (1843–1925), one finds a more theologically sophisticated interpretation of Christ as the moral ideal. This theme is set in the context not only of Jesus' teaching of the Kingdom of God, but also in his work as the living Spirit in and through whom we have our God-consciousness.[4] But since ethics is defined for Smyth primarily in terms of "ideals," Jesus Christ as the moral ideal *par excellence* is a persistent theme.

Ethics is basically the study of the *summum bonum*. The personal ethical question becomes, "What is your ideal of life?" Indeed, the distinction between man and the lower forms of life lies in his "moral power for forming ideals."[5] The Christian ideal "was no new speculation of the philosophers, no dream of the wise man, no prophetic imagination even of the glory of the Highest. The Christian Ideal was given to men in an historical embodiment of its glory," that is, in Jesus Christ. "We start in Christian ethics not to walk on the clouds; we find firm footing in the historical realization of the divine idea of man in the person of Jesus of Nazareth."[6] In Jesus we have "both an original, and an originative, moral power. The moral ideal which we

---

[4] The selection of Smyth, a New Haven pastor, as an example of a thinker for whom Christ is the moral ideal is not capricious. He represents a flowering of the liberal tradition on the American scene. He had thoroughly studied the German sources of liberal theology and ethics, as both his key concepts and his many references to and quotations from such theologians as Schleiermacher, Rothe, Dorner, Martensen, and the biblical critics indicate. Equal erudition is shown by his familiarity with nineteenth-century English moral philosophy. He is one of the last of the pastor-theologians of a New England Congregational tradition. Ethical concerns were united with apologetics in the light of growing historical and natural sciences. He was also associated with Bishop Brent in the earliest days of the ecumenical movement. Although Smyth is not important for his historical significance, he is an interesting representative of an important tradition.

[5] Smyth, *Christian Ethics* (New York, 1892), p. 50.

[6] *Ibid*., pp. 51–52.

discover in Jesus was original in him, and it has been creative of a new morality in his name."[7] The moral uniqueness of Christian ethics rests in its unique historical cause, the incarnation of its ideal in the Lord Christ. Thus Christian ethics is "the unfolding and application to human life in all its spheres and relations of the divinely human Ideal which has been historically given in Christ."[8]

Christian ethics becomes dominantly an ethic of ends, a teleological ethic, in this view. While Christ as the Spirit who gives power and Christ as the revelation of God are not lost from sight, the Christian life is described less in terms of living out our justification, or witnessing to the Reality, Christ. It is described more in terms of achievement of the *summum bonum*. Christ is the content of the ideal. But this must be said in terms of its correlates in human historical goals, or in terms of inferences that can be drawn from it for historical goals. "In general" Smyth writes, the Christian Ideal means "the good which it is Christian to desire as the supreme end of life."[9] The task is that of "Christianizing the idea of the *summum bonum*, the supreme good."[10] The Christian ideal of the supreme good can be described for both individuals and society, and the means for its progressive realization can be defined.

Its content is drawn from both the person and the teaching of Jesus. Jesus' doctrine of the Kingdom of God means an ideal good that has already begun in the life of Christ; it implies a "spiritual positiveness," a personal development into "Christlike" character, a "Christian humanitarianism," a "gradual spiritualization of life." Jesus' admonition to be perfect as the Father in heaven is perfect and his teaching of eternal life add to the content of the ideal. Man is to have a "moral love" of life, to have full and complete personal relationships, holiness, righteousness, benevolence, love, blessedness. But no definitions are complete, for the ideal is personal. It is personally realized in Christ and personally operative in his Spirit. Our moral nature is aroused and receives new energy in our personal relation of trust in, and loyalty to, Christ. But the methodical discipline of imitation of Christ in resisting evil and overcoming evil with good provides "the open way to progress towards the moral ideal."[11] This

[7] *Ibid.*, pp. 53–54.
[8] *Ibid.*, p. 57.
[9] *Ibid.*, p. 83.
[10] *Ibid.*, p. 88.
[11] *Ibid.*, p. 241.

means "conflict" with evil, cooperative service to others, increasing spiritual use of nature and the common life in all spheres—the personal, the family, the state, and the Church.

Following after Christ impregnates the conscience; Christ is our example for a "sense of personal responsibility," for freedom from a sense of duty and freedom to "a service of delight." Christ is our example of love and truth-seeking, of a perfect unity of life and absolute personal worth, of honorableness. His giving of his life for the world is an example of the "power of moral heroism."[12]

The fact that Christ has been a moral ideal for many morally sensitive and saintly persons cannot be denied. Whether this is the proper emphasis in Christian ethics, and, indeed, whether it belongs there at all, is disputed. Most contemporary theologians would either omit it or set it in a wider Christological frame. Without regard to whatever authority such a consensus may have, what is to be said about Christ as moral ideal? Can the earnest Christian find here some assistance in, if not the solution of, his moral inquiry?

For those who seek a model to which they can conform their action, Christ as a moral ideal is one option. Though the portrait cannot be clearly drawn, in spite of all the inspirational books on the life of Jesus, the figure of the Son of Man in the Gospel stories appeals to the consciences of many men. His loving deeds, his gentleness, his anger at injustice, his compelling charismatic and moral power stand as a model worthy of emulation, if one must have an ideal or an example. For many, Christ stands as *the* ideal man, and a host of men who have been inspired by him in the past, for example St. Francis and Jefferson, and the present, for examples, Gandhi and Schweitzer, are the cloud of witnesses to the absoluteness of his life and love. Why take Christ as model, and not Lenin or not the Buddha? The question will be answered variously. Christ is world-affirming through love and good will, Lenin is world-affirming through violence, and the Buddha is world-denying. Christ manifests love, and love is the highest good. Or Christ is part of our tradition, he is the head of the Church. Or Christ who saves me through his

---

12 This selection of strains from Smyth distorts the balance of his whole book, but is in keeping with our effort to deal with themes, and not the full theology of writers. Smyth knew the reality of sin, and the need for love to take the form of justice, though it is fair to say that in this and his division of duties, the ethos of liberal theology is dominant. Men no longer write about "the adorable Christ-likeness of God."

cross allows me to follow him as a model for the new life. To have Christ as a model, it can be argued, is not a mark of weakness, but of courage and strength, for to follow him is to be out of step with the herd morality.

Christ is a life model, and not a bloodless abstraction like Kant's definitions of the imperative, or Marx's theory of history. Persons can be charismatic, whereas abstractions and even imaginary pictures of an ideal have an aloofness and unreality about them. A massive biography of Lincoln is more compelling in its picture of his greatness and weakness than a reduction of his "philosophy of life" to a few pages, assuming the latter would be even possible. So the Christ who not only taught the double commandment to love, and gave us the sayings of the Sermon on the Mount, but also lived them out in his own life, is more compelling. He humbles men, indeed convicts them of their weakness and duplicity, he inspires them and draws them to him in an inviting life. The fact that Jesus Christ was a person enables us to have a personal relation to him; this is for many a more meaningful way to live than a life devoted to intellectual and moral principles.

Christ as an ideal for the moral life is persuasive to some because of the anticipated and real moral consequences of following him. This was the inspiration of Sheldon's fiction; it is the inspiration of some pacifism. "Was Jesus a pacifist?" becomes a threatening question to many, for they assume he was one and that their witness is modeled by his life. The "higher way" that is presented by the Christ-ideal may be hopefully assumed to be a means of national policy (as many did hope in the 1920's and 1930's) or it may be a personal witness to the consequences of the vision of a community of peace and love. Comparably in other areas, it is expected that by doing what Jesus would do, not only would the highest ethical motives be manifest, but also that the true temporal good would be realized. A certain moral nobility cannot be denied in the actions and their consequences of some of those who follow Jesus as the highest ideal of human moral life.

But is this the meaning of Christ? Is this what the disciples saw him to be, a moral ideal? Is it what he meant to be? By these questions again one is turned primarily to the task of exegesis and doctrine. Clearly a reduction of Christ to only an example is inadequate to both the New Testament and to the meaning of Christ in the life of the Church. But is it a legitimate part of the faith and life of the Church? Perhaps Christ as *example* is proper, whereas Christ as moral *ideal* is not. The tone of "ideals" is dissonant with the gospel; it implies too readily a striving for perfection out of the will-power and strength of man alone, and tends to deny God's gracious presence and power in and among men. As we have seen, and shall see further, the notion of Jesus Christ as example, set within a fuller Christology, is believed viable by many whose antipathy to the language of ideals borders on passionate disdain. But our focus is not on Christology *per se*, but on the moral life.

The morally earnest man may ask, quite rightly, "Which Jesus Christ is the ideal?" "To whose portrait of him should I adhere?" As the pictorial images of Jesus vary from Sallman's popular "Son of Man" to Thorvaldsen's beckoning Jesus saying, "Come unto me" in the Copenhagen Cathedral, to the tortured, suffering Christ of Rouault's Miserere drawings, so the image of the ideal is varied. Perhaps most of those who center on Jesus as the ideal have his earthly ministry in mind. Indeed, many would set Jesus Christ as the model for *all* men to follow, whether or not they believe anything more about him than that he was a noble moral hero. The language of "revelation" and "faith" in any traditional sense is an appendage the Church has attached which does nothing but distort the simple picture of one who stands with Socrates and Schweitzer as worthy of universal emulation. (Thus George Bernard Shaw could admire what he called "Christianity" and heap words of scorn on the accrued "Churchianity.") But the reconstruction of the earthly life of Jesus, not to mention an even more difficult issue of his self-consciousness of what he meant to be, has become historically problematic. Myth and legend enshroud "fact"; projections of general humanitarian morals invade the story, and the result is often inspiring but distorted.

Even within the Gospel narratives we have a many-sided person, whose actions are indeed surprising. The contemptuous language in which Jesus addressed the Syrophoenician woman who begged his help for her daughter possessed by a demon, ". . . it is not right to take the children's bread and throw it to the dogs" (Mark 7:27), can be made to sound gentle and kindly only by circuitous exposition of Jesus' intention. The ideal Jesus is drawn more commonly as the one who took children to his knees; the offensive Jesus is left out or explained away.

Assuming, however, that a defensible portrait can be drawn, what are its implications for moral action? How can a moral ideal from one century be effective nineteen centuries later? Are certain aspects of the life of Jesus suitable to one occasion and other aspects to another? Does one adapt the ideal person of Christ to the contemporary situation of man? How does one avoid a legalistic form of moral idealism, an "ethic of conscience" by which loyalty to an ideal divorces one from the problems at actual issue in a given time and place? Is Jesus Christ as the moral ideal meaningful in our time?

Many moral ideals, such as pure justice, are almost completely formal in character. One cannot avoid pouring into them the meanings and data of a given situation; indeed, one must do this. Jesus Christ, however, is not so devoid of detail; the story of his ideal life is drawn from the Gospels. But a life ideal, given in some detail, is bound to mirror both the more trivial characteristics of the time from which it is drawn, and the more significant determinative patterns that emerge from its particular definitions of issues. For example, does the following of Jesus as moral ideal require that one dress as men did in Judea and Galilee at that time? Obviously, no. But does the picture of Jesus require that the follower dress simply, without expensive adornment, without luxury? Is simplicity in manner and style of life the proper inference for those who would follow one who had no place to lay his head, and who told his disciples to take but one tunic with them in their ministry? If it is, the Christian moral ideal in our time would run strongly against the cultural and economic stream which presses more and more consumer goods into life, without regard for simplicity, not to mention self-denial.

One might make the relation between the moral ideal of Jesus and contemporary life more congenial to present modes by suggesting that in matters of dress and food Jesus conformed to prevailing customs except where a crucial moral and religious issue was involved. Thus to realize this ideal now requires a definition of what issues are morally crucial, and what realms of life are morally indifferent, and thus permissiveness can rule in them. For example, Christ broke the Sabbath as it was customarily observed. Does this imply that Sunday was made for recreation? Or does the life ideal applied to present Sabbath customs suggest quite another consequence for Christians now, e.g., churchgoing and a day of quiet? Jesus' Sabbath-breaking was a witness against a legalism which seemed to believe that man's relation to God was at issue in his keeping of Sabbath rules. Jesus obviously was not showing that an ideal way to spend Sunday is to thresh grain. The crucial issue was not the custom, but what it had come to mean. Thus the ideal applied to the present time gives ambiguous counsel. If Sabbath keeping is a rigid manifestation of works-righteousness, break it. It is essentially not significant in itself, but only in its religious import for those who keep or break it. But when Sunday recreation and work become a substitute for divine service, what does the ideal imply? Churchgoing can be legalistic, and Sunday work and recreation may manifest one's Christian vocation.[13]

As one interprets Christ in terms of a moral ideal, the potential legalism of the language of ideals and their application to less than ideal situations becomes clear. The Christian life becomes enmeshed in calculating the precise ways to actualize the ideal in a given situation, or in the schemes by which one may build up a life that will closely approximate "Christlikeness." The very freedom which Jesus himself demonstrated becomes lost in the process. Christians can be classified by degrees of achievement; men can hardly avoid making judgments upon those who are markedly successful and markedly failures.

Even where it is set in the framework of Christ's redeeming work, the language of Christ-ideal is unsatisfactory. Does the power of God's grace, or of my "God-consciousness" make it possible for me to achieve an ideal? Is grace infused to help me become perfect as Christ the ideal was? The language of ideals makes the human achievement of moral and religious perfection the end toward which men strive, even when they depend upon grace to help them along. It is one thing to discipline one's life so that it can take a Christlike form as its goal, and quite another to express in a life of simplicity, love, and freedom, a life of faith and trust in Christ. At least two issues are always involved: One is the import of the figure of Jesus Christ—as an ideal to be realized he is one thing, as a figure who appropriately shows forth a life of faith he is another. The second is the character of our relation to Jesus Christ—emulation of him as an ideal is usually self-centered and offers temptations to the subtle forms of pride and sin; faith and trust in him through which we

---

[13] I am reminded of certain Swedish pietists who believed that total abstinence from strong drink led to works-righteousness and to Pharisaism. Thus they took one drink to spite the Pharisees, but not so many as to spite the devil!

know we are forgiven, free, and have a new life may be expressed in simplicity, love, and obedience like his. The understanding of man's needs is quite different if, on the one hand, one assumes that having the proper ideals is the means of the achievement of the temporal good as well as eternal blessedness, and, on the other, that man must be freed from self-consciousness, self-awareness, self-glorying in order to live as God wills him to live. The former pictures a moral life of human striving, the latter a moral life showing forth what God has done for man. Thus there are theologians who deny that Jesus Christ is a moral ideal of human life, and who yet take him with utmost seriousness as a pattern or an example.

CHRIST—OBEDIENT, SUFFERING, LOWLY

"What ought I to do," asks the Christian. Follow Jesus Christ, not as moral ideal, not as the heroic image of what man might become, but as the Son of God who came in lowliness and humility, who was obedient unto death, who suffered at the hands of the world. It is the obedient one, the suffering Christ, the lowly Christ who calls you to be his disciple, to follow him. It is the God-man who claims our trust and our faith, who invites us with gentle words, "Come unto me." It is he who offers us joy in our humiliation, inner exaltation in our outer lowliness, and also the way of the cross in our obedience to him, in our following him. No earthly good is guaranteed, no personal or social higher righteousness that can be measured by the ethical calculists is guaranteed to be forthcoming. Indeed, in the eyes of the Church and the world, with their cheap grace and Christian culture, may come division and scorn, and suffering. But it is this Christ who bids us follow him; the obedient, suffering, lowly Christ.

The distinction between Christ as an example for the life of faith and Christ as a moral ideal is often sharper in definition than in actual function. The *relationship* of man to Christ is the principal point of distinction; as ideal he appears to stand off somewhere depending upon our efforts to be actualized. This, however, is a caricature of men who think in terms of Christian moral ideals, for they are often firm and enthusiastic confessors of the life-giving reality of his Spirit. As we have seen in Schleiermacher's thought, the language of ideals and the language of sanctification are sometimes used together. With this qualification, however, Christ as ideal still rings foreign to the New Testament witness as a whole; and especially when this ideal becomes the achievement of temporal earthly perfection and good, the witness of Christ is distorted. Christ as example, as model or pattern, by some contemporary writers is set within the prior reality of God's action for man's forgiveness and redemption in him. One's life may have some of the same characteristics as Christ's, because God has judged, saved, and claimed one's life. Man is to be conformed to Christ by the power of Christ's transformation of man. Christ's life is the pattern of life in faith.

With the difference in relationship to Christ that can be seen in the language of ideal and the language of example, there tends also to be a difference in the picture of Christ. Moral idealists, as we have noted, tend to stress Jesus' earthly actions, principally because they are interested foremost in the increase of good among men, the betterment of earthly life. They place Jesus in this wider concern; thus the cross becomes an *ideal* of self-denial, absolute loyalty to an ideal, and moral heroism. The language of example or pattern tends to stress the inner relationship of Jesus Christ to the Father (if one can avoid some of the connotations that Herrmann's use of the "inner life of Jesus" brings to mind—though they may be more akin to the idea of some contemporaries than they would care to admit). Thus obedience is a key word; conformity to Christ is a life of obedience; suffering and lowliness are other key terms. Self-denial is an expression, not of the achievement of our ideal, but of obedience to Jesus Christ; it is the way of the cross.[14]

Christ as example does stand before one, as Kierkegaard noted, beckoning one on, as well as behind one, driving him. While he may not be an ideal of man, he is a living reality standing over against man, judging, leading, and giving character to our actions. Though our command to follow him may be essentially "permission," and though our conformity to him is conformity to lowliness and suffering, he stands as one whom we follow. The Christian life bears the mark of the person, Jesus Christ.

When Calvin wrote about the Christian life, he did not hesitate to

---

14 One can be "crucified" for clinging tenaciously to an unpopular ideal, for being a radical moral nonconformist. Those who stress moral idealism in Christianity often equate "crucifixion" for moral tenacity and stubbornness in an "ethic of conscience" with obedience to God's power and will. The basic relationship and meaning of the two are quite different.

use the medieval words "imitation of Christ."[15] A believer, a disciple of Christ, is called to a life of self-denial, to a life of cross-bearing. The gracious rule of God is sovereign over our lives. The opening paragraph of Calvin's discussion of the Christian life contains the memorable and moving passage, "We are not our own. . . . " Discipleship begins with the affirmation, "We are God's; to him, therefore, let us live and die. We are God's; therefore let his wisdom and will preside in all our actions. We are God's; towards him, therefore, as our only legitimate end, let every part of our lives be directed."[16] In specifying the meaning of self-denial, Calvin's statements, taken from their widest theological context, echo medieval piety. For example, true meekness is to be achieved by imbuing one's heart with "self-abasement and a respect for others." The idea of respect and service to others as an act of self-denial, however, marks strongly the movement from meritorious self-mortification to action that demonstrates love and glorifies God. Indeed, actions of self-denial "ought to be pursued for this sole reason, because they are pleasing to him."[17]

The Christian's conformity to Christ has a deeper mark of Christ's own life, namely, bearing the cross. Those whom God has called "ought to prepare themselves for a life, hard, laborious, unquiet, and replete with numerous and various calamities."[18] We partake in Christ's sufferings, even though we shall partake also in his glory. We must live under a continuous cross to show our obedience to God, just as Christ's cross testified to and proves his obedience. Suffering and obedience show the imbecility of self-reliance, and create a reliance and confidence in God. For the believer, all afflictions remind him that nothing happens "without the appointment and providence of God," indeed, without showing his "systematic justice."[19] But in faith, our lives of cross-bearing are not only oppressed with affliction and suffering, but they are also "dilated with spiritual joy."

The testimony of a double character of discipleship of Christ the pattern runs in various ways through the writings of those who stress

[15] Passages from Calvin's commentaries using this language are cited by W. Niesel, *The Theology of Calvin* (London, 1956), pp, 143–51.
[16] Calvin, *Institutes*, III, 7, 1 (Allen trans.), Vol. I, p. 752.
[17] *Ibid.*, III, 7, 2, p. 753.
[18] *Ibid.*, III, 8, 1, p. 765.
[19] *Ibid.*, III, 8, 11, p. 775.

this theme. Kierkegaard, like Calvin, indicates that hidden exaltation
accompanies the lowliness and humiliation of the faithful life,
though he is not as willing to guarantee the dilation of joy and to
assuage the cost of discipleship with the promise of partaking in
Christ's glory as Calvin did.[20] Indeed, in various discourses Kierkegaard draws one of the most awesome, demanding, and unrelenting
pictures in modern theological literature of what Jesus Christ means
as our pattern, and what our life of following him costs. He turns his
gifts for irony and scathing sarcasm on those who would weaken the
demands of the Christian life.

The one who bids us, "Come unto me," and who is our pattern, is
"the humiliated Jesus Christ, the lowly man, born of a despised
maiden, His father a carpenter, His kindred people of the lowest
class, the lowly man who at the same time (like pouring oil upon
fire) declared He was God."[21] To follow him is to be humiliated in
the eyes of the world, to suffer in his likeness, to be despised and
rejected for living the truth. To examine oneself in the light of the
Pattern is to reflect upon one's obedience to the truth. Christ calls
not admirers, but followers.

To follow Christ is to suffer. Suffering in Christ's likeness is not
merely a patient forbearance in the face of unavoidable events; it is
not Stoicism. Christ suffered "because He was the truth and would
not be anything other than He was, namely, the truth."[22] Our
suffering is at the hands of men as we also live the truth, Christ, as
we strive after the Good. As we follow Christ in his deepest humiliation, we hear an inexorable command. "Thou *shalt* suffer with Him."
To avoid suffering one need only to cease to follow Christ, to cease to
will the Good. Christ is the Way, the Truth, and the Life. Thus we
are to be followers, and not admirers; to follow implies "the deepest
and most inward agreement with what He constantly said about
Himself or declared Himself to be. . . ."[23] He does not merely
deliver a doctrine "as that he might be content with hearers who
accepted it—although in life they treated it as nothing, or 'let five be
an even number.'" He does not want "admirers, admiring wor-

---

[20] See Kierkegaard, *Training in Christianity* (Princeton, 1941), pp. 195–96,
232.
[21] *Ibid.*, p. 40.
[22] *Ibid.*, p. 173; see pp. 172 ff., 200 ff., *et passim.*
[23] *Ibid.*, p. 231.

shippers, adherents." Discipleship does not mean adherence to a doctrine, but following a life of humiliation and lowliness.[24] Self-denial in the Christian sense is suffering for one's belief in Christ, for the sake of this faith. It is following one who is gentleness and love in a world which rejects him, and in a Church which also rejects him. To follow him is to be despised by the world, to look imprudent and foolish in the eyes of all respectable men of the culture: the clergy, the members of parliament, the businessmen, the lawyers. They all admire Christ, but to follow him seriously is ascribed only to fanaticism. For Kierkegaard, as is well known, the struggle of life was to become a Christian in Christendom, to be obedient to Jesus Christ, to the truth, in a society that had absorbed and diluted the truth to a consistency congenial to the masses of men.[25]

No program of personal or social morality is involved in Kierkegaard's extraordinarily powerful portrait of the Pattern and what it means to follow him. Indeed, since Christ is truth, and we are also to live this truth, the concern for man's temporal good is irrelevant. In a culture which is hostile to following Christ seriously, the truth suffers. This is its indirect and important moral consequence, namely, an undeniable condemnation of morality, Christendom, and all things which reduce the truth to expediency. Christ is not the Pattern because in following him human welfare will be enhanced, or because merit will accrue to the Christian. He is the Pattern because he is the God-man, the Truth. Temporal moral consequences are irrelevant, and the very concern to calculate them is the beginning of the denial of the Truth. Following Christ, the Example, is not a moral duty, nor is it a means to a moral end. But it has a temporal

[24] *Ibid.* See also pp. 183, 186–89, *et passim*; also *For Self-Examination* (Minneapolis, 1940), *passim.*

[25] One of the most ironic passages in Christian literature is in the section "The Inviter," in *Training*, pp. 40–56, in which Kierkegaard puts various typical responses to taking Jesus seriously in the mouth of wise and prudent men of the world.

Luther's use of Christ as example also stresses humility and suffering. He is, of course, gift before he is example. On the significance of the notion for Luther's whole outlook, as on almost every other point, there is much argument among Luther scholars. His Advent and Christmas sermons, and early Psalms expositions use the ideas of *Vorbild* and *Nachfolge* frequently. Among other literature, see E. Vogelsang, *Der Angefochtene Christi bei Luther* (Berlin and Leipzig, 1932), pp. 52 ff.; A. Gyllenkrok, *Rechtfertigung und Heiligung* (Uppsala, 1952), pp. 42 f.; H. Ivarsson, *Predikans Uppgift* (Lund, 1956), pp. 113 ff. Major references to the ideas of example and discipleship in Luther's works are cited by these men.

effect, namely, to undercut the smugness, complacency, and satisfaction of all that men deem to be the "good life," and particularly to put the ax deep to the root of the Church's own acquiescence in and support of Christendom. Christ invites us, "Come unto me," and in consequence we hear "and thou shalt suffer."

Kierkegaard's witness to the Pattern was not only through his pen, but with his life, though the latter was so indirectly communicated that he was taken to be frivolous by many. The twentieth century has produced its document on the seriousness of discipleship through another whose witness is both verbal and personal, Dietrich Bonhoeffer.[26] The Christian life is life in conformation with the Incarnate; it is a life of discipleship, of costly grace, for Bonhoeffer.

But what does it mean to follow Christ? "To follow in His steps is something which is void of all content. It gives us no intelligible programme for a way of life, no goal or ideal to strive after." It is a call to a new life. "Discipleship means Jesus Christ, and Him alone." "We are summoned to an exclusive attachment to His person."[27] He is the living Christ, the Mediator, the God-man. We are to be bound to him alone, and must be freed from all earthly ties. The call is to faith and obedience, for "only he who believes is obedient, and only he who is obedient believes."[28] The pattern of life is obedience to Christ; it is sharing his suffering and rejection; it means the cross. The old man must die; attachment to the world must be abandoned. "Suffering, then, is the badge of the true Christian."[29] The Christian life requires a breach with fathers and mothers, brothers and sisters, society and nation. The break may be external and open, or hidden and secret, but only in making it do we become obedient to Christ. What this life implies is seen in the Sermon on the Mount as well as in the living Christ.

For Bonhoeffer, and for Barth, the Christ who calls us is not a picture, a story, a law, or an ideal. Rather he is the living Christ, who

---

[26] Barth notes in his most recent discussion of discipleship, "Easily the best that has been written on this subject is to be found in *The Cost of Discipleship*, by Dietrich Bonhoeffer. . . . For I cannot hope to say anything better on the subject than what is said here by a man who, having written on discipleship, was ready to achieve it in his own life, and did in his own way achieve it even to the point of death" (*Church Dogmatics*, IV/2, pp. 533–34).

[27] D. Bonhoeffer, *The Cost of Discipleship* (1948 ed.), p. 51.

[28] *Ibid.*, p. 56.

[29] *Ibid.*, p. 74.

is and was obedient. Thus the life of discipleship is the life of obedience to the obedient one. Our obedience is "simple obedience"; it "is simple when we do just what we are told—nothing more, nothing less, and nothing different."[30] Christ destroys all supposed natural orders and historical forces, which have obtruded themselves as authorities. We are to conform to Jesus and his commandments.

Clearly, Bonhoeffer is not as taken by the lowliness of the man Jesus as Kierkegaard was. The Christ is the living Lord. Nevertheless the consequences of being called to follow him are the same: suffering, obedience, and the cross. Together with the teaching of Jesus, from which much of the content of the moral life can be drawn, this living Christ presents himself as a commanding and demanding person. God's grace through him is costly; Christianity without obedient discipleship is Christianity without Christ. Grace and discipleship are given together in Christ. The Christian life is a following of Jesus. But this following is more clearly moral in its implications for Bonhoeffer than for Kierkegaard.

What can be said about the moral life of the man who follows Jesus, the lowly, suffering, obedient one? Is there any counsel here for the morally serious believer? Perhaps the first meaning, in power and importance, is one that has come to the fore in previous chapters as well, namely, that faith and trust in Christ are prior to concern for the temporal and earthly good. The sharpest distinction between Jesus Christ as moral ideal and as pattern, toward which we have been pointing, lies here. Christ as moral ideal makes either the ethical function prior in importance to, or of equal importance with, the presence of the living God in Jesus Christ. Conformity to Christ for Kierkegaard and Bonhoeffer (to cite but two) is conformity to one whose very obedience, lowliness, humility and suffering show forth the presence and power of God. Christ's lowliness is not first of all concerned to effect the increase of earthly welfare, the sum total of moral goodness, the moral uprightness of individuals, and the demonstration of a moral way of life. What Kierkegaard says of lowliness must be seen in relation to the Eternal One coming into time, the One who is exalted becoming man. To follow him first of all is offensive because it is ridiculous in the light of all prudence; it is a scandal provoking either faith or unbelief. Then to be conformed

---

[30] Barth, *Church Dogmatics*, IV/2, pp. 540 ff., also II/2, pp. 569 ff.

to Christ means not the affirmation of values of the world, not the development of virtues, but living this truth because it is Truth. It is Truth whose living is despised by worldly wisdom; indeed whenever this truth becomes a means to morality or to Christendom its very essence as Truth is betrayed. Thus the moral witness that may be an ingredient of life after the Pattern is a witness first of all *against* false gods, falsely absolutized relativities, and Christendom with its concern for this life. The Christian life bears witness against morality itself, and promises no exaltation, no resolution of moral dilemmas, no rules of conduct, no increment of earthly good. There may be a concealed exaltation, and there is a promise of eternal blessedness or happiness, but these are not to be the objects of our striving and intentions. The witness to the Pattern is not without importance, for the Truth is important, but its consequences are not measured in ethical terms.

The object of our discipleship, Bonhoeffer suggested, is void of all moral content; he offers no plans, ideals, or hopes. Christ calls us, rather, to obedience and to suffering. Its moral implications can be drawn from Jesus' teaching, in part. It means a life of external discipline, for example. "By practicing self-control we show the world how different the Christian life is from its own. If there is no element of asceticism in our lives, . . . we shall find it hard to train for the service of Christ."[31] The Christian life means nonresistance to evil. "The only way to overcome evil is to let it run its course, so that it does not find the resistance it is looking for."[32] But such expressions of the Christian life as asceticism and nonresistance cannot be made into general principles for secular moral life. They have their validity and power only in trust in the presence of the living Jesus Christ, in discipleship to him. Like love of enemy, asceticism and nonresistance are not done for the sake of morality, the temporal good, the cultivation of virtue. Rather, they are simply things that Christians *do*.

Thus the Christian man is invited to come unto Christ, trust in him, follow him in faith and life, to live his truth. What then is the moral counsel? It comes only in and through and after faith. Then, in the setting of God's presence in Christ, his revelation in Christ, it is fitting to be conformed to Jesus. He is the Way, the Truth, and the Life. But one does not look to him for rational calculation of the

[31] Bonhoeffer, *The Cost of Discipleship*, p. 146.
[32] *Ibid.*, p. 122.

utility of actions, the increment of good and earthly value. Rather, one simply follows him; one is obedient in lowliness. It is self-denial. One suffers. The call to the Christian life is no less than this call. Moral consequences are incidental fruits to obedience to Christ. In moral quandary and perplexity, simply follow Christ.

This may appear empty, as indeed it is claimed to be. But the crucial point is (as in our discussion of the reality of the Christ, the Lord who is Redeemer and Creator) the living reality of Christ for Bonhoeffer, or for Kierkegaard the acceptance of Jesus Christ as the God-man. Faith is the determining factor in the Christian life; here, faith in this person, Jesus Christ, this historical figure. The authority he has as pattern is not a universal moral authority in the sense of a law of nature; it is the authority of a life in faith; it is given in our belief and trust. Its content is the form of God's manifestation itself, that is, in the form of obedience, suffering, and lowliness. Its implications are self-denial and separation, inner if not outer, from the world, witnessing to a life and truth denied by the world. Indeed, it is cross-bearing. What this life means in each moment is not for another to decide; it is the living, believing self, trusting in the living God, being conformed to his historical presence in Jesus Christ, who must determine his action. But the outer form will be determined by the relation to Christ, to lowliness, suffering, the cross. "Come unto me," Jesus says; we hear, "Thou shalt suffer." Even Thorvaldsen's warmly beckoning Jesus bears the nail prints in his hands. Suffering is the badge of the Christian.

CHRIST—THE FORM OF GOD'S ACTION

The Christian asks, "What ought I to do?" And he is answered, "Follow Jesus Christ." Be Christ to the neighbor is what this means. Reduplicate in your own life the pattern of God's action in Jesus Christ. To follow Christ means to commune with him, to participate in him. He is not a life-type, nor a pietistically oriented pattern of suffering and humiliation. He is the one who is the gift of God's election and grace, who becomes man, who dies, who is resurrected. We are to participate in him, the engendering deed, and in our own relations to show forth the action of God in Christ. As Christ died and was resurrected, so in him our old man is dead and the new creature has come to life. The Christian life, then, is discipleship, which means living as a new creature in Christ in our relations to other men.[33]

Perhaps the inspiring text for this view of following Christ is found in Luther's engaging treatise on Christian liberty. "Just as our neighbor is in need and lacks that in which we abound, so we also have been in need before God and have lacked His mercy. Hence, as our heavenly Father has in Christ freely come to our help, we also ought freely to help our neighbor through our body and its works, and each should become as it were a Christ to the other, that we may be Christs to one another and Christ may be the same in all; that is, that we may be truly Christians."[34] To be a Christian is to be for others what Christ is for us; it is to do, as it were, for others what Christ has done for us. This is what following Jesus means.

Not the life of Jesus as a life of obedience and self-denial, nor as moral ideal, but the "shape" of God's action in and through Christ is the model. But it is not an external model, it is not an objective life-type drawn for our imitation. Rather, we have an intimate, personal relation to him whom we follow; there is clearly a common third between us. We are to live by the shape of Christ's life because his action and love, in which we participate, shape our lives. The imperative of the Christian life is derived from, empowered, governed, and shaped by the action of God in Christ. The Johannine text, "Beloved, if God so loved us, we also ought to love one another" (I John 4:11) and the paragraph from which it is taken point to what is meant. Our life is to be patterned after the example of Christ because God has loved us in him, because God's love empowers and flows through our lives, because it shapes our actions. God's work in Christ shapes our deeds; our deeds are to be *shaped* according to the pattern of the divine activity in Jesus Christ. The author of Ephesians says, "And walk in love, as Christ loved us and gave himself up

[33] We have noted that Bonhoeffer's view of discipleship also includes obedience to the living Christ. But as it is spelled out, the life of discipleship for him, as for Kierkegaard and for Calvin, has many overtones characteristic of pietism in its Protestant and Catholic forms. Suffering, humiliation, and death become the notes; cross-bearing is the sign. There is no joy in the overcoming of death by Christ, no living forth the resurrection, no participation in exaltation, in the risen Christ. The inclusion of following Christ in new creaturehood in him changes the outlook on moral life. Barth, in his spongy inclusiveness, can keep cross-bearing within the joyous new life in Christ, as does Bonhoeffer in this later book, *Ethics.*

[34] *Three Treatises* (Philadelphia, 1943), p. 279.

for us" (Eph. 5:2). Jesus Christ is our example; we are to do for others what he has done for us; we can do for others what he has done for us precisely *because* he has done it for us. Christ was forgiving; we ought to be forgiving, we can be forgiving because in Christ we are forgiven. Christ gave loving care to those in need; we ought to love those in need; we can love those in need because Christ has loved us in our need.

Professor Gustaf Wingren has stated this general point of view in a brief but inclusive article.[35] The command "Follow me" is not superfluous to a tradition that stresses justification by faith, and thus is sensitive to the potential dangers of works-righteousness in Catholic and Protestant pietism. Rather, it is set in the context of our "communion" with Christ, or our "participation" in Christ. We participate in an event, Christ's death and resurrection; we die and are resurrected in him. Christ goes on to build through death and new life, and we follow our Lord. Following Jesus Christ in this meaning can lead to primarily religious or dogmatic expressions of life, for example, to the sacrament and the death and resurrection that take place there. But it is clearly ethical in its intention. It means sacrifice. Even foot-washing can be a meaningful example of a life of sacrifice; self-will and care must be sacrificed for the sake of the neighbor. To follow Christ means obedience; Christ's death is obedience; so now if our life be conformed to his, we must be obedient. The old man must die. It means service to the neighbor; I have washed your feet, so you should wash the feet of others.

Thus, discipleship is first a gift of our communion with Christ; it includes the entire transformation of life through our partaking in and showing forth the death and resurrection of Christ; it is expressed in deeds of love to the neighbor. The center of the conformation is *more religious than ethical* in character. The shape and order of God's activity in Christ, described in the inclusive (yet specific) terms of death and resurrection, are the pattern. Yet, in a sense, the idea of pattern at this point is inaccurate, for we partake in Christ's death and resurrection; we have communion with him. Our communion leads to more distinctively ethical attitudes and actions,

[35] "Was bedeutet die Forderung der Nachfolge Christi in evangelische Ethik?" *Theologische Literaturzeitung*, Vol. 75 (1950), pp. 385–91. See also, Helmut Thielicke, *Theologische Ethik*, Vol. I (Tübingen, 1958), pp. 309 ff. He interprets imitation of Christ as participation in him as he participated in humanity.

namely obedience and deeds of love. But again, we do not so much
initiate our discipleship or conformity to Christ as we *are conformed*
to him by our sharing in his obedience, partaking in God's love.
the gift of discipleship is the primary fact; the pattern of life that is
consequent is an appropriate expression, not of an ideal, but of a life
participating in Christ.

In his brief essay on ethics, filled with suggestive literary allusions,
Joseph Sittler develops something of the same point of view without
specific reference to the traditional language of the imitation of
Christ, or discipleship.[36] The Bible is the story of God's doing, his
acting. The language of the Bible is the language of relatedness, not
of static substances or properties. Echoing Luther, Sittler says, "ethics
is faith-doing," it is a function of "the living continuity between man-
in-God and man-among-men." The Christian life is a "living unity of
faithful obedience," and not abstract counsels, duties, and obligations.[37] This life is engendered by God's deed; there is a shape to this
deed that is drawn in the biblical account. God's "loving will-to-
restoration" has taken the form of a servant in Christ, and "having
swept down into the nadir of the human situation in time and place,
sweeps on, and through, and beyond it."[38] The shape of this deed
refers to both what God does in his action in Christ and what this
action accomplishes in the believer. Thus, "the Christian life is . . .
a re-enactment from below on the part of men of the shape of the
revelatory drama of God's holy will in Jesus Christ." It is "this same
shape of grace," a recapitulation in the life of the believer and the
community, of suffering, death, burial, resurrection, new life. These
"are actualities which plot out the arc of God's self-giving deed in
Christ's descent and death and ascension."[39] The terms "re-enactment" and "recapitulation" seem to be equivalent to the idea of
"conformity." The Christian life is conformity to, re-enactment of,
the shape of the engendering deed. But the shape that is re-enacted is
the shape of the *deed* that *engenders* our re-enactment, and thus

[36] Sittler, *The Structure of Christian Ethics* (Baton Rouge, 1958).
[37] *Ibid.*, p. 15.
[38] *Ibid.*, p. 31.
[39] *Ibid.*, p. 36. Cf. Augustine, *The Enchiridion*, 53: "All the events, then, of
Christ's crucifixion, of His burial, of His resurrection the third day, of His
ascension into heaven, of His sitting down at the right hand of the Father, were
so ordered, that the life which the Christian leads here might be modelled upon
them, not merely in a mystical sense, but in reality" (Chicago, 1961), pp. 63–64.

engenders our deed. We are conformed to that by which we are
formed. We act or do in accordance with that which enacts or
enables us. In this sense, Christian ethics is Christological. Ethical
counsel and the teachings and life of Jesus are to be seen within the
continuity of the Christ act and the Christian life. They are para-
digms of a "style" of life. The content of our response and re-
enactment "is disclosed in ever new and fresh ways as men's actual
situations are confronted by God's revelation in Christ."[40] The
moral decision is generated between "the two poles of faith and the
facts of life."[41] Every decision is a concrete actualization of justification and involves risks, approximations of the wholly desirable, and so
faith. Thus all action is done in repentance, faith, and hope. But this,
too, is possible because of God's engendering deed. With the given
facts of our situation, we live out the shape of God's action in Christ,
his love, and will-to-restoration.

Christ as moral ideal creates the dilemmas of legalism and casuistry
for the morally earnest Christian, and sometimes assumes that morality is the main purpose of Christian life. As the "engendering deed"
another dilemma is created, namely, What act is right? Obedience
and love are the expressions of our being brought to faith by God's
righteousness. But the decision in the concrete cannot be prejudged
or even externally counseled. Self-denial, even, is at best a paradigm,
just as foot-washing and other actions of love are. Our relation to
Christ is not established for its moral potential, but moral expression
of it is both an outgrowth and a requirement of it.

To understand conformity to God's action rightly it must be seen
in relation to God's righteousness or justification. The fruit of God's
redemption is our freedom from bondage to human codes of cult and
morals, freedom from oppressive self-examination and calculation of
sins and virtues, freedom to live a new life in love and obedience.
The very nature of our inner freedom, the consequence of God's
deed, is antithetical to prescriptive Christian ethics, whether they be
in terms of imitation of a moral ideal, zealous counsel to self-denial,
or literal obedience to the teachings of Jesus. The positive nature of
the moral life, then, has a redemptive and morally creative quality to
it. We participate in God's redeeming righteousness, we are brought
through the death of the old man in us to new life, new creature-

[40] *The Structure of Christian Ethics*, p. 69.
[41] *Ibid.*, p. 74.

hood. Now we are free to be loving, to find the shape of the current facts of our situation which conforms to the shape of our redemption. Christ affects our outlook, our attitude, our style, first of all. Thus we have an ethic closely related to the themes of justification and new life. But his effect is to mold our deeds according to the deeds that mold us. As Christ loved us, we are to love; as our needs are met in his acts, so we are to meet the needs of others. We have been freely helped; we ought freely to help. The content of our decision is the stuff of our time and place; we can shape it in obedience and love, in faith and in hope, seeking what counsel we can find from the Bible, but also from life. But our actions are not primarily conformations to counsels, principles, goals, or even historical persons as life patterns of humility and suffering. They are conformed to what forms them: God's action in Jesus Christ.

CHRIST—THE PATTERN OF SELF-MORTIFICATION

The call to follow Jesus, as we have noted, is often seen to be a call to humility, self-denial, and suffering. In Calvin, Kierkegaard, Bonhoeffer, and others this is the case. The same pattern of interpretation, i.e., self-denial, set within the context of some forms of Catholic and Protestant piety, however, means something quite different. The purpose of self-denial, for example, for Calvin was to devote one's energy to those things which are pleasing to God; not in order to win salvation, but in order to show forth God's glory. Set in the context of practical devotional literature which has had wide churchly influence, however, the dominant note is self-mortification for the sake of gaining merit. To follow Jesus is to mortify the flesh, to be separated from the pleasures of the senses, to become a "spiritual" man.

An ethic is both explicit and implicit in this outlook on the Christian life, and a theology that is debatable on many grounds impregnates it. The ethic, our chief concern, becomes detailed guidance about what behavior is desirable and undesirable as a Christian. It is an ethic of upbuilding certain personal virtues through the exercise of disciplines which mortify the flesh. Even service to others tends to be viewed as a means of self-improvement, as a method for accruing merit. While the new birth in Christ, and the sacrifice of the cross are by no means lost sight of, the implications that they have are a disciplined, directed overcoming of the "flesh." The life of the body, of the senses, is seen as an evil from which man must free himself through his own efforts, or in cooperation with God's grace. The imitation of Christ is a life of mortifying the flesh. The Christian life is a discipline of sanctification, as we have seen in Wesley and others.

The most widely known Catholic tract of such devotion and discipline is Thomas a Kempis' *On the Imitation of Christ*. Its popularity can be seen by its numerous editions and translations, and its use by Protestants as well as Catholics. The one who follows Christ takes pains to bring his entire life in conformity to Christ's (Book I, 1, 2). He will strive to withdraw from love of visible things and to transfer his affection to the invisible, for to follow sensual inclinations will stain the conscience (I, 1, 5). He will find true inward peace by resisting the fleshly passions (I, 1 and 2). If we were stricter with ourselves, and not entangled in outward things, we could taste of divine things (I, 11, 3). Suffering and grief are good for us, for they protect us from vain-glory and teach us not to hope in earthly things (II, 12, 1). Self-discipline is called for; one ought to root out one evil habit each year (I, 11, 5); "Keep your eye upon yourself in the first place, and especially admonish yourself in preference to admonishing all your friends" (I, 21, 3).[42] We are to be anxious about ourselves, to grieve for our sins, so that we will be safe on judgment day (I, 24, 4). Indeed "the more violence you do to yourself, the greater will be your growth in grace" (I, 25, 10).

Men are to be true lovers of Jesus, contemplating on his Passion, dwelling with delight in his sacred wounds (II, 1, 4). By loving Jesus we can raise ourselves above ourselves in spirit (II, 1, 6). The imitation of Christ is the way of the cross; in order to go into life everlasting man must take up the cross and follow Jesus (II, 12 passim). "There is no other way to life, and to true inward peace save the way of the Holy Cross, and of daily mortification" (II, 12, 3).

To be sure, there are many passages about divine grace which aids us in the life of imitation, just as there are in the Wesleyan sermons that admonish men to perfection. Salvation is in the cross, we are to rely upon "the subduing power of Jesus Christ" (I, 14, 3), to cite but one phrasing of Thomas' affirmation of the saving power that is objective to our discipline. We are to desire ardently the sacrament and ministration of the Church. But to what ends? One, to the end of our inward peace and joy in life, through our separation from

[42] Quotations are from an edition translated and edited by W. H. Hutchings, London, 1884.

things of the flesh. Two, to the end of our eternal happiness.[43] The love to which we are admonished is love *to* Christ; it is not first Christ's love to man. Thus Nygren rightly sets Thomas a Kempis on the *eros* side of his typology of love.[44] Jesus is the example of self-mortification; the Christian life imitates his mortification, his presumed ascetic and monastic-like discipline, his presumed flight from the senses to the realm of spirit.

The Anglican tradition has had its coworkers with Catholic imitation-of-Christ piety. William Law, whose influence on Wesley was great, especially before Wesley's conversion at Aldersgate (though it by no means ended then), is a major figure among them.[45] Two works of Law's are important counsels to imitation of Christ, the widely reprinted *A Serious Call to a Devout and Holy Life*, and the less widely read, *A Practical Treatise on Christian Perfection* (1726). Law was not devoid of evangelical foundations for the Christian life. We are to be converted; it is a soul *"born again of the Spirit*, that tends with one full Bent to a Perfection and Happiness in the Enjoyment of God."[46] Christ's sacrifice is sufficient, it could not be made more complete, "yet we should much mistake the Scripture, if we should think, that because he is our Holiness, therefore we need not endeavor to be Holy ourselves." "A State of Self-denial and Suffering is the proper State of this Life."[47] Self-denial and suffering "recommend us to God, as Holiness and Purity recommend us, by their own Nature and intrinsic Fitness."[48] "This is that Self-Denial, Holy Discipline, Daily-cross, to which all Christians are called; that by thus losing their Lives, that is, thus ceasing to live the Life of this World, they may purchase to themselves a Life of endless Happiness in another State."[49]

[43] Kierkegaard is very close to this point of view on occasion. He treasured both the inner exaltation of self-denial and the expectation of eternal happiness.
[44] Anders Nygren, *Agape and Eros* (London, 1953), pp. 662–64.
[45] For Law's impact on Wesley, see, among other books, Harold Lindström, *Wesley and Sanctification* (Stockholm, 1946), pp. 161 ff.; also N. Flew, *The Idea of Perfection* (London, 1934), pp. 293 ff.
[46] *A Practical Treatise*, in *The Works of William Law*, Vol. III (London, 1893), p. 35.
[47] *Ibid.*, p. 81.
[48] *Ibid.*, p. 84.
[49] *Ibid.*, p. 91. See also Ch. 11 and 12 of *A Serious Call*, for a description of the rewards of peace and happiness forthcoming from a life of devotion and self-denial.

Indeed, self-denial is not only a manifestation of the calling of the Christian in Christ's work; it becomes itself a means *to* grace. We have an "absolute Necessity of this Divine Assistance," i.e., grace. Self-denial, temperance, meekness, lowliness, all "*fit* and *prepare* our Minds to hear and receive, to comprehend and relish the Instructions and Doctrines which come from the Spirit of God." "So far, therefore, as we *prepare* ourselves by Self-denial, for this Change of Heart and Mind, so far we *invite* the Assistance and concur in the Inspirations of the Holy Spirit."[50] Here self-denial precedes and prepares for grace.

The imitation of Christ is the imitation of the "Greatness of his Spirit and Temper,"[51] his meekness and lowliness. "We are to be like him in Heart and Mind, to act by the same Rule, to look towards the same End, and to govern our Lives by the same Spirit. This is the Imitation of Jesus Christ which is as necessary to Salvation, as it is necessary to believe in his Name."[52] We are to strive after "utmost Perfection," for while the Christian religion is a covenant of mercy for frail and imperfect men, we cannot say we are within this mercy until we strive as hard as we can within our imperfection. God favors none "who do not labour to be as Perfect as they can be."[53]

The fact of admonition to self-denial is not as singularly important for our attention as its intention and purpose. We have seen from other writers how self-denial is a pattern of life that is both the gift and the command of the gracious God who has redeemed us. It is an expression of life in faith. The theological wellspring of grace and mercy given by the divine initiative affects the flavor and color of the life of self-denial. Even when the admonitions border on detailed counsel, as they do in some passages of Bonhoeffer, the awareness that God's power is more important than men's rules and models keeps the idea of the Christian life free from legalism and from the accrual of merit. The language of "perfection" in its moral context is somewhat strange to this more evangelical interpretation.

The opposite of self-denial as an expression of grace would be self-denial as a means of earning grace. Catholic piety and its Protestant cousins often appear to make this assumption. But it is so unbiblical,

---

[50] Law, *A Practical Treatise*, pp. 134 ff., 138, 142.
[51] *Ibid.*, p. 224.
[52] *Ibid.*, p.216.
[53] *Ibid.*, p. 241, see pp. 240–41.

so devoid of acknowledgment that God has acted for man's salvation in Jesus Christ, that its baldest form is not defended theologically or even devotionally. One is hard pressed to find any informed writer who is totally unaware of the importance of God's gracious initiative, and who sees human perfection and salvation as achievable purely by human imitation of Christ.

One question that is addressed to the "imitation" literature, then, pertains to the source and consequently the goal of self-denial. From Thomas a Kempis and William Law one gains the overwhelming impression that the fundamental source of the Christian life, though not the exclusive source, is human striving toward the model of perfection. Thus the goal is the most complete approximation of human moral and religious perfection that can be achieved. God's work in the cross is an "assistance" and makes our achievement possible, for the work of the cross could not be more complete, and we are to rely upon the "subduing power of Christ." But the seriousness with which the implications of this acknowledgment are taken is not great. Our own striving comes prior to the assistance from God; he helps those who work hard to earn his help. Thus the Christian life takes on a grim determination to achieve peace and happiness through self-mortification. Set in contrast to the imitation of God's saving, freeing love and righteousness in which we partake in Christ, the picture grows darker. We hear, not "Freely you have received, freely give" but, "Work hard to free yourself from the passions of the body through cross-bearing and suffering so that you may earn God's love and peace." Thus the detailed counsel about how best to achieve this goal is appropriate: what times of the day to pray, how to root out evil thoughts and habits, and many more.

The goal becomes egocentric, and of dubious moral value. We do not joyously witness to God's love and will for all men, with the outgoing, giving, moral consequences and implications of this. Neighbor love is not an important theme. We do not strive for an ideal that is the highest social as well as individual good; the perfection in view is not a universal Kingdom of peace and righteousness, but the peace and happiness of the self. Our self-denial is not a witness of obedience to Christ who calls us into his service; our suffering is not a consequence of our living the Truth in this world. Rather, self-denial and suffering become techniques and means to the true life. While we are to be separate from the world, it is not so much a witness against the idols of the world as it is a way to our own individual perfection and salvation.

The Christ who is imitated is hardly one we recognize in the Gospels or the rest of the New Testament. Rather, the spiritual artists have projected their own image of perfection onto the basic lines and features of Christ. It is not a perfection that redeems all things God has created, but a separation from the flesh and the world.

It rests on a view of the world that is as hard to find in the New Testament as is the language of lofty moral ideals. This is a view of a deep cleavage between the realm of the spirit—peace, true joy, the soul, all that is good; and the realm of the flesh—passions, senses, "the world," and all that is evil. Thus its picture of Jesus Christ, the object of imitation, is the one of a man whose mortification of the flesh, especially in the bloody passion of the cross, is the supreme example of the successful struggle for perfection.

The ethics of this pious imitation, like that of ideals, is finally an ethics of ends. But the *summum bonum* is severely egocentric. It is not achieving perfection to show forth the glory of God, or to establish a just society. Rather, the highest good is my peace and happiness now and in eternity. The implications of this view of the Christian life leave much to be desired, from both a theological and a moral standpoint. A continuing protest against such tendencies has rightfully been a part of the Church's history.

SOME REFLECTIONS ON CHRIST THE PATTERN

Certain questions have guided the discussion of Christ the Pattern. Two principal ones are involved in an evaluation of the theme. One, what picture or story of Christ is appropriate, and more important, valid? Two, what is the relation of the believer to the Pattern? For example, is it the achievement of a goal? Or is it witnessing to a pattern? Around these two are many subsidiary questions.

The full meaning of Christ for moral life escapes us if we make him exclusively a pattern, just as it does if he becomes exclusively the Redeemer-Lord, the Sanctifier, or the Justifier. This may be self-evident, but its meaning is not as easily avoided as one suspects it might be. One suspects that popular efforts to attract men to Jesus, the example, as a moral solution to all problems is loaded with this exclusivism. Whenever Jesus becomes, in function or in exhortation, primarily a pattern for a universally valid moral way of life, his meaning is distorted. For one reason, it has not been the claim of the gospel to publish primarily a moral example. Jesus was concerned with the forgiveness of sins, the graciousness of God's redeeming love, as much as he was with the achievement of a new moral life. The Church has been concerned with the new communion with God that is man's because of the revelation in Jesus Christ as much as it has with the establishment of the temporal good. The other side of this, however, cannot be ignored, namely, that there is a moral universality both claimed and experienced by the followers of Jesus. This is especially so when it is defined in terms of the love which he both manifests and commands. Many have been attracted to Jesus, his person and his teaching, by his moral persuasiveness. Jefferson and Lincoln, Gandhi and Martin Luther King, Jr., as well as Bonhoeffer and Kierkegaard, are attached to his person. One decisive question about the moral life is whether Jesus has this universal moral significance apart from faith in him as more than an example. Another is whether those who admire and follow him as moral example know the full moral significance of his person.

It has been argued through the ages, with some propriety, that while many admire Jesus as example for all to follow, the element of power to follow him is lacking for those who have no other form of confidence in him. He becomes another moral hero to strive after, like all the others of history and the present age. Repentance and grace are missing. Christ as moral example finally becomes only our judge, the norm in the light of which we are aware of our imperfections, whether we confess them as sin or not. It cannot be denied that important moral consequences have followed from the actions of many who have taken Jesus as their life model and are inspired by him. Passive resistance as a means of social change in human society is one example, with its good fruits in India and the United States. But the testimony of men in the New Testament and the Church, and of Christian experience, tells us Christ is more than, if not other than, a universal moral ideal.

Christ is more than Ideal. Through him the Church and those in its communion know and experience the God who creates, orders, and redeems life, the theme of the first part of this book. Through him the Church and its members experience freedom from bondage to sin, law, and death, and the new life in which redeeming and creative moral possibilities are opened up, the theme of the second part of this book. Christ reveals the nature of moral, and, indeed, of all life in its relation to God. Christ is a means of life which in turn has moral expression. Thus the Christian ethic is in its fullest sense a way and pattern of life for those whose faith in God has Jesus Christ as its center. It is not first of all a universally valid objective model of morality. This it may provide, but only as an expression of God's way to man in Jesus Christ.

If this be the case, what can be said about Christ the Pattern? The critical remarks in this chapter have pointed to an answer. Christ as moral ideal is hard to expound persuasively, either in the sense of a goal for a better self and world, or in the sense of the pattern for mortification and thus inner peace and eternal happiness. Newman Smyth's ideal has the ethical merit of being concerned for the greatest good in a universal sense; Thomas a Kempis and William Law appear to commend a mode of life that is severely egocentric in its intention. But the crucial difficulty lies not so much in the picture that is drawn (though there are many problems there too), but in the fact that the end, purpose, goal of the Christian life is moral or spiritual perfection. Our relation to God in communion with him, in the sacraments and contemplation of the cross, is relegated to a means to this moral and spiritual end.

The moral life, of course, always deals with human, moral ends. But the Christian life has its integrity in relation to God, and its moral concerns are grounded in that relation. The Christian life is not less moral because it is not primarily moral. It expresses morally, as well as in worship, what God has given to man in Christ—the gifts of love and forgiveness, and the gifts of commandments and teaching. The *personal center* of the Christian life is not the goal of individual peace and happiness, not the goal of the greatest moral good. The personal center is in God, his work, will, and love in Jesus Christ.

In what sense, then, is Christ the Pattern? As self-denial and cross-bearing, and as the shape of God's saving love. But self-denial, like redeeming love, is the outcome of confidence in the goodness and mercy of God, and not of *imitation* or even *following after* Jesus.

Self-denial, taking the sufferings of others upon oneself, inner if not outer separation from the world—all is part of the Christian life because it has a center not bound to the world, and a center which empowers and counsels the self to live this personal truth and loyalty. As self-denial in Jesus Christ was an expression of his obedience to God, of God's love to man disclosed in him, and thus an expression of his Godliness, so our self-denial is an expression of our obedience to God in Jesus Christ, of being his disciple and witness in our concrete, prosperous, other-directed world. We do not separate ourselves from the world in order to mortify the flesh, and receive whatever self-gratification of peace and joy in the promise that may come from that. Nor do we deny ourselves in conformity to an external pattern of humility, suffering, and lowliness. Jesus Christ is the pattern, but not in an objective external way; he is the pattern because he is the center through and in whom we understand the world and ourselves, through and in whom we live and act.

The absence of self-denial, of cross-bearing, of lowliness and suffering may indicate the weakness and the sickness of Christian lives. It may indicate that they have a center other than God, other than Jesus Christ. To be both inwardly and outwardly joined to the world, participating in its sickness, its prosperity, its pride, may be a testimony to a loyalty that is finally culture-centered and self-centered. The crucial aspect is the *character of our relation* to the world or, in other words, the *function* of the world in our lives. The world contains the good gifts of God's creation, preservation, and redemption. God's love and care are manifest in what the world provides, its beauty but also its technology, its order but also the disruptions of contemporary revolutions, its pleasantness but also the bitterness and suffering of existence. If our relation to these things—beauty and technology, for examples—is such that they function as objects of ultimate trust and loyalty, as the final source of our hope and expectation of redemption, then we are weak and sick indeed. Self-denial is not necessarily always outward—we are not uniformly called to deny ourselves the pleasure of symphonies or of automobiles—but it is appropriately inward. It is being related to the world in such a way that we both care for it and yet are indifferent to it; that we are good stewards of it, using what is given for the benefit of man, and yet aware that the fundamental issues of life are not solved by the preservation of the body or by the extension of man's world to the wider and wider margins of outer space.

This inner separation from the world, from persons and things, nature and culture, is one aspect of the Christian life. It is part of the

witness to the Truth we have in Jesus Christ that is neither the truth
that governs the social relations of organization men nor faith in the
expansion of consumer-minded economies and the diplomacy of
brinkmanship. The expression of our personal truth in Jesus Christ is
appropriately not only a denial of the world, but an inward denial of
the self that seeks its security and strength in the world.

But what of external, visible self-denial? Again the key is its *function,* and our relation to it. Self-denial can be a means of pride and an
expression of psychological masochism. This must be acknowledged in
the full force of its truth. But it may also show, in those called to
such a life, that lowliness and simplicity are ample and suitable
modes of life in faith. Jesus' attraction to the people-of-the-land,
without much property and status, his simplicity of earthly life, his
indifference to the external marks of prestige and respectability—
these are all fitting expressions of his Godliness, of the life and
witness that he bore to God the Father. The contemporary expressions of the same spirit, grounded in our relation to God the Father
and Christ the Son, are equally fitting. Again, Christ is not pattern by
being an external authority. He is pattern because of the integrity and
coherence of his obedience and faith as the Son of God, and his life
among men in a particular time and culture. He is our pattern by
virtue of the overpowering subjective truth of his life—both in its
faithful obedience and its outer expressions.

But self-denial includes cross-bearing. This is not Stoic patience in
physical affliction, though affliction may be a cross. It is not only
denying oneself as a manifestation of a truth that is indifferent to the
world. It is also taking upon oneself the world with its cares and
aspirations, its suffering and its healing, its injustice and its victories.
It is an inner identification with the downtrodden and disinherited in
their struggles for justice and a better life, with those who suffer
incarceration for the sake of the gospel and human liberty, with the
emptiness and loneliness of men driven to flight from life in suicide,
alcohol, or other ways. Cross-bearing is neighbor-love through inner
communion with his concrete suffering and need. It is taking upon
oneself the responsibility for the causes and relief of various forms of
affliction. But it is not only inward. It is outward. Action appropriate
to the inner unity is fitting and normal. Thus the Christian life is a
sharing in both the ills of the world and the movements, actions, and
powers appropriate to heal them. It is not only inwardly costly

through the sharing of pain and sorrow, but outwardly costly in the expressions appropriate to the occasion—identification and support of unpopular causes, speaking out against the voices of self-satisfaction and tyranny, taking risks of one's own earthly security and prestige.

Again, Christ is pattern not by external authority, but by the subjective truth of his own life, suffering, and death. We do not bear crosses because of an example given us to follow; we bear crosses because God has disclosed in Jesus Christ that cross-bearing is a way of love and life. Cross-bearing is not a form of pride or masochism. It has a moral power and beauty as the outward side of a life of love.

Thus cross-bearing, in a sense, joins self-denial to the pattern of life Sittler calls "re-enactment" of the "shape of the engendering deed." Self-denial and cross-bearing are fruits of a life in relation to Christ as its personal center, in relation to all that is given and disclosed in him. In a sense, in our lives they are a "re-enactment" or "re-duplication" of God's redeeming and revealing action. But the deed does not stop with suffering and death, as many pious Protestants and Catholics seem to believe. We live also the life of victory over sin and death. Christ is the Pattern of the new life, the life of hope, joy, redeeming love, and renewal, the life of seeking the neighbor's good, the social good. Christ is the Pattern for a life of victory over sin and death, of redeeming and creative moral possibilities.

The new life, victorious and hopeful, tells us less of what we ought to do and be in detail than even the life of self-denial and cross-bearing does. Our conformation is to love that forms us and thus that is exhibited in and through our actions. It is, as we have seen in the discussions of Christ the Justifier and the Sanctifier, a life of freedom from the rigidities of morals and customs, freedom to do the unexpected, to violate the herd morality, to create new good in new forms. The Pattern we have to follow is more clearly a pattern of outlook and disposition than a pattern of action. It does not define precisely what the particular historical goal of action ought to be. It does not give us a political way to follow. The very nature of our new life centered in Christ makes for an "open morality," to use Bergson's phrase, for "ethics of creativity," to use Berdyaev's phrase. Christ's overcoming of death testifies to power, life, and hope that are not bound to the common expectations of men. It testifies to life unprecedented in relation to the morals, beliefs, and behavior of men.

No universal lines of social morality can be formulated and deduced; social ethics remains pragmatic to a great extent. But one living in a society with all its closed character is given courage, life, and hope to break through accepted levels of custom and social pattern, to bring new possibilities and life to bear.

Those who seek in Jesus Christ a complete moral blueprint by which they can build their lives, or a detailed moral map by which they can arrive at a better human community, will not find in him what they seek. The Christian life must draw upon the blueprints and maps of philosophy, social and political sciences, and general wisdom to find its way from time to time and place to place. Christ is not all-sufficient as a source of moral guidance. He did not mean to be, and he was not meant to be. But he is the Pattern in the sense that his life was the exhibition, expression, and manifestation of his Godliness, of God's disclosure through this man Jesus Christ. Our lives in faith partake of his Godliness, and like his can manifest, express, and exhibit moral seriousness and moral action, self-denial, cross-bearing, and love as the fruits of God's work. He is Pattern for us as we are patterned by him. Not all we need for moral life and action is found in him, but Christians find in him the center, the root of life, including moral life.

Yet if what God has done for man in Christ has a story that is the appropriate historical manifestation of it, a story to be found in the Gospel narratives, this story does give some shape and specification to what human purposes, actions, and orders are appropriate expressions of man's own sharing in Christ's life. Thus we turn to the teachings of Jesus.

VI ⎰ JESUS CHRIST,

The Teacher

And when Jesus finished these sayings, the crowds were astonished at his teaching, for he taught them as one who had authority, and not as their scribes.

MATTHEW 7:28–29

[Nicodemus] came to Jesus by night and said to him, "Rabbi, we know that you are a teacher come from God."

JOHN 3:2

Take my yoke upon you and learn from me. . . .

MATTHEW 11:29

There are two ways, one of life and one of death; and great is the difference between the two ways. This is the way of life: "First, you shall love God who made you, secondly, your neighbor as yourself, and whatever you would not like done to you, do not to another."

Didache, 1:1–2

The ideal picture of human life which Jesus draws in what he has to say about morals, is a picture of life in the Kingdom of God on earth, life as it may be lived by men who acknowledged one supreme loyalty, in whose hearts one supreme passion burns; and it is only as we hear the call to that loyalty and feel that passion that the moral teaching of Jesus grows luminous.

T. W. MANSON. The Teaching of Jesus, p. 286

We must reduce our volume to the simple Evangelists; select, even from them, the very words only of Jesus, paring off the amphibologisms into which they have been led, by forgetting often, or not understanding, what had fallen from Him, by giving their own misconceptions as his dicta, and expressing unintelligibly for others what they had not understood themselves. There will be found remaining the most sublime and benevolent code of morals which has ever been offered to man.

THOMAS JEFFERSON, in a letter to John Adams (1813)

The good is the will of God, not the self-realization of humanity, not man's endowment. . . . His ethic also is strictly opposed to every humanistic and value ethic; it is an ethic of obedience: He sees the meaning of human action not in the development toward an ideal of man which is founded on the human spirit, nor in the realization of an ideal human society through human action. He has no so-called individual or social ethics; the concept of an ideal or end is foreign to him. . . . Conduct moreover is not significant because a value is achieved or realized through action; the action as such is obedience or disobedience; thus Jesus has no system of values. This really means that *Jesus teaches no ethics at all* in the sense of an intelligible theory valid for all men concerning what should be done and left undone.

RUDOLF BULTMANN, *Jesus and the Word*, p. 84

The ethic of Jesus is the perfect fruit of prophetic religion. Its ideal of love has the same relation to the facts and necessities of human experience as God of prophetic faith has to the world. It is drawn from, and relevant to, every moral experience. It is immanent in life as God is immanent in the world. It transcends the possibilities of human life in its final pinnacle as God transcends the world.

REINHOLD NIEBUHR, *An Interpretation
of Christian Ethics*, p. 37

The Sermon on the Mount . . . is primarily and decisively a notification, a proclamation, a description and a program. Its imperatives, too, have primarily and decisively the character of indicating a position and laying a foundation. The position indicated and the foundation laid are the kingdom, Jesus, the new man. . . . The Sermon on the Mount proclaims the consummation of the covenant of grace, and therefore the *telos* of the Law and the Ten Commandments.

KARL BARTH, *Church Dogmatics*, II/2, p. 688.

The sermon which Our Lord delivered on the mountain contains the whole formation of the life of a Christian. Therein man's interior movements are ordered.

St. Thomas Aquinas, *Summa Theologica*
First Part of Second Part, Q. 108, Art. 3

WE HAVE SEEN IN THE PREVIOUS CHAPTER HOW CHRISTIANS HAVE been admonished to follow Jesus in answer to their question, "What ought I to do?" Indeed, the ethics of discipleship can only be artificially divided between following the person and following his teachings. This could be seen if one chose to study further two very different books referred to extensively in that chapter. Newman Smyth fills out the content of the moral ideal with extensive reference to the teachings of Jesus; Dietrich Bonhoeffer's *Cost of Discipleship* contains moving expositions of Matt. 5–7 as a way of fleshing out the content of the radical obedience to which Christ calls men. Indeed, in one sense this chapter is but a subdivision of the previous chapter.

In seeking an answer to their moral quests, Christians have often been counseled to follow the teachings of Jesus. Our quotations at the beginning of this chapter indicate both some of the reasons why they are so counseled, and something of what this counsel is to achieve for them. Early in the life of the Church, *The Didache*, or "Teachings of the Twelve Apostles," in its first chapters drew a contrast between the way of life and the way of death. To go the way of life is to live out the teachings of Jesus, to go the way of death is to live the life of those who manifest all the vices from which Christian faith saves men—fornication, self-centeredness, and many more. To be in the way of life is to follow the teachings of Jesus.[1]

Thomas Jefferson's personal compendium from the New Testament, which he called "The Life and Morals of Jesus of Nazareth" was typical of other enlightened men's response to the Christian faith in the eighteenth century. No salvific issue was at stake, no issue of life or death; nor did he wish to lend credence to the teachings on the

---

[1] See *The Didache*, Chs. 1–6; in *The Fathers of the Church, The Apostolic Fathers* (New York, 1947), pp. 171–76.

basis of some verbal inspiration of the Bible. He was no more concerned to give an interpretation of the revelation of God in the
person of Jesus Christ than he was to prop up the importance of the
teachings with arguments about biblical inspiration. Rather, the
import of the teaching was almost self-evident to Jefferson: it was
"the most sublime and benevolent code of morals . . . ever . . .
offered to man."[2] The sublimity of the "code" itself was persuasive
to the rational man. Tolstoi, a century later, had more of a sense of
the religious than did Jefferson, but in both *The Teaching of Jesus*
which he compiled and supplemented for the edification of children,
and in *The Christian Teaching*, the significance is the revelation of a
superior moral life which led to a basic peace and happiness. After
struggling to the point of despair to find a sense of well-being, Tolstoi
found the "presence of truth" in the Gospel teachings, a truth different from that taught by the churches.

At length this solution became perfectly clear, and not only clear, but
incontestable as well; because, firstly, it harmonized entirely with the demands of my reason and heart, and secondly, when I came to understand
it, I saw that this was not my exclusive interpretation of the Gospel (as it
might appear), nor even the exclusive revelation of Christ, but the very
solution of the problem given more or less explicitly by the best among
men both before and after the Gospel was given.

Who were these men? Moses, Isaiah, Confucius, the early Greeks,
Buddha, Pascal, Spinoza, Fichte, Feuerbach, and "all those . . .
who, taking no teachings on trust, thought and spoke sincerely upon
the meaning of life."[3] For Tolstoi as for Jefferson, there was a self-
authenticating and persuasive power in the teachings of Jesus.

A radically different authorization is claimed by the contemporary
conservative evangelical author, Carl F. H. Henry. Writing of not
only the teachings of Jesus, he says, "The first emphasis of Hebrew-
Christian ethics must always be the absolute uniqueness of its revealed character. Every attempt to explain Christian ethics as being
merely a more complex development of the insights of general ethics
either conceals or minimizes the basis it has in special revelation."[4]

---

[2] From a letter to John Adams, quoted in the editor's "Foreword" to Jefferson, *The Life and Morals of Jesus of Nazareth* (New York, 1940), p. vii.
[3] Leo Tolstoi, *The Christian Teaching* (New York, 1898), pp. xi–xii; see also
Tolstoi, *The Teaching of Jesus* (New York, 1908).
[4] C. F. H. Henry, *Christian Personal Ethics* (Grand Rapids, 1957), p. 146.

"The Christian ethic is a specially revealed morality—not merely a religious ethics. It gains its reality in and through supernatural disclosure."[5] Within this view of special revelation, then, the Sermon on the Mount is a "particularization of the will of God." One might say that for Henry and others, the teachings of Jesus have ethical importance only because they are in the Bible; if they were found among a collection of newly discovered manuscripts in Greece they would not have any authority. The authority attributed to the Bible is the basis for their importance.

The question of the authority of the teachings of Jesus for morality in general, and even for Christian morality, has become much more complex in the past few decades for a number of reasons. Among these, three seem to be of greatest importance.

First, the biblical scholars raised serious questions about the ethicists' assumption that the teachings were of timeless applicability. The profound impact that the idea of the Kingdom of God had on the social gospel writers is a well-known case in point. The idea of the Kingdom in the teachings of Jesus was translated into more or less relevant terms to endorse a growing democratization, cooperation, and socialization of American life. The petition, "Thy Kingdom come" was meant to stir men on to greater efforts to build or achieve the Kingdom on earth. But what if the Kingdom does not refer to the establishment of a just and loving social order on earth? What if, in the light of such chapters as Mark 13, Jesus expected God to bring in the Kingdom by divine intervention in an apocalyptic event? What if those "hard sayings" of Jesus have reference to an "interim ethic," not appropriate for American society, but the kind of life to be lived because historical responsibility was to be altered by God's imminent forceful reign? Such questions raised by Schweitzer and others created an uncertainty from which ethicists have never been relieved.[6]

Second, the form-critical scholars, in a sense continuing the work of their antecedents, proceeded to seek to determine which words were authentically those of Jesus and which were not. This effort was not new; Thomas Jefferson, among others, did an editing job, "ar-

[5] *Ibid.*, p. 193.
[6] For one account of the discussion and of where it leaves the issue of the use of the ethics of Jesus, see Amos Wilder, *Eschatology and Ethics in the Teaching of Jesus* (New York, 1950).

ranging the material which is evidently his and which is as easily distinguished as diamonds in a dung-hill."[7] The work of Dibelius and Bultmann that has now evolved into the "new quest for the historical Jesus" raised radically the question of whether or not verifiable historical authenticity could be a ground for the authority of much that was attributed to Jesus by the nonscientific writers of the Gospel narratives. The question raised for the ethicist became one of what reliance and authority the so-called teachings of Jesus could carry if they were not the words or teachings of Jesus himself. To say that at least the texts we have represent the consensus of the apostolic community about what is at least attributable or harmonious with the memory of that community does not satisfy the profound quest for the proper answer to the question of whether faith and ethics in the Christian community have to rest on verifiable historical evidence. Again, the ethicists have not got out of uncertainty; nor can they wait for the New Testament scholars to achieve unanimity.[8]

Third, in the theological revival of 1920–60, for various reasons it was affirmed among Protestants that the revelation given in the Bible was one basically of the deeds of God, and not of a morality. The account of God's ways with man was the story told—in creation of man, his judgment as well as sustaining care of man, his redemption of man. Jesus Christ then is to be seen primarily as the one in and through whom God made himself known, and not as the ideal life pattern or the giver of a sublime moral code. The Bible became the basis for interpretations of the meanings of events, or the basis for developing great theological themes. We have seen in previous chapters that the Bible has always and for most writers had a theological significance, and its ethical significance resting on the theology has referred to more than just the moral teachings contained in it. The teachings of Jesus have had to be seen in relation to the theological significance of Jesus; in recent decades this has been brought sharply to the awareness of ethicists, whose immediate forebears in the field had built such large edifices on the foundation of Jesus' teachings.[9]

[7] Jefferson, *op. cit.*, pp. vii-viii.

[8] See, for example, Rudolf Bultmann, *The History of the Synoptic Tradition* (New York, 1963).

[9] For a discussion of the significance of this for American Christian ethics, see my chapter, "Christian Ethics," in Paul Ramsey, ed., *Religion* (Englewood Cliffs, 1965), pp. 309–25.

What ought I to do? Follow the teachings of Jesus. But this is meaningless apart from the experience of faith. Indeed, the message of Jesus is the message of faith, of trust in the goodness and mercy of God. This is not only the message of the teachings of Jesus, but of his life. The teachings are themselves a call to perfect and complete trust in God; their importance is not in what they say that appears to be of moral importance, but in the relationship that they both indicate and call forth as the proper relation to God. Or, God in Jesus shows what he wills his relation to man to be—one of love, of caring for man. The message in turn is that men should so be related to God and to their neighbors. What is given us in Jesus' teaching, as part of the whole revelation, is the evocation and beckoning to a basic attitude, or basic disposition. We are called to an attitude of obedience, of trust, of love. We are to be disposed toward God in obedience and to obey him in our relations to others. We are to be disposed toward God in love, and in turn to be affirmative toward others in love since God has loved us. What do the teachings of Jesus make clear to men in faith? They are to be obedient, to be loving, to have a basic disposition in accord with the gift of God in Jesus Christ.

What ought I to do? I ought to have a basic purpose or intention in accord with Jesus' teaching, for his teaching is in accord with God's purpose and intention for man revealed in the gospel. The teachings give us the *telos*, the ultimate end of God's will and law. They give us the basic direction for our new life in Christ. They are not so important for their moral details, for the specific rules and precepts, but for the direction and way that they show Christians to go. Our own intentions and direction of life ought to be in accord with the basic direction of Jesus' teaching.

What ought I to do? Some say we are to follow the teachings of Jesus as a new moral code. This moral code is authorized, as we have seen above, by some on the basis of its apparent reasonableness, its intrinsic moral appeal. To follow this moral code would be to order life, personal and social, in such a way that peace and good will would take place in our common life.

The moral code is also authorized as the revelation of the new law, as the outer, written precepts that are in accord with the new law of life and love written on the heart. The teachings, for those who are converted, provide the explication of the will of God. For some this conversion is the work of the Spirit through preaching and a dramatic repentance and experience; for some it is the work of being drawn into Christ through the sacraments and other ministries of the Church. The new law in precept form is to be obeyed because the new law is written on the heart. To obey the new law is to show forth the new life, to lead one on the way to one's final end.

What ought I to do? Seek to achieve the ideals given in the teachings of Jesus. As in the language of the law, so in the language of ideals they can be judged appealing on the basis of the kind of fulfilling human consequences they would have if only men would follow them. They have an intrinsic moral appeal to some humane consciences. But others are clear that the ideals make no sense apart from the kind of loyalty, faith, and trust out of which they were born in Jesus' own life and ministry. The ideals of Jesus can be fulfilled by those who have a kind of passion and loyalty to God that Jesus had.

What ought I to do? In serious moral judgments consider teachings of Jesus as norms that illuminate options and are authoritative in the determination of choices. The teachings of Jesus are not easily applicable as a norm, but must be brought to bear together with other considerations and principles derived from them in one's decisions. They are the new law to be obeyed or applied by Christians in their judgments and actions.

Thus we see that the teachings are used to make various kinds of religious and ethical points. Their commendations and prohibitions reinforce the call to a basic attitude or disposition; they are also seen to indicate the way, the basic direction of the moral life of the faithful community; and they are believed to be a new law or a new set of ideals, either self-recommending on the basis of moral appeal, or in some way part of God's revelation.

THE TEACHINGS OF JESUS—AN ATTITUDE

What is taught or evoked by the teachings of Jesus in the interpretation of some writers is basically an attitude, or a determination of the will. To make this point, Rudolf Bultmann finds in, or imposes upon, the teachings of Jesus a view that rules out all ethics of idealism, development, and authoritative moral norms. He seems to wish to make it clear that the main if not only point to what men call the ethical teachings of Jesus is a call to radical obedience, to self-sacrifice, and to love as "an attitude of the will." Bultmann would be properly uneasy about much elaboration of what obedience or willingness to self-sacrifice might be as a "lasting disposition" (*habitus* in St. Thomas), for that would violate the prime focus placed upon the decision to be obedient, the decision to love. It would assume that the teachings of Jesus have to do with the formation of character traits, with the development of qualities of life—an interpretation he explicitly rejects. But one does not force the word "attitude" excessively to suggest that the teachings of Jesus for Bultmann evoke a disposition to be obedient, to be loving, to be self-sacrificing, particularly if this can be contrasted with the moral purposes and ideals that some other writers find there. The teachings relate not to goals, ideals, or moral laws, but to the basic stance of the believer, to his willingness to be obedient.

Certainly Bultmann would be severe in his criticism of other writers who wish to elaborate on the qualities of life or the disposition engendered and taught by Jesus. When Lindsay Dewar tells us that certain qualities of life are commended by Jesus, such as "unwillingness to cause scandal," he has approached the teachings of "Our Lord," as Anglicans are wont to call him, in a radically different way from Bultmann's. Or when L. H. Marshall expounds a commonplace interpretation of the teaching, that for Jesus "conduct is determined by character and not character by conduct," Bultmann would shudder. The differences between him and these authors are profound, for they read the Gospel with different exegetical and philosophical principles in view. Indeed, Dewar and Marshall believe that Jesus taught ethics in the ordinary usage of that word, and one aspect (not the only one) of that ethics is that men are to have certain good qualities of life, certain good dispositions. For all the differences between Bultmann and these authors about what is taught or evoked, how it comes into being, and what the biblical historical authorization for it is, they all stress a stance or attitude of the human self.

"So then by their fruits you will know them." These words of Jesus mean, for L. H. Marshall, "when a man's disposition is good, that is, when a man with his whole heart wills what God wills, his conduct is good."[10] While Aristotle's theory of the formation of virtues by habituation, in Marshall's view, argues that doing good deeds makes a

---

[10] L. H. Marshall, *The Challenge of New Testament Ethics* (London, 1946), p. 68.

man good in character, Jesus clearly understood, as Kant did, that the disposition of the will was at the heart of morality. This is what Jesus' "internalization" of morality—from obedience to external codes to a willingness of the heart—discloses. Conduct is "the natural and inevitable expression of a good disposition."[11] For Marshall the law of God is to be written on the heart, so there is an internalized norm that is joyously and spontaneously followed. This is the point of the account in Matt. 12 of the parable of the unclean spirit. It may find the house swept clean, but unless the good enters to fill the house, seven other unclean spirits are likely to dwell there. Those who follow Christ's teaching acquire "moral genius." The Christian, he quotes from Sir John Seeley, "must . . . cherish a peculiar temperament, such that every combination of circumstances involving moral considerations may instantly affect him in a peculiar way and excite peculiar feelings in him." He is to arrive at the right practical conclusion "by an instantaneous impulse." This, Marshall endorses as a "perfect description of the way in which the moral sense of the Christian at his best always works. . . . It is real moral genius."[12]

The features of this good disposition were described by Jesus in the Beatitudes. They set forth "the tone and temper and quality of spirit" of those who have the Kingdom of God within them. Some attention to Marshall's interpretation of them needs to be given to see how one interpreter of the teachings of Jesus visualizes their challenge. "Blessed are the poor" (Luke's form) tells us that "the hard-working poor are more likely to find in their spiritual goods their most precious possessions, to spend themselves in the service of others, to be humble-minded, self-sacrificing, compassionate, kind, tender. . . ."[13] "Blessed are they that mourn" reminds us that men and women rarely achieve noble and strong character unless they have suffered. "Blessed are the gentle" (meek) indicates the importance of forbearance and consideration of others, of willingness to forgo one's own interests for the sake of others, of those qualities that are opposites of arrogance, violence, and domination. Mercifulness, purity of heart, peacefulness and "enthusiasm for humanity," steadfastness in holding fast to virtue, humility, willingness to forgive are

---

[11] *Ibid.*, p. 70.
[12] The first quotation is from Sir John Seeley, *Ecce Homo* (Boston, 1900), p. 344, cited by Marshall, *op. cit.*, pp. 71–72. The second quotation is also p. 72.
[13] Marshall, *op. cit.*, pp. 76, 77.

all features of the good disposition that characterizes the new humanity.

What Marshall calls "features" of the good disposition, Lindsay Dewar, in *An Outline of New Testament Ethics*, calls "qualities" that are "commended by Christ."[14] Among them is faith as trust, trust in God that includes within it the virtue of courage. Dewar sees both Jesus' rebuke of the disciples for their lack of faith on the occasion of their fear during the storm on the Sea of Galilee and his rebuke of cowardice in Mark 4:20 as grounds for affirming that faith (which the disciples did not have) has implicitly in it the virtue of courage. Another quality commended by Jesus, says Dewar, is that of "forgivingness." "Here, indeed, as in the case of the word *agape*, we have a new word for a new virtue."[15] Jesus' stress on the importance of this virtue is to be seen in the petition of the Lord's Prayer where forgiveness and forgivingness are linked, and in many of the parables. It is to be seen in what Jesus says about freedom from vindictiveness. Jesus teaches us also not to will to cause scandal, as in Mark 9:42. "Whoever causes one of these little ones who believe in me to sin, it would be better for him if a great millstone were hung round his neck and he were thrown into the sea." Just as certain qualities were commended, so others received special condemnation by Jesus, such as lustfulness, covetousness, hypocrisy, and various forms of foolishness.

To amplify the descriptions of the attitudes, dispositions, and "traits of character" that Jesus is believed to have commended is not a difficult task. One need only to read the Gospels looking for such, and to remember dozens of sermons he has read, heard, and preached, in order to indicate how the Christian religious consciousness has believed that such dispositions are not only the fruits of sanctifying grace, but also commended by the teaching of Jesus. Freedom from anger, the spirit of reconciliation, honesty, willingness to turn the other cheek and go the second mile, freedom from anxiety about the matters of eat and drink, and absence of judgmental attitudes can all be sifted out of the Sermon on the Mount as proper aspects of the disposition of the believer. Certainly love has

---

[14] Lindsay Dewar, *An Outline of New Testament Ethics* (London, 1949), pp. 62 ff.

[15] *Ibid.*, p. 65.

been considered to be pre-eminent among all the attitudes and dispositions commended by Jesus.

Indeed, for many Christians, the distinguishing characteristic of the ethics of their community has been the notion that morality has become something of the "heart" and not rules and laws imposed from without. Christians are supposed to be characterized by an inward disposition that governs their relations to others; they are to be loving. In popular piety certainly some of the most remembered persons are those who seemed to have embodied the attitude that Jesus seems to have embodied—St. Francis with his carefree concern for the needs of others, his humility, his joy, his childlike trust, or Albert Schweitzer with his "reverence for life." The internalization of certain values so that the words and deeds of Christians are expressions of that disposition is highly commended in many Christian groups.

Even Karl Barth, who is hardly guilty of pious sentimentalism about Jesus, states that as the Christian corresponds to God's gracious action, there are definite *attitudes* and acts that can be found. These are "all in line with Matt. 5:48." "You, therefore, must be perfect as your heavenly Father is perfect." Boldly stated, these attitudes and the actions that express them are a *readiness* to forgive, to be compassionate, to bear each other's burdens, to be helpful. A "persistent kindness," humility, and love are proper. Barth makes no careful distinctions between attitudes, acts, demands, and commands, but it is safe to say that the gracious power of God commands definite attitudes as proper for those who endorse this grace in their lives. Jesus' teachings specify what these are and ought to be.[16]

Bultmann, though he is concerned to show that Jesus' teaching is not primarily ethical in the ordinary usages of that word, nonetheless in my opinion ends up stipulating a dispositional ethic as the characterization of Jesus' teaching. The message of Jesus, according to him, as was noted in Chapter IV, is not primarily, or even in an important way, ethical. The "Kingdom of God," which had become the ideal or the paradigm for a just social order in liberal Protestantism, is a message of eschatological deliverance, which ends all earthly things, and not a message of morality. "Thus it is meaningless to call the Kingdom of God the 'highest value,' if by this is meant the culmina-

[16] Karl Barth, *Church Dogmatics*, II/2, p. 578.

tion of all that men consider good." It is *"no 'highest good' in the ethical sense.* It is not a good toward which the will and action of men is directed, not an ideal which is in any sense realized through human conduct. . . ."[17]

This line of interpretation continues with reference to the teachings of Jesus in general and to particular aspects of them. "Jesus expresses no conception of a human ideal, no thought of a development of human capacities, no idea of something valuable in man as such, no conception of the spirit in the modern sense. Of the spirit in our sense of its life or experience, Jesus does not speak at all." "Jesus . . . differentiates his thought sharply from the *idealistic ethic.* He knows nothing of *doing good for good's sake.* . . ." "His ethic . . . is strictly opposed to every humanistic ethic and value ethic. . . ." "This view also parts company with the *idea of development,* according to which the moral judgment of man develops or the man himself develops and perfects himself." ". . . It is misleading to set Jesus' moral teaching as an 'ethic of intention' " in contrast to an ethic of works. The significance of obedience, though it may appear to be like an ethic of intention, "is not that it is a habit of man's inner life, an attribute of man which gives him as such a moral quality."[18]

Obviously, Bultmann wishes to differentiate the heart of the matter in Jesus' ethical teaching from most of the common types or styles of ethical theory, including an ethic of dispositions in man's inner life. This is because he views man as radically free, making his decisions and commitments, not out of habits, internalized values, or following of ideals, but in his radical freedom. What is demanded in Jesus' teaching is a decision. The message of the Kingdom of God "signifies for man the ultimate Either-Or, which constrains him to decision."[19] "Jesus sees man as standing here and now under the necessity of decision, with the possibility of decision through his own free act. Only what a man now does gives him his value." Man's worth is not determined by his qualities of human life, or by the character of his spiritual life, but by his decision.[20] Similarly, when Bultmann speaks of love, it is not a quality of actions, nor is it a rule

[17] Bultmann, *Jesus and the Word,* pp. 35–36.
[18] *Ibid.,* pp. 53, 79, 84, 85, 86.
[19] *Ibid.,* pp. 40–41.
[20] *Ibid.,* p. 54.

or ideal, but it is a commandment to obey, to renounce one's own claim. "Jesus does not support his demand for love by referring to the value of other men as human beings, and love of enemies is not the high point of universal love of humanity, but the high point of overcoming the self, the surrender of one's own claim."[21] These quotations make it clear that if Bultmann's view of Jesus' ethical teaching is that it calls forth an attitude, or a disposition, this is different from the "good disposition" or the "qualities" that Marshall and Dewar find commended there.

Yet the outcome of Bultmann's interpretation is finally to indicate that what the teachings require is basically attitudinal or dispositional in character. What Jesus' teachings demand is an attitude of the will. One can find the word "attitude" used sparingly by Bultmann in this regard. "Jesus knows only one attitude toward God—*obedience*. Since he sees man standing at the point of decision, the essential part of man for him is the will, the free act. . . ."[22] Indeed, the great commandment of love suggests, as Bultmann interprets it, the relation between one's attitude toward God and one's attitude toward the neighbor. "The chief command is this: love God, bow your own will in obedience to God's. And this first command defines the meaning of the second—the attitude which I take toward my neighbor is determined by the attitude which I take before God; as obedient to God, setting aside my selfish will, renouncing my own claims, I stand before my neighbor, prepared for sacrifice for my neighbor as for God."[23] Love is not an emotion or a desire for reunion of the estranged; it is "an attitude of the will," and thus subject to command.

The weight of the evidence for suggesting that Bultmann sees Jesus' teaching to command an attitude does not rest solely upon the fact that he used the word in a few significant places, though that is important. It rests more in what one comes to by a process of elimination in which Bultmann himself engages. To what do the ethical teachings not refer? What kinds of ethics are they not? In Bultmann's effort to systematize Jesus' perspective he indicates how many types of ethical theory can be contrasted with Jesus'.[24] We

---

[21] *Ibid.*, p. 112.

[22] *Ibid.*, p. 48.

[23] *Ibid.*, p .114.

[24] This whole process seems a bit strange to me. Jesus did not know an idealistic ethic from an ethic of habituation, and certainly also he was not aware

have seen in Bultmann's own words what he believes Jesus does not intend to teach—a conception of the human ideal, development of human capacities, the value of man *qua* man, the flowering of the human spirit, value theory, habituation in virtue, etc. The net effect of this process of elimination is that Jesus' ethical teachings refer ultimately to the man who is being addressed rather than a conception of a morally good world. And they refer to man's disposition toward God and neighbor, but not in the sense of *habitus,* lasting dispositions acquired by practice and grace. That distinction is important; in a sense Dewar and Marshall see Jesus endorsing qualities or traits of character without formulating a theory of the virtues such as one finds in St. Thomas to explain such traits. Bultmann's interpretation rules out lasting dispositions which are the condition out of which intentions and actions come because such a view would mitigate the severity of the call for an either-or decision for obedience. Bultmann's normative view of man, which he believes was also Jesus' view, emphasizes man's capacity to make decisions in his radical freedom from moment to moment, and thus does not take as seriously as others the continuities of experience that predispose a man to respond in a given moment in a particular way. Thus attitude for him cannot be used as a predisposition formed by prior acts. Nonetheless, he sees Jesus calling for an attitude—that of obedience to God, and that of willingness to sacrifice for the neighbor. What Jesus teaches is that man must be willing to obey, willing to sacrifice himself for the sake of the other. But this is not a general willingness, as if it were a habit. It is an attitude evoked in the moment.

Jesus teaches what the self ought to do in the moment of decision. The direction is not to the neighbor for the sake of his good, not to the society for the sake of its good, but to the self. Love of God seems to mean, "Obey God," and the attitude of obedience seems to be the prime object of attention. Love of neighbor seems to mean, "Renounce your own claim," and this attitude of renunciation seems to be the prime object of attention. It teaches "the *readiness* to *forgive* one's neighbor, and this readiness characterizes most dis-

---

of the existentialist alternative. Bultmann strikes me as forcing a consistency of ethical theory, developed in modern philosophy, on Jesus, who probably cared not a whit about what theory of ethics (idealism, intention, etc.) he was offering, especially since he was not schooled in such matters.

tinctly the love which is here demanded."[25] Note that love is characterized by a "readiness" of the self, a disposition of the self.[26]

We see that Bultmann interprets Jesus' ethical teaching to be directed toward the attitude, the readiness of the Christian. It is not a quality of life, not a good disposition with certain features, but an attitude of the will. Whether one follows the path of Marshall or Bultmann in exposition is a matter of importance, and involves technical judgments about proper exegetical and interpretative procedures on which not only ethicists but also New Testament scholars disagree. How novel Jesus' stress on disposition is in the history of Jewish ethics is also a question that does not have to be adjudicated here. The point to be stressed is that the teachings suggest the propriety of certain attitudes or dispositions as appropriate for Christians. Jesus in his teaching evokes, commends, and commands a readiness, a stance toward God and neighbor. It would be hard to read the teachings attributed to Jesus in the Gospels without receiving the profound impression that for him the inner disposition or attitude of will is a significant part of the moral life as he spoke about it. There is, whether it be absolutely novel or not, a profound sense of the internalization of morality. Not only is this the case with the obvious stress on one's intent (whoever looks on a woman with lust in his heart has already committed adultery), but also with the commendation of trust, obedience, and love. Perhaps the language of "qualities" and of "features" of a good character is not well-chosen to describe this dimension of the morality commended and commanded to the disciples. Whatever words are chosen need to point to the way in which those who followed Jesus were to be disposed to love, to obey, to trust, to be humble and merciful. There is a determination of will and disposition that is in accord with Jesus' message. It is by no means improper to use that message, those teachings, to suggest

[25] Bultmann, *Jesus and the Word*, p. 116; italics for "readiness" are mine; for "forgive," Bultmann's.

[26] Bultmann has learned from Kierkegaard's *Works of Love* on these points. Kierkegaard's concern is more with the self, the inward self that develops in obedience to the command to love than it is with the neighbor who is to be loved. For example, "If it were not a duty to love, then the concept of neighbor would not exist, but only when one loves one's neighbor, only then is the selfish partiality eradicated, and the equality of the eternal preserved" (Swenson trans.; Princeton, 1946), p. 37. Kierkegaard is more concerned to eradicate selfish partiality in the self than he is to meet the neighbor's need.

aspects of the interior readiness of the Christian to act in accord with the gospel.

THE TEACHINGS OF JESUS—A DIRECTION

For many Christians, Jesus not only commends or evokes an attitude, or set of attitudes; he also shows the basic way, direction, line, which their moral lives are to follow. Jesus' teachings are, in a sense, pointers; they show the direction in which human behavior that is consistent with the message of salvation will go. They are not to be seen as rules absolutely authoritative and immediately applicable in every situation. They do not provide the sole norms in the light of which moral action is to be judged and guided. Rather, their authority is more instructional than legal, more informing than prescriptive. The teachings do not call for copying; one does not model his life *after them in an external way*. Rather, just as the particular commands of Jesus are consistent with the message of God's love, God's Kingdom, God's election of men in Christ, so also the deeds of Christians ought to be consistent with the message of God's grace. The teachings of Jesus point to the kinds of behavior that will be consistent with the message of redemption.

This way of using the teachings of Jesus seeks to maintain the priority of the message of God's grace without losing the imperative character of the commands of Jesus. The authorization of the imperative lies within the gospel, the message. No doubt this is true for those who stress attitude as well, but the distinctive note I wish to indicate here is that the imperative shows the way, it has moral content and is not merely a formal command to obey, to love. In a sense, if a Christian should ask, "What should I do to show my obedience, to show my love?" the answer would be, "Read the Bible, and particularly the teachings of Jesus, and you will get a sense of the purposes, the ends, the deeds that are fitting expressions of your disposition to obey and to love." The answer would not be, "Do what Jesus said to do," or "Do what Jesus did," in the form of external imitation. Nor would it be, "From the teachings of Jesus, you can distill a rule that you ought rationally to apply"; nor would it be, "Follow the sublime moral code that Jesus gives." The use of the teachings as direction is more by way of analogy than deduction, more by way of illustration than application, more through how they help one to perceive and understand what action is appropriate than through explicit definition or delineation of appropriate action.

Karl Barth, in my judgment, uses the teachings of Jesus in Christian ethics in this way, as was noted in Chapter II. When Barth writes about Jesus Christ giving men direction, however, he is indicating something more important than just the instruction of Jesus' teachings. He is first, in the order of importance, indicating that it is the work of the Holy Spirit, "the living Lord Jesus Christ Himself in the work of the sanctification of his particular people in the world," that gives direction.[27] True to his theological principles, in which it is the gracious determination of the work of God that moves men in faith and in the faithful life, Barth attributes the direction to the sanctifying work of God himself. Some attention needs to be given to this work of sanctifying grace if we are to see the teachings of Jesus in their proper theological context. The Holy Spirit, he says, "creates saints by giving them direction." By this, Barth does not mean something "weak and external" but, rather, suggests that direction "speaks meaningfully and dynamically . . . of man's indication to a particular and new situation, of the correction which he must receive in it, and of the instruction which he is thereby given to adopt a particular attitude." It is not the kind of instruction or direction one man gives another man. "It is the direction of the royal man Jesus, who is the one true Son of God." "Thus . . . it falls, as it were, vertically into the lives of those to whom it is given. It is thus effective with divine power. It is the sowing and the developing seed of new life. It crushes and breaks and destroys that which resists it. It constitutes itself the ruling and determinative factor in the whole being of those to whom it is given . . . It becomes their wisdom." Christians hear the direction as a determinative and effective call to obedience. Their sin is limited by the presence of the Spirit. They participate in Jesus Christ.[28]

This direction of the Holy Spirit, this sanctification of man, is a call to a life of discipleship, a call to follow Jesus Christ. It is within this call to discipleship, to obedience, that the teachings of Jesus function to give certain "prominent lines," or to give a direction to the lives of Christians. The Sermon on the Mount, Barth can write, is "the order which constitutes the life of the people of God." In it,

[27] Karl Barth, *Church Dogmatics*, IV/2, p. 522.
[28] *Ibid.*, p. 523.

Jesus himself "defines, in the form of comprehensive positive and negative directions, the *sphere* in which He is present with His own, . . . the sphere of His care for them and lordship over them."[29] While one cannot use the Sermon to draw a picture of the Christian life, it is "a notification, a proclamation, a description, and a program. Its imperatives . . . have primarily and decisively the character of indicating a position and laying a foundation."[30] The words are carefully chosen to suggest several things. The Sermon is part of the declaration of what Christ is doing for man; it is not instruction apart from God's deeds. It nonetheless shows what the order of life Christ brings is, it lays a foundation and indicates a position. It proclaims the new manhood that Christ gives and yet at the same time is "instruction and exhortation, the training and exercise of man. Every 'Thou shalt!' and 'Thou shalt not!' is seriously meant as an intensified indicative which has the force of an intensified imperative."[31] The demand is a gift, the gift is a demand. "Grace must be lived out, or it is not grace."[32] "These demands denote modes of conduct which can become possible and necessary even in their literal sense for those who will hear and do the words of Jesus."[33] This is not to say that what God commands in a concrete situation is precisely what is said in the Sermon on the Mount, as we saw in the discussion of Barth in Chapter II. The Spirit leads men into new truth; the command can be a new command. But the voice of the Holy Spirit "in repetition and confirmation, in elucidation and application of the Word of the Sermon on the Mount . . . will lead them into all truth and from one truth to another." It appears that God's command, that the voice of the Spirit, will be consistent with the order of the people of God given in Jesus' teachings. Indeed, "a man can be obedient to the Sermon on the Mount only in so far as he is ready and prepared for acts of the most specific obedience on the lines it indicates and as God demands them from every man in his own hour and situation; only in so far, that is, as man is content to fill the position it requires and therefore to feel that he has *no other choice but to direct his life according to its claims*."[34]

---

29 Karl Barth, *Church Dogmatics*, II/2, p. 687. Italics added.
30 *Ibid.*, p. 688.
31 *Ibid.*, p. 694.
32 *Ibid.*, p. 695.
33 *Ibid.*, p. 697.
34 *Ibid.*, p. 699. Italics added.

Barth chooses the words "prominent lines" as another way of suggesting the directionality that the teachings of Jesus provide for his disciples. "The truth is . . . that what the Gospel sayings . . . really preserve are certain prominent lines along which the concrete commanding of Jesus, with its demand for concrete obedience, always moved in relation to individuals, characterizing it as His commanding in distinction from that of all other lords." Those who are called to obedience to Christ may be called to be different things in different times and places, but Christ's command "always moves along one or more of these prominent lines." Indeed there is no commitment to Christ "if the action of the disciple is not along one or more of these great lines."[35] These "lines of instruction" are to be found in the Sermon on the Mount and elsewhere. How Barth works with specific sayings is instructive, not only for the moral specification, but for the procedures that he uses.

There are a number of sayings that have to do with human possessions. "Give to him who begs from you, and do not refuse him who would borrow from you" (Matt. 5:42). "Lend, expecting nothing in return" (Luke 6:35). "If any one would sue you and take your coat, let him have your cloak as well" (Matt. 5:40). "Do not lay up for yourself treasures on earth . . ." (Matt. 6:19). "Take no gold, nor silver, nor copper in your belts, no bag for your journey, nor two tunics, nor sandals, nor a staff . . ." (Matt. 10:9). What is the "prominent line" to be discerned in these and other passages that deal with human possessions? It is not, in Barth's interpretation, a call to realize an "ideal or principle of poverty as it was later assumed into the monastic rule." Nor is it "the basis of a new society freed from the principle of private property." Nor can it "be reduced to a normative technical rule for dealing with possessions." Indeed, when one reads these sayings of Jesus "it is palpable that these are specific directions given to specific men at specific times and to be specifically followed, not in a formalized or spiritualized, but a literal sense." But one can discern "the drift of them"; they challenge and cut across the self-evident attachment that men have to things. The direction then is clear: the disciple of Jesus "does not only think and feel but acts (here and now, in this particular encounter with the neighbor) as one who is freed from this attachment. He not only can but does let go that which is his."[36]

[35] Karl Barth, *Church Dogmatics*, IV/2, p. 547.
[36] *Ibid.*, p. 548.

Barth discerns other such "lines of instruction" given by Jesus to those whom he calls to discipleship. From various texts that are similar to Matt. 20:26, "Whoever would be great among you must be your servant," such as Matt. 5:11, Matt. 5:39, Matt. 23:6 f., John 13:14 f., the following direction is discerned: "The disciple of Jesus can descend from the throne—the little throne perhaps—which even he may be allotted in human society." He does this because he is commanded to do so, for he undergoes a transvaluation of values through the ruling grace of God that frees him from the "constraint of ordinary conceptions of what constitutes social status and dignity and importance."[37] Both an attitude and a direction are commanded by such passages. The Christian, just as he is called to be freed from his concern with possessions, is also called to be freed from his concern for earthly status; this is the evocation of a disposition or attitude. But these sayings attributed to Jesus command those acts that are in accord with the disposition; they show the direction of behavior. The Kingdom of God transcends the earthly rules and common sense, thus, "If anyone strikes you on the right cheek, turn to him the other also" (Matt. 5:39). "If I then, your Lord and Teacher, have washed your feet, you also ought to wash one another's feet. For I have given you an example, that you should do as I have done to you" (John 13:14–15). There is a "prominent line" to these specific commandments.

Another line deals with the use of force. Careful to be consistent with his general method in ethics, Barth says that "According to the sense of the New Testament we cannot be pacifists in principle, only in practice." If men are called to discipleship, they must "consider very closely whether . . . we can avoid being practical pacifists, or fail to be so." This "is a concrete and incontestable direction which has to be carried out exactly as it is given." This direction, once again, is not a "general rule, a Christian system confronting that of the world, in competition with it, and in some way to be brought into harmony with it."[38] Rather it is the direction given in specific sayings of Jesus.

There is an order to Barth's thinking on this point that maintains

---

[37] *Ibid.*, p. 549.
[38] *Ibid.*, p. 550. For a remarkable critical study of Barth on the point of pacifism, see John Howard Yoder, *Karl Barth and Christian Pacifism* (Basel; mimeographed, n.d.).

the sense of the "intensified indicative which has the force of an intensified imperative." Those called to discipleship are not to fear force brought against them, "for at the very worst their enemies could kill only the body and not the soul. Their true and inward selves would remain inviolate." They are not to be anxious about their lives, for they are "under the care of the fatherly assistance and protection of God" who even cares for the sparrows, and for the very hairs on the head of every man[39] (Matt. 10:26 ff., also Matt. 5:25 ff.). "Fear not, therefore: you are of more value than many sparrows" (Matt. 10:31).

If the followers of Jesus are not to fear force (the intensified indicative), surely they are not to exercise force (the intensified imperative). In Luke 9:5 ff., there is an account of the disciples' disappointment when they were turned away by Samaritan villagers to whom Jesus had sent them. James and John said, "Lord, do you want us to bid fire come down from heaven and consume them?" But Jesus, who came not to destroy men's lives but to save them, rebuked the disciples.

At the Garden of Gethsemane, Jesus again prohibited the use of force (Matt. 26:47 ff.). The crowd came with Judas with swords and clubs, as if to seize a man of violence. When Jesus was taken, the narrative indicates that "one of those who were with Jesus stretched out his hand and drew his sword, and struck the slave of the high priest." But Jesus said, "Put your sword back into its place; for all who take the sword will perish by the sword." Jesus, who could have called twelve legions of angels to his defense, does not use that kind of protection, and thus certainly the disciple who draws his sword ought not to be drawn into the vicious circle of violence.[40] Life is not to be lived according to the law of retaliation, an eye for an eye. Rather, one's enemies are to be loved. The whole view of "friend-foe relationships" is transvalued, for when one loves his enemy, he is no longer an enemy. There is "a concrete and uncontestable direction which has to be carried out exactly as it is given." If one is a follower of Jesus, he has to consider very closely whether he can avoid being a practical pacifist.

Barth names three other prominent lines, one of which—taking up one's cross—he reserves for extensive discussion until the final (as yet unpublished) subsection of the *Church Dogmatics*. The other two

[39] *Ibid.*, p. 549.
[40] *Ibid.*

lines deal with the dissolution of self-evident attachments, such as to family ("Let the dead bury the dead," etc.) and the restraint of outward marks of piety and moral righteousness. In both of these instances the procedure for the usage is roughly parallel to the way he develops the "line" on property and on force.

Though he rehearses the stricture against general rules over and over again, Barth nonetheless wishes the teachings of Jesus to have a profound impact upon the lives of Christians. We can in our time envisage from the Gospel narratives about Jesus and the disciples the situations in which they were commanded and in which they rendered concrete obedience. "The picture of these men and the way in which they were concretely ordered and concretely obeyed is one which ought to impress itself upon us." The commands are part of the *kerygma* itself. "The reason why we have to bring out these main lines along which it takes concrete shape is that the call to discipleship as it comes to us *will always be shaped also by this correlated picture*" (italics added). Yet, as their call was concrete in their time and place, so will ours be in our time and place. The specific content of our call is not fixed by the specific content of their call. Barth becomes increasingly cautious to hedge against misinterpretation as he tries to claim much and not much at once for the direction we receive from Jesus. On the negative side, Jesus is not "confined as it were to the sequence of His previous encounters," nor does his command move "only in the circle of His previous commanding." "It is not for us simply to reproduce those pictures." We are not to "identify ourselves directly with those who were called then,"[41] and thus we do not learn *directly* from what they were commanded what we are commanded. We are not "merely to copy in our activity the outlines" of the obedience of the disciples; indeed, it might be disobedience to be content to imitate them.

On the positive side he states that "It is now our affair to render obedience without discussion or reserve, quite literally, in the same unity of the inward and the outward, and *in exact correspondence* to the New Testament witness to His encounter with them. There can certainly be *no question of a deviation from these main lines*" (Italics added). Indeed, "there will always be reason for distrust against ourselves if we think that what may be required of us along these lines

[41] All quotations from *ibid.*, p. 552.

will be something less, or easier, or more comfortable than what was required of them."[42]

Barth's gyrations are necessary for him in order to preserve his basic model of a concrete command of God to a concrete individual, a model which he believes to be true to the revelation in Scripture. Nonetheless, he wants to maintain that God's command to us will be in line with, correspond with, Jesus' commands to his disciples. One needs to be as concerned with this framework as Barth is to appreciate the general point that he is making. What God has done for man is made known in the record not only of the events of Jesus' life, but also in the teachings attributed to him by the Gospel writers. There is, first of all, in the order of generation, the declaration of the Kingdom of God, of his grace and his righteousness. But this is also at the same time an "intensified imperative"; it shows the way, the direction that faithful men will follow. We go beyond attitude and disposition here; men are not only commanded to have faith and to obey, to be loving and have courage; there are indicators of the kinds of actions that are appropriate for those who are called to discipleship. These are not models to be copied, not general rules to be followed, but give a direction in accord with which Christians are to act. The relationship to these "lines" is one of being in correspondence with them, instructed by them. Present-day Christians find in them an informing directionality, purpose, and intentionality that is their own in faithful obedience.

THE TEACHINGS OF JESUS—LAW, IDEAL, NORM

The persistent warnings of modern biblical and theological scholarship that the teachings of Jesus do not constitute a new law in the sense of authoritative moral prescriptions, a new set of ideals, or even a moral norm, do not blot out the memory of times and places when they were so used. Indeed, these warnings in themselves are subtle, as we have seen in analyzing the usage of the teachings in Barth and in Bultmann. Christian theologians are reluctant to abolish all authority of these teachings, whether their attacks on the kinds of usage they have had in ethics come from biblical criticism or from dogmatic perspectives.

There has been a long tradition in the Church that has viewed the

[42] *Ibid.*, p. 553.

teachings of Jesus as the new law. In what senses it is new and in what senses it is law have been subject to much discussion. Certainly as early as the writing of *The Didache* there was present in the Church a strong tendency to identify the teachings of Jesus with the Way of Life, or in the *Letter of Barnabas* with the Way of Light. These moral teachings prescribed the rule and pattern of life that those who were in the community were to follow. Historians have interpreted the rise of monasticism as a movement toward securing an exemplary rigorism of Christian conduct, following the teachings of self-denial, within the whole body of Christ. The rigors of the new law were not for all believers to follow, but provided the higher way of exemplary conduct and an approach to perfection to those who had received a special vocation. The teachings became identified as "counsels of perfection," and thus were not necessarily applicable to all Christians. One of the marks of some sect movements in Christian history, as Troeltsch indicates, is a return to the costly world-denying discipleship on the part of a whole community of Christians in obedience to the pattern and teaching of Jesus. What was deemed laxity in the Church was countered by not only a new intensification of faith and devotion, but also by a new radical obedience to Jesus Christ, an obedience that was shaped by the Gospel accounts of his words and deeds. And to the emancipated mentality of enlightened men, as we have noted in the citation of Jefferson, what is given is a "sublime moral code," a rule of life that appeals to reason, and if universalized would bring concord among men.

But the new law is not merely external precept for most of the Christian tradition. As we saw in Chapter III, theologians cite Jeremiah and Paul to indicate that it is a law written on the heart, it is the law of the Spirit of life. The Christian experience is one of grace bringing a newness of life, of an internalization of the principles of conduct appropriate to that life. But for many Christians this law written on the heart does not exclude the significance of the new law in its form of precepts. The precepts continue to be authoritative as articulations of the new law, and thus are binding upon the consciences of Christians.

The language of law and the language of ideals have often been used indiscriminately by Christian writers. Many writers have not been conscious of the kinds of distinction that the two words seem to suggest to some theologians and philosophers. Though the distinctions have achieved a currency in very recent times in Christian circles as a result of H. R. Niebuhr's typology of man the maker (ideals), man the citizen (law), and man the responder,[43] they have a much longer history. In modern Protestant ethics, for example, Schleiermacher self-consciously developed an ethic of the highest good in contrast to an ethic of the law.

This distinction I have in mind is of practical value in distinguishing nuances in the usage of the teachings of Jesus. As new law, the teachings are seen dominantly as a set of prescribed mandates, rules, or precepts to which Christians are to be obedient, which they are to follow. As a moral ideal, they are seen dominantly as a standard to be realized, an end to be fulfilled, a goal to be achieved. A Protestant tendency in the last century has been to see the teachings to represent a high moral idea.

As an ideal, the teachings present a goal for attainment, or at least for approximation, in man's historical social experience. The Kingdom of God becomes a moral ideal, a notion of the highest good that human social order can approximate. It represents a possibility that is given to graced men, to the Christian community. As such it has caught the imagination of many Protestants, and an abundant popular literature was written to propagate the ideal and to stimulate a desire to move toward its realization. The Kingdom of God is "the great social ideal" of Christianity.

The teachings can be cast not only into the terms of social idealism, but also into a personal or individual idealism. The Beatitudes, for an example, can be interpreted to represent the ideal life of the believer; they provide a picture of what life can become for those who have sincere faith and trust. The parable of the Good Samaritan has provided a pattern of the ideal behavior of the loving man, the follower of Jesus.

With the demise of the idealistic interpretation of the teachings of Jesus, there has emerged an alternative that still has acknowledged their authority but cast it in somewhat different terms. The teachings, like the self-sacrificial death of Jesus, function as a norm to be brought to bear upon various moral situations. They become a touchstone for judgment that has applicability through various procedures to situations that are not simply susceptible to their full realization.

[43] H. Richard Niebuhr, *The Responsible Self* (New York, 1963), pp. 48 ff.

Jesus' teaching about love is a case in point. The complexities of human life in both its interpersonal and its highly institutionalized forms do not bend readily to the radical teachings of Jesus about love, to the radical exhortations of the Sermon on the Mount, such as turning the other cheek. The law of love finds no simple obedience in human life; the ideal of love finds great resistance to its realization. Yet many Christian ethicists would not be prepared to say that Jesus' teaching about love is totally irrelevant to the complex moral situations of humanity; particularly, they might say that Christians are constrained to search out the import of that which is so central to their faith for the ways of life in the world. Thus, love functions as a norm, as a touchstone, as a principle involved in the ways in which they make judgments about what is to be done. It is not the only consideration, and it may take the form of secondary principles derived partially from it, but nonetheless it has normative significance.

THE NEW LAW

The interpretation of Jesus' teachings as a new law raises at least as many questions of biblical scholarship and theology as other interpretations do. The question of whether he meant to teach them as law is endemic to a Protestant approach that looks at Scripture through the Reformation and especially Luther's interpretation of St. Paul. Law seems to be antithetical to grace and to freedom, and these are what the gospel is all about. Such a view of the gospel puts a strain on the understanding of Jesus himself as a new lawgiver. Certain aspects of this Protestant perspective have already been noted in our discussions of Barth's "prominent line" view of the teachings and Bultmann's stress on obedience and love as attitudes of the will. The hornet's nest of contesting perspectives in New Testament scholarship can be opened a bit more by looking at two scholars, T. W. Manson and Hans Windisch, who on the whole in this outsider's judgment have at least as much in common with each other as either of them has with a scholar like Bultmann.

The issue is the similarity and difference between Jesus' teachings and that of other contemporary Jews. Very commonly, the difference is stated in terms of the motivation or disposition that Jesus calls forth, as we have seen. Thus T. W. Manson can say that in contrast to other Jews, "The moral demands of Jesus presuppose a changed nature and disposition in man: they imply a previous conversion."

Jesus is "chiefly concerned with the heart of man as the spring of conduct rather than with the Law as the regulative force in society. . . ." Or, "for Jesus good living is the spontaneous activity of a transformed character" or personality, rather than obedience to a discipline of law imposed from without.[44] If this is the heart of the matter in Jesus' teachings, one cannot consider them to be a new law, or if one does call them law they are law in a radically different sense from the commonsense usage of that term. They cannot have external authority; one's response to them cannot be that of obedience; they cannot be rules of conduct. They cannot be regarded "as a 'New Law' in the sense of a reformed and simplified exposition of the Old, or as a code of rules to take the place of the code of Moses and his successors." How, then, are they to be regarded? They are "but a number of illustrations of the way in which a transformed character will express itself in conduct."[45] Jesus refuses to legislate, Manson says, for he is concerned with the springs of character, the kindling of a light that shines in the heart, rather than with the outward act. Law tells men what they are to do; Jesus is concerned with moral character. His teachings present "only a rule of thumb" for guidance of those who already have the root of the matter in them.

This stance, so common not only among some New Testament scholars but also among Protestant ethicists, preachers, and laity, assumes an antithesis between inner disposition and law. "The antithesis," Windisch says (in contrast with Manson), "is false." The teachings of Jesus, and particularly the imperatives to be found in the fifth chapter of Matthew, are commandments, and thus "the customary view that Jesus brought a new attitude but not a new law cannot be correct."[46] It seems probable to Windisch (and with apparent good reason) that Jesus' words that take the form of commands were intended to be commands. Windisch takes quite directly the impact of Matt. 5:17-20, the passage that has its climax, "unless your righteousness exceeds that of the scribes and the Pharisees, you will never enter the kingdom of heaven." And just because the antitheses "You have heard that it was said, . . . but I say to

[44] T. W. Manson, *The Teaching of Jesus* (Cambridge, Eng., 1931), p. 299, p. 300.

[45] *Ibid.*, p. 301.

[46] Hans Windisch, *The Meaning of the Sermon on the Mount* (Philadelphia, 1951), p. 85.

you . . ." refer to something one can call an attitude or a disposition, they are no less commandments. "What is intended is: 'You shall not be angry; you shall not use any abusive language,' etc."[47] Emotions, passions, desires are subject to control, and ought to be controlled. Windisch does not say that there is not something different between Jesus' teaching and that of other Jews, but he does not wish to locate that difference between "character" and "law." Jesus teaches morality "as though it were a matter of jurisprudence." Sometimes Jesus' stress is on moral discipline rather than law, but it is not in contrast to law. Sometimes, as in the teaching on divorce (Matt. 5:31–32), there is a contrast of one legal regulation with another. But the teachings are in all cases commandments; the fact that we do not regard them as rules does not mean that in their own setting they were not to be so regarded. Certainly, against Manson's interpretation, Jesus is not talking about "the spontaneous act of a transformed personality."[48]

These contrasts between New Testament scholars set the stage for contrasts among writers in ethics, all of whom are their own biblical interpreters. We have noted that one can have a new law found in *The Life and Morals of Jesus*, a "sublime moral code" without either Manson's view of transformed personalities, or Windisch's sophistication about the Jewish law of Jesus' time. The fact that Jefferson believed that the fragments of Jesus' teaching "have come to us mutilated, misstated, and often unintelligible," and even worse, "have been still more disfigured by corruptions of schismatizing followers, who have found an interest in sophisticating and perverting the simple doctrines he taught by engrafting on them the mysticisms of a Grecian Sophist (Plato), frittering them into subtleties and obscuring them with jargon" did not keep him from claiming them to be the "most perfect" moral code ever taught.[49] The appeal is to the rational man.

Certainly one also finds the teachings becoming an authorization for not taking an oath, for nonviolence, and other quite particular

---

[47] *Ibid.*, p. 78.

[48] I refrain from succumbing to the temptation to follow through with comparisons on specific teachings. See, for example, Manson, pp. 297–99 on oath-taking, in comparison with Windisch, pp. 80–81.

[49] From a "Syllabus of an estimate of the doctrines of Jesus, compared with those of others," pp. 15–16, in a 1902 ed. of Jefferson's *Life and Morals of Jesus of Nazareth*.

behavior in the radical Protestant sectarian tradition. For example, in the record of the trial and martyrdom of Michael Sattler (1490–1527), which discloses Sattler's defense against a number of charges on which he was convicted, he stated, "We hold that we are not to swear before the authorities, for the Lord says [Matt. 5:34]: Swear not, but let your communication be, Yea, yea; nay, nay." And, "if the Turks come, we ought not to resist them. For it is written [Matt. 5:21]: Thou shalt not kill. We must not defend ourselves against the Turks and others of our persecutors, but are to beseech God with earnest prayer to repel and resist them."[50] The teachings of Jesus are the law of life for such Christians, even when they are "impractical," and even when they lead to being despised by the world, to suffering, and to death. Indeed, the claim of Christ is to radical obedience in discipleship, to a life of potential suffering; Christians are to be prepared to go the way of the cross for their faith and their witness.

In main-line Protestantism and Catholicism, the teachings have never received the literal obedience they have got from the radical Reformers. Most churches have not followed the "higher way" view of exemplary obedience to the teachings of Jesus as their vocations.[51] Yet the idea of the "new law" has not been abandoned, or even neglected. For Catholic ethics, the discussion of it has come as part of the idea of the divine or revealed law within St. Thomas Aquinas' theory of law. For Protestants in the Reformation tradition, to some extent the discussion has occurred around the question of the "uses of the law," and particularly the "third use" as a guide for those who are in Christ to aid them in living out the Christian life. For illustrations of the place of the "new law" in the Catholic and broad Protestant streams we shall look at St. Thomas and at Calvin and Emil Brunner.

One of the most neglected aspects of St. Thomas' great "Treatise on Law" in the *Summa Theologica* is his discussion of the divine law, and particularly the new law within that discussion; yet in sheer bulk

[50] *Spiritual and Anabaptist Writers*, ed. George H. Williams and Angel M. Mengal (Philadelphia, 1957), p. 141.

[51] See Ernst Troeltsch's church-sect distinction which indicates in ideal-typical form the differences between the ethics, Christological emphases, and doctrines of the Church in two strands of Christian history; *The Social Teaching of the Christian Churches*, 2 vols. (New York, 1949), Vol. I, pp. 331 ff. See also H. Richard Niebuhr's chapter, "Christ against Culture," in *Christ and Culture* (New York, 1951), pp. 45–82.

of space the treatise attends at greatest length to the divine law, rather than to the eternal law, natural law, and human law. In Chapter III we looked at the discussion of new law under the aspect of the internal character of the new law, that is, the dwelling of the Holy Spirit in the heart. Here our concern is with the precepts of the divine new law, that is, with the use of the moral teachings of Jesus particularly, as part of the biblical revelation.[52]

Taking his cue from St. Augustine, St. Thomas writes that "the sermon which Our Lord delivered on the mountain contains the whole formation of the life of a Christian."[53] To see the place of this statement properly, one needs to remember that St. Thomas has made clear in previous sections that, while the new law is the law of the New Testament, it is first of all a law instilled in our hearts; it is preponderantly the grace of the Holy Spirit which is given through faith in Christ. He is not writing about an external law, to which man's relationship is a coercive bending of his will in an effort to form the Christian life. Only secondarily is the new law a written law, but yet it is important, since the faithful need instruction both by spoken and written word "both as to what they should believe and as to what they should do."[54] This new law is the law of perfection, the law of love. It is not like the old law, the decalogue and the Old Testament, a restraint of the hand, but rather it is an inner inclination of the self. It is the fulfilling of the old law in three senses: it explains the true sense of the law by addressing the "interior acts" as well as the overt deeds of man; it prescribes "the safest way of complying with the statutes of the Old Law," such as abstaining altogether from taking oaths as a way to avoid perjury; and it adds to the old law certain counsels of perfection, such as Jesus' words to the "rich young ruler," in Matt. 19:21, "If you would be perfect, go, sell what you possess and give to the poor. . . ."

The new law in its precept forms, as we have seen in Chapter III, prescribes some acts as in keeping with the promptings of grace, prohibits others as contrary to it, and leaves other acts to the discretion of the believer. These prescribed acts include the sacraments and

---

[52] Our sources are largely confined to Questions 106–108, *Summa Theologica*, I–II. The discussion of divine law runs from Question 98 to 108, of the other three forms, one question for each.

[53] Q. 108, Art. 3, *Basic Writings of St. Thomas Aquinas*, ed. A. Pegis (New York, 1945), Vol. II, p. 973.

[54] *Ibid.*, Q. 106, Art. 1, p. 950.

the works of love. Our interest is clearly in the moral aspect of the new law. What is it, then, specifically that the Sermon on the Mount in particular, orders as the new law? There is an ordering of man's "interior movements." First, Christ commands the will to refrain from the inner acts of sin and from the occasions of evil deeds; he orders man's intentions by teaching that our good deeds should not be done for the sakes of human praise or worldly riches. Second, in acts toward the neighbor we are forbidden to judge him rashly, and yet also forbidden to "entrust him too readily with sacred things if he is unworthy." Finally he teaches us to fulfill the teachings of the gospel, to strive to enter through the narrow door of perfect virtue. Christians are not merely to fulfill these "interior movements," but also to take seriously the "optional" counsels specifically given in the new law. By following the evangelical counsels, by giving up the goods of this world entirely, man can attain "more speedily" his eternal happiness.[55] But one must always remember that the law is first the indwelling of the Spirit, only second, precepts and written requirements.

When one looks at the new law in Protestant discussion, one's sight is directed to a thorny and continuing debate in theological ethics. In Chapter IV we indicated that the issue of law and gospel becomes crucial for Luther, and subsequently for much of Protestant theology and ethics. On two uses of the law, the so-called "political use" and so-called "theological use," there is a considerable measure of agreement among the Reformers and their descendants. That God's laws, indeed law and institutions, function to preserve order in a world in which chaos threatens, and that God's law leads to a personal awareness of one's imperfection and sin and thus to repentance, there is little to quarrel about. Whether there is a "third use" of the law is another matter, discussed at great length as a historical problem in Luther, and as a systematic problem in theology and ethics. The question is whether the law, old or new, is necessary

---

[55] *Ibid.*, Q. 108, pp. 967–78. Father Bernard Häring moves quickly from the particular commandments of the New Testament to their "essence," and sets the discussion typically in a more Pauline context. The new law is the law of the Spirit, as we have seen; Christ is himself the law to those whom the Spirit takes into Christ. This law is "the renewal of disposition" in the believer; it is, as with St. Thomas, the law of grace, the "perfect law of liberty," the law of the Spirit of life. This law of the Spirit "demands of us that in love we bring forth fruit unto God" (*Law of Christ*, Vol. I, pp. 257 ff.).

to guide Christians in the outworking of their faith and love in the world. Calvin not only had a third use, but said it was the most significant use. Among recent writers Emil Brunner clearly has a third use, as does the lesser known Swiss ethicist, Alfred de Quervain.[56]

"The Law," Emil Brunner writes, "even for faith itself, does not lose its significance; its significance, I mean, as the God-given exposition of what it means for our conduct to be 'in Christ.' " Belief alone does not lead automatically to unity with God's will, for even in faith God is "over against" us. We walk in the right way only if God guides us in it.[57] This, it need hardly be stated, does not mean that the law stands in its own autonomy for us to obey, but rather that the Holy Spirit expounds the law to men of faith. The isolated commandments of the law come to Christians as references to the first commandment, and to the basic law of love. They are, in a sense, deductions from and explications of the requirements of love. They do not preconceive what is right in all situations; the obedience to which the Christian is called is a particular one. It is not as if the Sermon on the Mount stated precisely what each man ought to do, "but this preconceived principle, based on the knowledge of the Sermon on the Mount as law, is not without significance; indeed, it is of highest significance as showing the right path, as demonstrating what the Good is 'in and for itself.' "[58]

But for Brunner the usual usage of the word "law" is radically

[56] De Quervain, in the first part of his *Ethik, Die Heiligung,* presents the most systematic exposition of the law in its third, or didactic, use in contemporary Protestant ethics. As the title indicates, the book is an exposition of the meaning of sanctification as the basis of ethics; the exposition of the law is in the context of the threefold office of Christ and the work of the Holy Spirit. Within this context, assuming that the gift of the Spirit is bound to the Word, the commandments become a consolation and not just a threat to faith. Sanctification does not make the law superfluous, but frees it from moral isolation and autonomy (pp. 249 ff.). The exposition of the law in this book is, however, limited to the Decalogue; de Quervain does not expound the teachings of Jesus. I cite it at length to indicate the way in which a theological framework can make a central place for the didactic use of law; it seems to me that an exposition of Jesus' teaching as new law within this framework is as plausible as an exposition of the Decalogue.

[57] Emil Brunner, *The Divine Imperative* (Philadelphia, 1947), p. 148.

[58] *Ibid.*, p. 149. Brunner earlier in the book makes a radically situational claim for how the command of God is heard, but like Barth with his practical casuistry and prominent lines, he gives back a great deal of what he ostensibly took away. Here, however, the author is willing to make his case under the third use of the law. The practical impact may not be very different in the two cases.

altered in faith. Indeed, the "law" in the Sermon on the Mount is not Christian ethics. Christian ethics, Brunner wrote, "is the science of human conduct as it is determined by Divine conduct";[59] it refers to the more open obedience to the actual command of God to do the loving thing. Faith alters our relation to God, and thus our relation to the law. It is in faith no longer the command to a slave, but the instruction of the father to the son. Thus the commands of God are for those who are in Christ, "regulations," "the directions for the route," "instructions for work." The "ethical sentiment" no longer resides in the law, but in faith. The function of the law, including the Sermon on the Mount, is a secondary technical one.

The spiritual and moral heirs of John Calvin have a legacy of the significance of the law that is not known to the descendants of Martin Luther. It is Calvin who says that the third, didactic, use of the law is the principal use for Christians. This didactic use, of course, is set in the framework of the graced life; it functions for those "in whose hearts the Spirit of God already lives and reigns." In its written form the law has a double advantage for those who already are animated to obey God: it gives them a surer and better understanding of God's will, confirming their knowledge of it, and it exhorts them to obedience, serving as a "whip," since even the spiritual man is like a "dull and tardy animal" who constantly needs to be goaded and spurred.[60] In faith the law is no longer a terror to the conscience, but by "admonition, reproof, and correction, forms and prepares us for every good work."[61]

Chiefly, the law that forms the Christian moral life for Calvin is the Decalogue; it is this that gives structure to his extensive exposition of the moral law which constitutes Chapter 8 of Book Two of *The Institutes*. But Calvin takes into account the fact that Jesus was himself an interpreter of the law, and while Calvin does not in his exposition of the moral law give detailed attention to the Sermon on the Mount or other teachings of Jesus, he does make certain claims for what Jesus Christ has indicated about the law.

For one, he makes it clear that Christ was not "another Moses," he was not "the giver of an evangelical law, which supplied the de-

[59] *Ibid.*, p. 86.
[60] Calvin, *The Institutes*, Book II, Ch. 7, 12 (Allen trans.), Vol. I, pp. 388–89.
[61] *Ibid.*, Bk. II, Ch. 7, 14, p. 391.

ficiencies of the law of Moses." He did not offer counsels of perfection optional to Christians, and binding on those who have special religious vocation. Rather, Christ is "the best interpreter" of the law, he "restored it to its genuine purity, by clearing it from the obscurities and blemishes which it had contracted from the falsehoods and leaven of the Pharisees."[62] Indeed, Calvin at one point says that Jesus is the "infallible expositor of the law."

Thus, the claim that Christ gives clearer perception of the law by restoring it to its purity suggests that in the formation of Christians the teachings of Jesus, as well as Christ as Pattern, have a significant function. The particularity of this restoration and perception of the law lies generally for Calvin in a more rigorous awareness of what a Thomist might call the "interior" part of action. Obedience is not mere external conformity to the external requirements of the law. Rather, Jesus pronounces "an unchaste look at a woman to be adultery; he declares them to be murderers, who hate a brother; he makes them 'in danger of judgment,' who have only conceived resentment in their hearts; them 'in danger of the council,' who in murmuring or quarrelling have discovered any sign of an angry mind," etc.[63] In his exposition of the commandment, "Thou shalt not kill," Calvin indicates in more detail both how he works with the Decalogue and how Christ gives a better perception of the law.

This sixth commandment is not to be interpreted only in a restrictive sense, nor does it apply only to the relations between two individuals for Calvin. Surely it means what common sense perceives it to mean, that is, that we ought to abstain from acts injurious to others, and from all desire to commit such acts. But it also has a positive implication; that "we should do every thing we possibly can toward the preservation of the life of our neighbor." Not only does God forbid man to injure his brother because he wishes the brother's life to be acknowledged as precious; he "at the same time requires of us all those offices of love which may contribute to the preservation of it."[64] This rule is, in the language of Christ, to govern the soul as well as the external act. "Mental homicide" is forbidden, and the "internal disposition" to preserve the life of the brother is commanded. Thus, you are to "examine whether you can be angry with

---

[62] *Ibid.*, Book II, Ch. 8, 7, p. 403.
[63] *Ibid.*
[64] *Ibid.*, Bk. II, Ch. 8, 9, p. 405.

your brother, without being inflamed with a desire of doing him injury." Obviously one cannot be angry without a disposition to do injury. Jesus, in Matt. 5:22, shows the true intention of the commandment, "But I say to you that every one who is angry with his brother shall be liable to judgment . . . ," and the "Holy Spirit" has said in I John 3:15, "Anyone who hates his brother is a murderer."[65] Thus the true meaning of the sixth commandment is both a restraint of the inner man, and a positive note of doing in love what the preservation of the neighbor requires.

In the double love commandment we have the whole summary of the law; love to God refers to the first table of the Decalogue, love to neighbor refers to the second. Jesus makes clear in this teaching that the "best and most holy life" is that one that is lived as little as possible for itself. Indeed, the Christian is commanded to transfer "to others that affection of love which we naturally restrict to ourselves." Love, which through our depravity has terminated with ourselves is to be "diffused abroad" to every man, even the greatest stranger and the enemy.[66]

Law is not abrogated in the Christian life, but it is the law of grace. In being "ingrafted" into Christ, men are delivered from the curse of law, and by the Spirit the law is written on the heart. But these affirmations only set the context for the third use of the law. "It is the Lord in whom we find strength: let him give what he commands, and let him command what he pleases."[67] Any who would avoid the law in the Christian life have failed to take account of Jesus' own words in Matt. 5:19, "Whoever then relaxes one of the least of these commandments and teaches men so, shall be called least in the Kingdom of heaven." "If God has declared his will in the law, whatever is contrary to the law displeases him."[68]

What one finds in Calvin is not a new law, and certainly not an evangelical law that is added to, or makes up for deficiencies in the

[65] *Ibid.*, Bk. II, Ch. 8, 39, pp. 436–37. Since Calvin has a polemical stance toward Anabaptist literalistic rigorism in adherence to the teachings, he has some difficulty in interpreting the saying against taking an oath as a literal, infallible exposition of the commandment against taking the Lord's name in vain. He satisfies himself that Jesus refers only to oaths "which transgress the rule of law." See *ibid.*, Book II, Ch. 8, 26, pp. 422–25.

[66] *Ibid.*, Bk. II, Ch. 8, 54–57, pp. 451–55.
[67] *Ibid.*, Bk. II, Ch. 8, 57, p. 455.
[68] *Ibid.*, Bk. II, Ch. 8, 59, p. 456.

Mosaic law but, rather, a true perception, understanding, and exposition of *the* moral law of God. The teachings of Jesus, then, restore the purity of the law from corruptions by contemporary Jewish movements. They function as instruction and admonition in the faith; they are the external precepts that goad the man ingrafted into Christ to live out his sanctification. The law teaches what Christ enables and requires man to be.

Clearly there are differences of some importance among writers for whom the teachings of Jesus function as the new law. The authorization that convinces the adherent is different: the teachings seem rationally persuasive to some; they are the literally recorded words of the Lord to others. They are to some the revealed law that enables man to achieve his true end more readily, and they are counsels of perfection beyond the expectations normally held. To others they are instruction that has a practical technical utility, or whips and teachings that move and direct the life of the Christian. For Christians in the main stream the law is not only precepts given in verbal form, but the law of the Spirit of life; it is inscribed in the heart. But for those who view the teachings with great authority, the precepts are given both as a help to feeble men who do not automatically know what they ought to do, and as good instructions, part of God's gracious gift itself, to console and direct human life.

For all writers who stress the teachings as law in some sense, as for all who view them as the representation of an ideal, or as a moral norm, the place of morality within the Christian life is perhaps larger and certainly more clearly defined than it is for those whose major fear is that morality becomes idolatrous, or falsely believed to be saving. Some specification and precision in moral law is not seen by men like Calvin to be the inevitable and irrevocable first step to a works-righteousness; rather, it is a gracious possibility and necessity. Also, those who feel at home writing about God's law do not hesitate to say, as Calvin does about honoring one's father and one's mother, "it ought not to be doubted that God here lays down a universal rule for our conduct. . . ."[69] They can conceive of God's providing something general or universal, and not necessarily being bound to addressing each man in each moment, as Barth insists. "Prominent lines" can be "laws" if one does not have to preserve the theological

[69] *Ibid.*, Bk. II, Ch. 8, 36, p. 433.

point that God in his freedom does not bind himself to universal moral rules. Perhaps a Calvin could say that God in his freedom chooses to reveal his will to men in laws. Finally, for Christian writers who think in terms of laws, sin is not just unfaith but transgression of God's law. The overcoming of sin is not only faith, but obedience to God's law.

Jesus in his teaching gives a new law; he instructs men in the ways that God would have them live. Men then are to conform to this law, to obey it, to be taught by it. But the teachings have also been set in the ethical framework of the language of ideals, a language more foreign to Scripture than the language of law, yet a language that had wide appeal within the past century.

THE MORAL IDEAL

We have seen in the previous chapter how Christ himself was interpreted to be the greatest good, and therefore the proper moral ideal for man. His teachings as well as his person constitute the substance of that ideal for Newman Smyth and many writers. One finds the language used not only by theologians but also by some biblical scholars as well. It is not necessary to rehearse the criticisms made of this usage of Jesus' teachings; the citations already given from Bultmann and Barth are only the beginning of what could be an extensive list that make the point. But if we are to see how the teachings have been used, it still is a worthwhile task to explore the ways men set them in the context of moral ideals.

T. W. Manson's work as a New Testament scholar moved into the issues of ethics throughout his career in at least two ways: he was interested in establishing what the ethical teachings of Jesus and the early church were, and he was interested in indicating their importance for the Christian community in modern times. To the reader of his work whose competence is in ethics and not in technical New Testament scholarship, there are palpable revisions in the ethical language he uses, with accompanying shifts in emphasis through his career. There is also a great technical apparatus for the interpretation of Jesus' teachings in relation to Jewish ethics that persists through his career that is beyond the scope of the present concern. This is mentioned, however, to indicate how selective the use of Manson's work is in this chapter.

Manson wrote about the teachings of Jesus in various ethical terms, none of which necessarily ought to exclude any other. He was concerned to show their inseparability from the religious loyalty that they both commanded and evoked; they imply a "conversion," a "changed nature and disposition in man." They are not a new law but a "number of illustrations," as we have earlier noted. The teachings present a "moral standard" rather than a "precept"; they are given sometimes in parabolic form that incites the moral imagination, and sometimes as principles that Jesus had clearly in mind. They are "rules of thumb." Sometimes he uses the word "precepts" to describe particular teachings, even though at other times he wishes to exclude its normative moral usage. But the teachings also present an ideal, as does the person of Christ himself.[70]

A summary statement shows how Manson could write about ideals in the context of other themes. "The ideal picture of human life which Jesus draws in what he has to say about morals, is a picture of life in the Kingdom of God on earth, life as it may be lived by men who acknowledge one supreme loyalty, in whose hearts one supreme passion burns; and it is only as we hear the call to that loyalty and feel that passion that the moral teaching of Jesus grows luminous."[71] The affirmation is significant for its claims, disputed as they are by other New Testament scholars and theologians. Jesus' sayings about morality contain an ideal picture of human life; it is the portrait of life in the Kingdom of God on earth. "The Kingdom of God is manifested on earth and in the present in the existence of human subjects who own God as their King, who look to him for protection, guidance, and a rule of life, who offer to him their absolute loyalty, complete trust, and willing obedience. That is the ideal."[72] One finds realizations of this ideal to some extent whenever there is a faithful remnant, whether in the history of the Old Israel or of the New. Thus this great ideal has a continuous history from its be-

[70] Manson, *The Teaching of Jesus*, pp. 285–312. In his posthumously published *Ethics and the Gospel* (New York, 1960), he sets forth "following Christ" as the foundation of Christian ethics, a theme that is also present in the earlier work. He uses the language of ideal less in the later work than in the earlier one used here. For example, the ethic of Jesus "is not merely an ideal: it is act and deed. It is the way Jesus carries out his life-work" (p. 63). Indeed, he makes the point early in the chapter, "To follow Christ is not to go in pursuit of an ideal but to share in the results of an achievement" (p. 59). As I have indicated, even in his earlier work, he did not neglect these extra-ideal notes.

[71] Manson, *The Teaching of Jesus*, p. 286.

[72] *Ibid.*, p. 234.

ginnings in Hebrew religion, through Christ and his teaching on into present times.

Christians, then, are people with a particular moral ideal, though they are more than this. This ideal "lies not in a code, nor in a social order." It lies ultimately in Jesus Christ, the man and his teaching, "in a life where love to God and man is the spring of every thought and word and action." The sum of all morality for Christians is "to have the same mind which was also in Christ Jesus."[73] The teachings and the man, the Kingdom of God that he taught and that he lived, are the ideal to be realized for Christians. This language of ideals is one way in which the teachings of Jesus have been commended to humanity.

In America the social gospel writers, as we have noted in the previous chapter, used the language of ideals with reference to the teachings of Jesus. Many writers in this broad movement could agree with Newman Smyth when he wrote that in part, "Jesus' Moral Ideal [is] disclosed in his doctrine of the Kingdom of God."[74] The ways in which this ideal, found in the notion of the Kingdom of God, was explicated varied somewhat from author to author. For Smyth Jesus' teaching could be adumbrated with several clear emphases. The Kingdom is now and it is here on earth, not something wholly future and remote from our present participation in it. It is the highest good, ideal and real, transcendent and immanent, an ideal surpassing all known good, and yet realized in any virtue. It is a message of "moral positiveness"; it has an "objectiveness" and a "calm certainty" about it. The supreme good that the Kingdom teachings reveal is a personal good as against an excessively collective or political good. "The Kingdom of God is constituted of persons, and has its glory in personal worths and fidelities. The kingdom is to be built of persons having Christ-like characters."[75] Yet the Kingdom is also a human good, a Kingdom of the society of men, a good to be secured for the "larger life of humanity." It "is no ideal of life to be attained by men individually, apart from the perfection of humanity." At the same time, the Kingdom is also something superhuman; it is God's Kingdom, a humanitarian idealism that is centered in "the light and radiant power of God" rather than in the greatest happiness of the greatest number of men. It is a Kingdom that has its own "law of

[73] *Ibid.*, p. 312.
[74] N. Smyth, *Christian Ethics*, p. 96.
[75] *Ibid.*, p. 101.

realization of the ideal good among men," namely sacrifice. The "ethical processes" by which the ideal is to be realized require consecration and suffering. Through these will come "the gradual spiritualization of life."[76]

The most widely known interpreter of the Christian ideal of the Kingdom of God is Walter Rauschenbusch. Jesus, of course, was heir to the doctrine of the Kingdom as this was present in Judaism; but in "sovereign freedom" he made corrections of the traditional conception so that in his teachings "we have pure Christian thought and not inherited Judaism." Rauschenbusch, in *Christianizing the Social Order*, enumerates the emphases he believes to shape "a distinctively Christian ideal of the Kingdom."[77] In contrast to the expectation that the Messiah would "hoist the flag of revolt and slay oppressors," Jesus repudiated the use of force. Thus, "this must be one of the differentiating marks of those who seek social salvation under the leadership of Jesus: to refuse violent means, however tempting, and to throw all fighting ardor into moral protest."[78] In contrast to the expectation of the triumph of Judaism, in Jesus' teaching about the Kingdom "we encounter the spirit that beats down the trammels of a narrow group to seek a wider allegiance; that reaches out beyond jingo patriotism toward the brotherhood of nations; that smites race pride and prejudice in the face in the name of humanity . . . That determined breadth of brotherhood is another permanent landmark of the Kingdom ideal as Jesus expressed it."[79]

Jesus contradicted the basically despotic and monarchical forms in which the Kingdom was expected, and laid down instead the law of service, the value of the human soul, and the idea of God as Father instead. It is in this context that Rauschenbusch wrote those oft-quoted words, "When Jesus spoke of God as our Father, he democratized God himself."[80] In distinction from punctilious obedience to the law as the hope of the Kingdom, Jesus' enthusiasm went toward "justice, mercy, and good will among men." His language of the Kingdom was the language of emancipation and social sympathy;

[76] This is a summary of *ibid.*, pp. 96–108. Smyth also discusses the Beatitudes and Jesus' teachings about eternal life in terms of moral ideals. I shall not elaborate on them here, since for my purposes the point of idealistic interpretation is sufficiently made on the basis of the Kingdom theme.

[77] W. Rauschenbusch, *Christianizing the Social Order* (New York, 1912), pp. 57–66.

[78] *Ibid.*, p. 59.

[79] *Ibid.*, p. 60.

[80] *Ibid.*, p. 61.

these are the things fitting to the Kingdom of God. While his conception of the Kingdom did not despise the physical needs of men, eating and drinking were not the ends of human life. "The socialists are right in emphasizing the economic basis of human society; but Jesus is also right in emphasizing its spiritual ends"; indeed, the spiritual values of human life are higher than the economic ones, and are the real ends to be sought.[81]

Jesus, in Rauschenbusch's interpretation of his teaching of the ideal of the Kingdom, discarded utopian elements, and had instead a "marked insistence on present duty." He combined "enthusiasm and sanity" by showing that the Kingdom would not come apocalyptically, but would slowly make its way against obstacles until it comes to organic maturity. Yet, while having a long outlook, Jesus felt the nearness of the Kingdom. It was already here, "germinating in their hearts, pulsating in their common thoughts, reversing their valuation of things, sweetening their relations, lifting the least of them above the highest representative of the old order, and quietly creating a new world."[82]

This great "social ideal" of Christianity was eclipsed in the history of the Church, in Rauschenbusch's judgment, and it is in the recovery of it that new hope could be found for both the Church and the world. With remarkable persuasiveness, this great social reformer then proceeded to show what inferences could be drawn from the ideal to formulate social goals that needed to be realized in the unjust society of men. As is widely known, he found that in the orders of family life, democratic political institutions, and public education considerable progress had been made in the process of "Christianization." The economic order remained intransigent, and for it Rauschenbusch wrote pages of criticism and counsel, some profound and some reflecting the more trivial moralism of his time. In his work the ideal of the Kingdom of God set forth in Jesus' teachings was not only stated; it was applied to the realities of social history, and the paths to its realization were mapped out in some detail.

The language of ideals has appropriate counterparts in the languages of "realization" and "approximation." Christians are to realize or approximate the moral ideal. We have seen how Jesus' teachings have been viewed as proposing a moral ideal, a language most contemporary theologians and biblical scholars believe to be foreign to

[81] *Ibid.*, p. 63.
[82] *Ibid.*, p. 65.

the Scripture itself. In the age in which it flourished, this language was no doubt deeply moving. As a correction to both moral and theological difficulties, it seems to me that a new way of using the teachings has emerged. That is as a norm in moral reflection, judgment-making, and action.

THE NORM

In American Christian social ethics, one finds the teachings of Jesus, and particularly the "law of love" used as a norm for ethical decisions and policy making. The language used is often the "law of love" or even the "ideal of love," but the way in which love is used is not one of radical literal obedience to the law of love and the teachings of Jesus, nor is it used as the basis for shaping moral ideals about the just and peaceful society. Both the radical literal obedience of the absolute pacifist and the utopian conjuring of the Christian idealist are avoided. The moral concern is for the possible, for that which is "relevant" to what is actually going on in history. It is for the achievement of a viable state of peace or equity within the moral ambiguities and conflicting historical forces that exist at a particular time. Unlike other Christians who would derive their ethics for society strictly from the natural law, or from the orders of creation, or from the political use of God's law, this American pattern of thinking insists that love is normative for, and applicable to, the realms of politics, economics, and even the conduct of warfare. The authorization for the norm of love is neither only nor always the teachings of Jesus in the double love commandment and elsewhere; it is also revealed in the self-sacrificial death of Christ on the cross. The way in which the norm is made relevant differs for different writers. For Paul Ramsey the procedure is to make love "in-principled," that is, to find those moral prescriptions that specify the proper inferences from the law of love for general problem areas such as war or sexual behavior. These principles in turn function as rules for conduct. In *War and the Christian Conscience*, one finds an example of this procedure. He states, for example, that in working out the just war theory, the church fathers did not "fall" from the pristine purity of Christian ethics, but were seeking to find what "responsible love and service of one's neighbor" required "in the texture of the common life." The limits placed on the just conduct of war, and the permission given for Christians to work within such limits, "bear significant traces of the fact that the norm of Christian love, and not natural justice only, was still the main source both of what the Christian could and should do and of what he could and should never do in military action." Love is the *source* of principles for Ramsey.[83] Ramsey is proposing neither a radical obedience to a simple interpretation of what the law of love demands nor that love provides an ideal end toward which a warring world can make a gradual approximation in history. Yet he is not ready to say that love is irrelevant to the problem of war. For Christians it is the norm, and as such is the source of inferences drawn with reference to the conduct of moral life.

John C. Bennett, in 1946, developed J. H. Oldham's term "middle axioms" as a procedure for moving between love as norm and the complexities of moral existence. These axioms are "more concrete than a universal ethical principle and less specific than a program that includes legislation and political strategy."[84] In a brief later essay Bennett indicates that a tension between the radical Christian ethical norm of love, on the one hand, and the public life of institutions and social policy, on the other, is inevitable in the lives of Christians. This tension ought not to be relieved by fleeing either into an adjustment to the prevailing secular culture, or into isolated "religious" communities. On the contrary, Christians ought to set forth the Christian ethic of love "in its fulness without dilution or compromise." This is the ethic of universal love which cares for the dignity and welfare of all persons; it is the ethic of costly sacrifice for others, the ethic of radical commitment to love of God with all our hearts and minds. This ethic gives the norm which judges all other norms of action in society. The responsibility of Christians, then, is to find the best course of action in the world in the light of the norm of love, on the one hand, and the norms that exist in society, on the other.[85] Here the radical love commandment functions not so much as a normative source of principles, as it does as a criterion for judgment that is relevant to decisions about policy through a more or less dialectical process with the actual situation of society. Christians consequently

---

[83] P. Ramsey, *War and the Christian Conscience* (Durham, N.C., 1961). The whole book works out this procedure; the quotation is from p. xviii. Love as a norm for Ramsey is a generalization derived from various aspects of the New Testament, and not from the teachings of Jesus alone.

[84] John C. Bennett, *Christian Ethics and Social Policy* (New York, 1946), p. 77.

[85] John C. Bennett, *et al.*, *Christian Values in Economic Life* (New York, 1954), pp. 202–7.

are called upon to live in the inevitable tension between the radical norm of love and the realities of experience with their limitations of what is possible.

In this procedure Bennett is close to the work of Reinhold Niebuhr, for whom *agape* is the norm of life, as we saw in Chapter IV. Here our attention is directed more toward his 1935 book, *An Interpretation of Christian Ethics*, than toward later writings in which the sophisticated love-justice dialectic is worked out in greater detail; for in these earlier "Rauschenbusch Lectures" it is the ethic taught by Jesus that provides the norm, more than the self-sacrificial death of Christ on the cross. Niebuhr, in these lectures, writes about love as ideal, as law, and as norm, using these words interchangeably, and the dominant language is the language of ideals. It is my conviction, however, that the structure of thinking is in accord with the conception of norms used in this section as much as it is in accord with a pattern of thinking about the realization of ideals, and that the dialectic that later becomes more explicit is foreshadowed clearly in this book.

The tension illustrated by John Bennett is starkly present in the setting of the problem in Niebuhr. The "immediate moral problem of every human life" is to arrange "some kind of armistice between various contending factions and forces." Man's life is taken up with "the relativities of politics and economics," with "the necessary balances of power which exist and must exist in even the most intimate social relationships." With these things the ethic of Jesus establishes no connection. "The absolutism and perfectionism of Jesus' love ethic sets itself uncompromisingly not only against the natural self-regarding impulses, but against the necessary prudent defenses of the self, required because of the egoism of others."[86] He teaches that God's love is indiscriminatingly shown to the just and the unjust (Matt. 5:46), and has no place for prudential calculations so necessary in social life. He admonishes men not to be concerned even for their physical existence (Matt. 6:25–32), again being abrasive to the "prudent conscience." Love of possessions is seen to be a form of self-assertion, and meets Jesus' rigorous attack (Matt. 6:19–24, and his counsel to the young ruler to go and sell all that he has). He over and over again excoriates pride and exalts humility (e.g., Luke 14:7–11). Whereas in the common life resentment against

[86] Reinhold Niebuhr, *An Interpretation of Christian Ethics* (New York, 1935), p. 39.

injustice is a basis for corrective justice, Jesus teaches men to love their enemies, to turn the other cheek, to "forgive, not seven times, but seventy times seven," and to bless those who curse one. Any effort to make this ethic into a practical social ethic inevitably blunts its force. "The love absolutism in the ethic of Jesus expresses itself in terms of universalism, set against all narrower forms of human sympathy, as well as in terms of a perfectionism which maintains a critical vigor against the most inevitable and subtle forms of self-assertion."[87] One cannot derive directly from Jesus' "pure religious ethic" a "prudential social ethic which deals with present realities."

This absolutism of love in Jesus' ethics, however, does not make it irrelevant to human life. Its relevance is obviously not simply as an ideal toward which the "spiritualization" or "Christianizing" of life is steadily moving. Its relevance for Niebuhr is of another sort. The radical ethic of love, the "law of love," which one must remember for Niebuhr is also the ultimate law of life, is the "*source* of the norms of justice" and "an ultimate *perspective* by which their limitations are discovered."[88] It is the norm of justice that is applicable to the concrete immediacies of human social life. The identification of what Jesus taught with the law of life that is dimly perceived and realized in only an inchoate way by most men is important in following Niebuhr's discussion. The radical norm is then not a totally alien norm. One finds evidences of its presence in even the most universal minimal standards, such as the prohibition of theft and murder. One finds its recognition in the acknowledged right to live and secure the goods needed to sustain life. Wherever the "ideal of equality" is present as the regulative principle of justice, "there is an echo of the law of love, 'Thou shalt love thy neighbor AS THYSELF.' "[89] Indeed, equality is a "rational, political version of the law of love." But even this justice can be exercised imaginatively, as it is where communities support refined standards of life. Thus one finds "an ascending scale of moral possibilities in which each succeeding step is a closer approximation of the law of love."[90] But these approximations of equality are limited; they are bound to "the recalcitrance of nature in historical existence." "The ideal of love, [however,] transcends all law,"[91] and as such provides a norm which shows the limitations of all rational

[87] *Ibid.*, p. 48. See the whole second chapter, "The Ethic of Jesus," pp. 37–61.
[88] *Ibid.*, p. 140. Italics added.
[89] *Ibid.*, p. 108.
[90] *Ibid.*, p. 110.
[91] *Ibid.*, p. 149.

justice. It provides that trans-historical, transcendent norm from which comes moral criticism of all historical orders. Apart from allegiance to this transcendent norm, and from critical interpretation in its light, the world of justice can slip into less than justice. Thus the norm of love functions critically and informatively in the moral life, showing both what man has failed to achieve, and providing the source for what he has been enabled to achieve. Niebuhr's language is partly that of "approximation of ideals," but his pattern of reflection is perhaps more dialectical than developmental. Achievements in history come from man's being cognizant of the transcendent absolute, which is both the teaching of Jesus and the law of life, on the one hand, and the realities of self-assertion, power, and sin in human life, on the other.

The theme that holds many contemporary writers together, who in many other respects differ, is the relevance of a norm that is in its pure and immediate application contrary to the counsels of prudence. This norm of love cannot be avoided by the adherent to the New Testament; it is present there in the teachings of Jesus, in his life and his death, in the writings of Paul, John, and many others. Nor can it be replaced, if one takes a traditional Protestant view of the authority of Scripture, by natural law, or by any other basis for ethics. Yet, men like Ramsey, Bennett, and Niebuhr are unwilling to make it the law that Christians obey directly without regard to consequences for history, just as they are unwilling to make it a historically actualizable ideal. Thus it becomes a norm: a source of principles and axioms, a "transcendent" point of criticism in living out the actualities and ambiguities of life in history.

SOME REFLECTIONS ON CHRIST THE TEACHER

C. H. Dodd once wrote, "Jesus certainly intended His precepts to be taken seriously." Just how seriously they were to be taken is a matter of centuries of discussion. Indeed, it has been a question of *how* they were to be taken, as well as how *seriously* they were to be taken. Dodd himself suggests "that we may regard each of these precepts as indicating . . . the *quality* and *direction* of action which shall conform to the standard set by the divine *agape*."[92] The two terms "quality" and "direction" are, in my judgment, aptly chosen to indicate something of the significance of the work of Christ, the

[92] C. H. Dodd, *Gospel and Law* (New York, 1951), p. 73.

teacher, for contemporary Christians. I should wish to add, in the sense developed above, that they are also *a* norm in the judgment-making of Christians.

Dodd uses the word "quality" with reference to actions; I would use it also with reference to the disposition which is a ground of action. Jesus certainly commended particular qualities of life, as various writers discussed in this chapter have indicated. The Beatitudes, the rest of the Sermon on the Mount, and many other teachings attributed to Jesus indicate some basic stances of life that are in accord with the trust in, and obedience to, God that he proclaimed. As banal as some treatments of these have become in Christian literature, one cannot avoid the evidence for them in the Gospels, or the attractiveness of them to a people who believe that love, mercy, and justice are proper words to attribute to God himself. There is, in St. Paul's words, "a manner of life" that is worthy of the good news, and this manner can be pointed to by paraphrases of Jesus teaching: freedom from anxiety about the daily cares of life, freedom from anger, envy, and lust, willingness to be reconciled with others, readiness to love rather than hate, concern for the good of the neighbor, humility, and many more. These indicate some of the contours of the dispositions that followers of Jesus Christ are called upon to have.

One need not argue for uniqueness either of the concern for such qualities of life or for the qualities that one can enumerate as characteristic of Jesus' teaching in order to make the point that the teachings commend certain dispositions which in turn are effective in moral actions. Nor does one have to find the historical verification for each saying to be convinced that the Gospels at least show some consistency in what they commend and what they generally disapprove in human life. One might desire to see all of these qualities as consistent with, or expressions of *agape*, but even here I do not believe Christians have much at stake in establishing a single reality as the touchstone of all other aspects of life.

Can such "qualities" be taught? In the sense that Jesus apparently did teach that they are worthy of approval, obviously they were taught. But whether they come into being by hearing them espoused is quite another question. Perhaps a Jefferson or even a Tolstoi thought that they would. But certainly Jesus was not concerned only to teach or even evoke certain moral attitudes; he was a religious man who had basically a religious message to preach. He was concerned with men's trust in God at least as much as he was concerned with their trustworthiness to each other. Indeed, as almost all writers dealing with the teachings indicate (though there is vast disagreement about most aspects of the point) the moral commendations make sense only in the context of the faith Jesus proclaimed, the expectations of the future he espoused, the basic loyalty that he evoked. The teachings, now as then, have such power and persuasiveness as they have within this religious and theological context. The point, then, is not whether these qualities can be taught apart from the religious faith and life of the community. They may be; but the convincing power of the teaching of them is enhanced by the wider context of which they are a part. Not only may trust in God who cares for the sparrows relieve the one who believes in such a God of some of his daily cares; it is appropriate to know that one ought not be anxious about the daily concerns if one trusts in God. The teaching is within the life of trust in God, expectation of his Kingdom, reliance on his goodness. The commandment to love the neighbor is not an imperative that is persuasive as a rational norm, though one might give extensive reasons why it is worthy of acceptance for its potential good consequences, universal applicability, and the like. Rather, the teaching is in the context of a proclamation of a God who loves both the neighbor and the self, and finds its home in a living faith in such a God. It is nonetheless appropriate to hear the teaching—a disposition to love the neighbor is both required and enabled in the followers of Jesus.

We have already moved somewhat from quality of life, a readiness and manner that can be described with modest efforts at precision and inclusiveness, to the direction of action. Direction is a useful term, since it avoids the connotations of specific compliance to specific precepts, on the one hand, and the reliance on expressions of attitudes without governance by any objective delineations of proper conduct, on the other hand. It indicates, as we shall see in the final chapter, a basic intention, a movement in a relatively clear way, toward certain ends. The direction of the teachings can have a validity that is more general than the specific statements made by Jesus under specific historical conditions that no longer prevail. Thus the kind of generalizations Barth makes in his "lines of instruction" or "prominent lines" is both legitimate and useful, though they can never become precise prescriptions applicable equally to all men and all occasions.

Again, the question of whether one can teach these directions as persuasive in their own moral terms has to be raised. Historically it is clear that Gandhi, for one example, learned his nonviolence in part from the teachings of Jesus, without confessing faith in the Kingdom Jesus proclaimed, not to mention faith in Jesus Christ as the mediator of God to man. For Christians, more than the effectiveness of a technique of social protest and social change, deemed right because it causes the least possible suffering, is involved in learning from Christ the teacher. There is a personal coherence between the faith Jesus proclaimed, the deeds attributed to him by the Gospel writers, and the teachings he is said to have given to men. In a parallel way, the faith of the Christian community in the God proclaimed by, and made known in, Christ requires a certain direction of activity as its concurrent behavior. The thought of the community is not so much that because Jesus said such-and-such about God, logically the following directions of behavior are entailed: . . . Rather the coherence is more personal than that; trust in God and in Kingdom evoke, enable, and require existentially a certain direction of behavior. The teachings of Jesus, as direction, make explicit these directions, make clear the way that is consonant with the faith he proclaimed, and the faith the Christians share.

The teachings can also function as norms, points of reference that have authority, not as literally inspired divine revelations of God's law, but as the relatively precise verbalizations about the manner of life and the deeds fitting for disciples of Jesus Christ. To suggest this is not to suggest that they are the only norms brought into moral judgment-making. But insofar as faithfulness to Jesus Christ is the commitment of Christian people, the teachings attributed to him will always have a point of judgment and self-criticism, and will always be brought to bear on the decisions and actions.[93]

When Christians ask, "What are we to do?" they can never fully avoid the teachings of Jesus, in spite of historical and theological difficulties about their accuracy and proper usage. They will always hear, "Take my yoke upon you, and learn from me . . ." (Matt. 11:29).

---

[93] This is not elaborated here, since in the final chapter the pattern involved here is given in greater detail.

VII ∫ CHRIST AND THE MORAL LIFE:

A Constructive Statement

DOES JESUS CHRIST MAKE ANY DIFFERENCE TO THE CHRISTIAN'S moral life? In the preceding chapters we have seen various ways in which this question has been asked and answered. The facets of the discussion have been many. The different understandings of Christ and the significance of his work for men have provided different ways of interpreting his significance for moral life. The subjective responses of Christians to him, as Revealer, as Justifier and Sanctifier, as Example and Teacher, vary. This chapter does not seek to bring all the previous material into a summary form but, rather, is a modest effort to address the question in a systematic way.[1]

Any constructive effort to answer the question of the difference that Jesus Christ makes in moral life must be given with scrupulous honesty and with caution. If the question is construed to be one that asks for historical evidences that the morality of Christians has been demonstrably better, more humane, and in actuality superior to the morality of other men, one's honest answer is at best ambiguous. Max Weber, in his comparative sociological studies of some of the great religions, has indicated that there appears to be a particularly positive attitude toward work in cultures that have been influenced by ancient Judaism and Christianity, and particularly Protestantism, when com-

---

[1] This systematic development will be continued in subsequent publication, in which I intend to explore further the idea of the virtues, and the ways in which Christians make moral judgments. On the latter, see my "Context vs. Principles: A Misplaced Debate in Christian Ethics," reprinted in Marty and Peerman, eds., *New Theology 3* (New York, 1966), pp. 69–102, and also the article "Moral Discernment in the Christian Life," in the symposium *Norm and Context in Christian Ethics*, eds. Paul Ramsey and Gene Outka (New York, 1968).

pared with a culture informed by Hindu religious life and ideas. But one can hardly make a case for the moral superiority of this attitude except from within an outlook that already places a highly positive value on the fruits of man's efforts to subdue himself and the creation; and with reference to some other values, the outworkings of this attitude in history have not always been morally salutary. John Wesley could return to Kingswood after a revival there in the eighteenth century and find that there was a great reduction in drunkenness, whore-mongering, and other vices. But whether these are the principal vices that faith in Christ is to overcome, and whether their counterpart virtues are the chief laudable marks of Christian action, is subject to debate.

Reinhold Niebuhr astutely warns us against looking to history for verification of the moral efficacy of the Christian faith. As we have noted earlier, he calls to our remembrance "the sorry annals of Christian fanaticism, of unholy religious hatreds, of sinful ambitions hiding behind the cloak of religious sanctity, or political power impulses compounded with pretensions of devotion to God." And Karl Barth, in a passage that penetrates the self-righteousness of any Christian, says, "Let us be honest. . . . What are we with our little conversion, our little repentance and reviving, our little ending and new beginning, our changed lives?"[2] No alert Christian needs to have eminent theologians raise the issue for him. Most Christians are readily put to shame by other men whose moral lives have brought the well-being of men into existence far beyond the measure of the efficacy of the activity of Christians. St. Paul speaks for all when he is aware of the good that he does not do, and the evil that he would not do which he does.

Christians are in no position to claim moral superiority over other men, or to make a case for the Christian faith on the grounds of verifiable evidence of its contribution to the moral well-being of the human community. Personal and historical evidence is not unambiguously on the Christian's side, even if one should choose to pursue such a defensive apologetic. Furthermore, the effort would hardly be in accord with the priorities of Scripture and of the Christian tradition in any case, since the message and the life of the Church have at least as much to do with man's deliverance, with God's saving work, with man in relation to God, as they have to do with morality.

[2] Reinhold Niebuhr, *Nature and Destiny of Man*, Vol. II, p. 122; Karl Barth, *Church Dogmatics*, IV/2, p. 582.

But even those who warn against claiming too much, in their own ways wish to make some claims for a morality that is peculiar to Christians, a morality that has beneficent effects for the human community. Without claiming that because Christ is Lord there are certain good consequences going on in history, or without claiming that because men trust in Jesus Christ certain moral effects are absolutely predictable, they still wish to show that the faith and loyalty of Christians evokes certain attitudes, dispositions, intentions, ends, and norms that are moral in character. Without articulating carefully and clearly what the "morphology" of faith and moral action is, they do infer that to trust in Christ is to have a new inner freedom, to be directed toward one's true end, to be governed by the law of love, to be disposed to do what is good for the neighbor.

In this chapter, as a response to the analyses given in previous chapters, and in a development of those analyses, I propose to explore a way of interpreting and explicating Christian moral life, regarding particularly some of the differences that faith in Jesus Christ *often does make, can make,* and *ought to make* in the moral lives of members of the Christian community. This is not a defense of the Christian faith or of Christian ethics, but an effort more clearly to understand in currently useful patterns of thinking what are some of the claims of Scripture and the theologians, and some of the experiences of Christian people. Thus the deliberately chosen terms: "often does make," "can make," and "ought to make." This interpretation, for purposes of arrangement, is divided into four parts. First, and inclusive of the other three, is a delineation of a perspective, a fundamental angle of vision and posture of life that the Christian gospel enables and requires. Second is an effort to portray certain salient aspects of the attitudes and dispositions that are evoked and shaped by loyalty to Jesus Christ. This is followed by an attempt to interpret some of the fundamental intentions, purposes, and ends that are consonant with Christian faith, and to see their moral significance. Finally, I shall indicate ways in which Christ and his teachings provide norms to be brought to bear in particular moral judgments of members of the Christian community.

PERSPECTIVE AND POSTURE IN THE CHRISTIAN MORAL LIFE

Christians are people with a common object of loyalty, Jesus Christ. What binds them together as a community is neither dogma nor piety, neither ecclesiastical institution nor standards of morality.[3] What Christ is to them is variously articulated: the revealer of God in the flesh, the God-man, the adopted Son of God, the One in whom the believer finds the key to the meaningfulness and goodness of existence, a center of moral and spiritual coherence, the revelation of what true manhood is, or some of these in various combinations with each other. How they worship is varied: through the divine liturgies of the Orthodox and Western Catholic communions, the lay Bible-reading and prayer cell of the conventicle, the rousing hymns of the revivalist tradition, the solemnity of Gregorian chants, in both private devotions and gathered congregations, or again in various combinations. The institutional forms of their community life differ from the imposing hierarchical structures of the Catholic and Anglican communions to the lay-dominated, radically democratic structures of the Free Churches. Their standards of morality diverge: there are pacifists, and believers that some wars are just; there are those who believe that poverty is part of obedience, and those for whom the stewardship of what one has is more important than the amount of goods that one has; there are those who stress the liberty of the Christian conscience, and those who stress the norms to which the Christian conscience is bound. Yet Christians have one point of common life, namely, the centrality of Jesus Christ as the One through whom the ultimate powers and realities of life are known and understood, the One who represents as an historical figure the origin of a continuing historical community of trust and loyalty.

Jesus Christ is the focal point of the integrity and the coherence, such as it is, of the Christian community, He is, or may be, the focal point of the integrity and coherence of the lives of those who are his followers. How this focal point of loyalty, integrity, and coherence affects the specific deeds and actions of men is difficult to delineate with precision, just as it is difficult to delineate how having a loyalty to one's nation and its historic values affects one's speech and deeds. Certainly it is not precisely predictable how such a center will affect what one says or does on every particular occasion of life. Nonetheless, the fact of a loyalty to a common Lord suggests that insofar as

[3] I am building here on a way of thinking that I learned from H. Richard Niebuhr, and from many of the theologians and philosophers who influenced him, though the way in which this chapter is developed might well have merited as much of his disfavor as of his approval. See also my *Treasure in Earthen Vessels: The Church as a Human Community* (New York, 1961).

this loyalty has the marks of an inner commitment, of a meaningful subjective relationship, it is possible to suggest some of its characteristic consequences in and for those who share it. Christ as Lord, as Master, for Christians often does, can, and ought to give them a particular perspective on life, a particular posture toward life.

The words "perspective" and "posture" at best only point to some aspects of what is very basic in the Christian life. The word "perspective" is drawn from the sphere of its normal usage, that is, visual experience, and suggests that the point from which things are seen and observed determines what is seen and what is not seen, which aspects of what is seen are outstanding, which are shadowed and which are clear, what attracts attention and what is subdued in attention. It has come to be used to refer to more than strictly visual experience as well. Perspective is used to refer to the state of the observing subject; to his preferences for certain things, to his fundamental vocabulary for describing and evaluating what he observes, his criteria for rational judgment, and his values that determine his affective responses. Sometimes the word "understanding" has been used to cover these things, and this is fitting and proper if it is used in such a way that the affections are included together with the intellect. This notion of "perspective" or "understanding" has been used, and still can be used, with care to interpret a basic aspect of the Christian moral life.

The word "posture" has its normal use in the description of the physical aspects of a body, the arrangement of some of its parts relative to each other. But it has come to be used also to suggest the basic characteristic of a person, his fundamental "state" or his "frame of mind." In this less precise usage it suggests more than one's intellectual delineation of where he stands in life; it can refer also to the orientation of one's affections, sensibilities, and value preferences. Indeed, the word "orientation" is another that in common usage points to a basic state and direction of the self. We wish to suggest here that it is meaningful to affirm that Christians often have, can have, and ought to have a characteristic posture or orientation toward the world.

The suggestiveness of this language has the merits not only of referring to the "whole man," but also of permitting latitude and variation within something that has fundamental integrity and coherence. To say that Christ gives the believer a perspective is not to say that every believer has absolutely the same perspective, that every Christian has exactly the same value perferences, the same values, the same understanding of himself and the world. To say that Christians have a certain posture toward the world is not to claim empirical evidence for the presence of a uniform characteristic, or uniform "state" or "frame of mind" in all Christians. The variations are often more impressive than the consistency is to the eye of the observer, and the claim for such a perspective perhaps has to be cast more in terms of "can have" and "ought to have" than "actually have." Other fundamental loyalties and commitments to self, to family, to vocation, to nation, and to certain means of conduct are not related to the trust in and loyalty to Jesus Christ in the same way in all Christians. Social and cultural conditioning as well as the factors that influence the development of the individual personality all qualify the posture and perspective of the Christian. The particularly religious contexts in which Christians are formed and live, further shape differences within the basic loyalty and perspective. The "spirituality" of the Russian Orthodox believer is different from that of a Western Catholic and a Presbyterian. Theological traditions, with their varying emphases and polemics, as well as the personal religious beliefs of persons within these traditions create variations in posture and perspective. There are also great differences in the religious faithfulness and loyalty of people; there are those who for various reasons make their loyalty to Christ more central in their speech and actions, and those who find such a loyalty to be peripheral. And there is the presence of warring tendencies within the same person over time, so that the same person may in some words and deeds express his Christian posture more than he does at other times. There is also the reality of untrust and disloyalty to Jesus Christ, of primary orientation to the gods of self, or family, or nation, that alters perspective and posture.

To delineate all the facets of the posture and perspective toward one's self, toward others, and toward the world which Christ enables those who are his loyal disciples to have is a much more extensive task than can be executed in this chapter. I will isolate a most salient aspect of that perspective here to show how it functions in human moral experience. That aspect is confidence in God, in the goodness of the ultimate power and source of life, and in the power of goodness. This confidence, one readily acknowledges, can be evoked by other than loyalty to Jesus Christ, and indeed, it is present in the religious and moral faith that Jesus himself shared as a good Jew.

One can get a glimpse of the significance of this confidence by rehearsing in a brief and unscholarly way the differences that are often drawn between an Augustinian and a Manichean view of history. The Augustinian view is grounded in the conviction that the good has in principle triumphed over evil, that men can live in the affirmation of the goodness of God and his creation, rather than in a devastating fear of the negation of good and the destructive power of evil. The Manichean view is grounded in the conviction of an ongoing struggle and warfare between good and evil powers, with clear delineations between them. Christ is a revelation and a symbol of the reality of the power of goodness; his teaching, his deeds, and the interpretation given to his significance in the Church all point to the Augustinian view as a central theme. Christ becomes, then, the basis of Augustinian perspective or a posture toward oneself, toward others, and toward the world. If one believes that the goodness of God and the goodness of life as created, governed, and redeemed by God are ultimately and really greater than any particular occasion of evil, or all occasions of evil collected, one will move with a fundamental confidence in the world, with an openness toward the world, with a sensitivity to change and the opportunities it provides, and without a debilitating despair. If one believes that evil has a status and a power equal to the good, one will move from fear to a crusading mentality that forecloses sensitivity to the changing constellations out of which new good can emerge, that seeks to destroy the evil rather than reform it, that seeks to abolish rather than to reconcile. Jesus Christ makes possible a confidence in the power of the good; he provides a basic posture and perspective to those who are loyal to him.

The Gospels bear witness to Jesus' own confidence in the goodness and mercy of God, his indiscriminating care for the just and the unjust. The deeds of Jesus narrated in the Gospels testify to his faith that renewal, healing, and reconciliation are possible for all men: for those who have fallen into degradation, those who are without respectable status, those who serve the human oppressors, those who are sick, those who are one's enemies. Christians find in Jesus Christ, both in the faith he proclaimed and in his own life and death and resurrection, a confidence in the goodness, mercy, and power of God.

This is not to assert that no one trusts in the power of goodness apart from an explicit faith in, and a committed loyalty to, Jesus Christ. Nor is it to say that Christians suffer from illusions about corruption and evil in the world that have to be historically and personally overcome. There are many experiences of men, mature and childlike, that tend to lead to confidence in the reality of the good. And there are many occasions to remind Christians that their trust in God as good has not led them to assume a perspective and posture that seems to be the human correlate of such a faith.

Jesus Christ provides a clue to, an insight into, a knowledge and confirmation of the goodness of God, and thus a confidence in the power of the good. In part this is what the great New Testament Christological texts proclaim as the writers have interpreted the significance of Jesus Christ. "In the beginning was the Word, and the Word was with God, and the Word was God. All things were made through him, and without him was not anything made that was made. In him was life, and the life was the light of men. The Light shines in the darkness, and the darkness has not overcome it" (John 1:1–5). "He is the image of the invisible God, the first-born of all creation; for in him all things were created, in heaven and on earth; visible and invisible, whether thrones or dominions or principalities or authorities—all things were created through him and for him" (Col. 1:15–17). What has been made known in Jesus points beyond itself to assertions that what can be said about him is in accord with the purpose and will of the Creator; indeed, in Christ the goodness of the Creator and Sustainer of the world is made known.

Human experience also testifies somewhat to the sustaining goodness of life. Life in the family gives the child some understanding and experience of a sustaining love, of the goodness and reliability of others and of life itself, of the fact that there are beings in whom one can trust. But the shocks of human experience put to test the limits of this reliability and love; the experiences of rejection, and the betrayal of trust, of the finiteness and decay of created things, of death and evil, all make clear the limitations of created things to evoke a sense of reliability. The confidence that is engendered and sustained by human beings and by other created things is always relative, for it is evoked by finite and relative goods.

The biblical testimony is to a universal power in which men can trust, a power that sustains even when trust in men and created

objects is betrayed. The Old Testament story of the covenant of a
faithful God of Israel who evokes their trust is part of what is confirmed in the Christian's faith in Jesus Christ. Their faith in God was
partially confirmed by their understanding of the way in which he led
them through their history, his deliverance of them from their
oppressors and their enemies. But it was also faith in the promise of
an ultimate deliverer and deliverance, and a fulfillment that was
anticipated rather than confirmed. The God in whom they trusted
was the ground for a confidence and a hope that could not be oblit-
erated by the vicissitudes and disappointments of the experience of
any one man, or a whole people. The New Testament acclamations
that in Christ sin and death, the powers that threaten the supremacy
and goodness of life, are overcome is further testimony to the
ultimate reliability and trustworthiness of God, a reliability that
persists in the midst of all that threatens the goodness of life.

These convictions, confirmed in Jesus Christ and symbolized by
him, provide a perspective and a posture toward oneself, others, and
the world. Theologians who have accented these convictions have
had, as we have seen, a particular word to say about the moral life in
Christ. Knowledge of the goodness of God, and of the goodness of
created and redeemed life, has been given in Jesus Christ. In him is
confirmed the faith of Israel, and the human experiences of human
love and trust. Moral life takes place, then, in the perspective of this
affirmation. We have seen how Karl Barth proceeds to answer the
moral question, "What ought we to do?" by asserting that "In Him
the realization of the good corresponding to the divine election has
already taken place—and so completely that we, for our part, have
actually nothing to add, but only to endorse this event by our
action."[4] One need not endorse the whole of Barth's ethics in order
to appreciate a perspective elucidated here that is evoked by Jesus
Christ. It is not man's task to create human moral good out of
nothing, or even to bring into being on his own the goodness that is
latent in the stuff of experience in which he is embedded. It is not
man's task to exaggerate the presence of evil in the world, and to
recruit a mighty army to cast it out as if it were some thing, some
embodiment, that could be destroyed. It is not man's task glumly to
face the world, and to build it into a fitting kingdom for his residence

---

[4] *Church Dogmatics*, II/2, p. 540.

as if he had to rely only upon himself. No, the good has been realized and confirmed; the power and source of life is good; it corresponds to what men know in God's goodness toward them in Christ Jesus. Human action can assume a reality and potentiality for moral good that already exists; it can attest to the fact that life and the giver of life enable humane life to be sustained and cultivated; it can give shape and character to the world in the confidence that it is fundamentally good.

F. D. Maurice sounded a similar note when he wrote, "I may bid [each peasant and beggar in the land] rejoice, and give thanks, and sing merry songs to God who made him because there is nothing created which his Lord and Master has not redeemed, of which He is not the King. . . ."[5] The fundamental assertion about life is not about the powers of evil in the world, though they are present with imposing reality, nor about the absolute goodness of finite human beings and the created world, but about the status of everything that is, before God. There is nothing created which God has not redeemed; there is nothing over which he does not exercise his rule. This kind of affirmation gives a perspective and posture to the moral life: even in adversity and human destructiveness, there is still a goodness that can be realized, a possibility for reconciliation and renewal, a basis for confidence. Thus, in Maurice's terms, we are called to "witness to the Light," to affirm the moral possibilities present in all things in human experience. This perspective does not lose sight of the threats to the moral well-being of man. "I ask no one to pronounce, for I dare not pronounce myself, what are the possibilities of resistance in a human will to the loving will of God. There are times when they seem to me—thinking of myself more than others—almost infinite. But I know that there is something which must be infinite. I am obliged to believe in an abyss of love which is deeper than the abyss of death: I dare not lose faith in that love. I sink into death, eternal death, if I do. I must feel that this love is compassing the universe. More about it I cannot know. But God knows. I leave myself and all to Him."[6] The abyss of God's love is deeper even than the abyss of death. Such a conviction, even though Maurice seemed to have to cajole himself into affirming it sometimes against the evidence of experience, provides a perspective and posture

[5] Maurice, *Theological Essays* (1957 ed), p. 123.
[6] *Ibid.*, p. 323.

for the Christian moral life. Jesus Christ is both a source and a symbol of that affirmation. Moral life becomes a testimony to Him; human experience is responded to from the perspective of such an affirmation. Why not sing merry songs, rejoice and be thankful, even while seeking to restrain and reform those forces that debilitate the good creation, for God the Lord of life is good? The life which he created is good, and he has acted to redeem it from its corruptions.

Much more could be said about other facets of the perspective and posture that Christ evokes in those who are loyal to him, for more can be said about what Christians affirm about God, and his judgment of, and care for, the world. And variations can be made on this perspective, in the light of theological qualifications and nuances not discussed in this brief account. But surely close to a universal assent can be given by the Christian community to the testimony that in Christ men come to have confidence in the goodness of God, of the ultimate power of life. And surely this conviction evokes and commends a perspective, a posture toward the self, others, and the world.

DISPOSITION OF THE CHRISTIAN MORAL SELF

This perspective gives shape and movement to a certain disposition, or set of dispositions, in the moral lives of Christians. By disposition I wish to suggest a "manner of life," a "lasting or persisting tendency," a "bearing toward one another and the world," a "readiness to act in a certain way." Dispositions are in continuity with perspective and posture; I am not trying to formulate a new set of categories that would represent separate faculties or even distinct chronological stages in action. The distinction between perspective and disposition that I wish to make is as follows. Dispositions refer to the self's attitudes, its somewhat stable readiness to speak and to act in particular ways. Perspective and posture refer more to the fundamental points of orientation that are governed by convictions that one has about crucial matters. Dispositions are "habits" in the classical Roman Catholic usage of that term; not mechanical automatic responses to external stimuli, but persisting tendencies to act in such a way that one's action is directed in part by these lasting dispositions. Thus one can speak intelligibly about a "loving disposition," a "hopeful disposition," a "trusting disposition"; and one can speak about inner freedom, courage, temperance, justice, and prudence in a similar way. By using the word "disposition" in distinction from the word "intention," I wish to indicate that intentions have a greater degree of self-consciousness and rational specification than do dispositions.

The traditional language of virtue pointed toward this aspect of human experience. St. Thomas wrote that a virtue is a "lasting disposition" that is in accord with a being's true nature and true end. I do not wish to make a case in this chapter for a certain delineation of man's true nature and end, but to suggest that one can have lasting dispositions that are in accord with one's loyalty to Jesus Christ, and with the perspective and posture toward life that is evoked by this loyalty. I am convinced that St. Paul had something like this in mind when he wrote to the Christians in Philippi, "Only let your *manner of life* be worthy of the gospel of Christ," in Phil. 1:27, or "Let your bearing towards one another arise out of your life in Christ Jesus," as the New English Bible translates Phil. 2:5. The manner of life, and the bearing toward one another, is, to be sure, a "gift of the Spirit," but it is also a requirement of Christians, subject to their discipline and attention. They are to have a readiness to do what is loving; they are to have lasting dispositions of hope and trust; they are to have a willingness to be bold. These dispositions are part of what is given to them "in Christ Jesus," and yet they are also to be "worthy of the gospel of Christ," and thus there is an imperative note as well.

In this chapter I shall delineate only two aspects of what might more richly be included in the characteristics of the "Christian manner of life." These are hope and freedom. I will indicate some of the significance of these for the moral action of members of the Christian community. This leaves out much: love, trust, boldness, humility, and others. It also distorts hope and freedom to the extent that one cannot speak fully about one or two aspects of a manner of life without indicating both their coherence and their abrasiveness with other aspects of it. Nor am I making the claim that all Christians have or even ought to have the same disposition, or that every aspect of that disposition ought to be equally present in every action.[7]

Christians often are, can be, and ought to be disposed to be hopeful. Hope is part of their bearing toward one another and the

[7] A more detailed and inclusive presentation of the "virtues" will be given in subsequent publication.

world, it is part of the manner of life that is worthy of the gospel of Jesus Christ.[8] Hope is a disposition that correlates with trust in the goodness of God and the power of goodness in life. Hope is carried by the confidence that life is more reliable than unreliable, that the future is open, that new possibilities of life exist, that the present patterns of life are not fated by the blind god Necessity, but are susceptible to change, to a recombination of aspects and elements of the world. Hope also is carried by freedom. Without freedom one could not hope: freedom to become what one now is not, freedom to change the course of one's own life and the course of the social history of which one is a part, freedom to alter the patterns of life that oppress human dignity and human aspirations. Some facets of hope can be best seen by observing two aspects of the absence of hope: despair, and the sense of fatedness.

Despair is a sin against hope. It emerges where confidence is gone, where there are no signs of the possibility of a human and moral good coming into being in personal and communal experience, where there is no confidence in the goodness of one's own life to break into meaningful and rewarding experience and relations. Despair is evoked not so much by the presence of visible and active forces that destroy the significance of life in some dramatic way as it is by degeneration of humaneness through the loss of vision of new possibilities, through lack of confidence that the future is open and worthy of trust. Despair is hopelessness.

The reality and presence of despair, and the knowledge that the basis for it is starkly present in the lives of many people in the human community, caution the Christian interpreter against excessively moralizing against those who are in despair and against a Pollyanna "pull yourself up by your own bootstraps" optimism. The presence of despair will not be overcome by bland assurances that the abyss of hope is deeper than the abyss of despair given to those for whom

[8] My reflections about hope have been stimulated by the writings of Gabriel Marcel, particularly, "Sketch of a Phenomenology and Metaphysic of Hope," *Homo Viator* (Chicago, 1951), pp. 29–67; by writings of Josiah Royce, particularly *The Problem of Christianity*, 2 vols. (New York, 1913); and most recently by Father William Lynch's *Images of Hope: Imagination as Healer of the Hopeless* (Baltimore, 1965), which I heartily commend for its penetrating insights into the significance of hope for the healing of spiritual and mental illness. Jürgen Moltmann's *Theology of Hope* (New York, 1967) came to my attention too late to be incorporated into this discussion.

there is little or no confirmation of the reliability of persons and communities, of the openness of the future. St. John and St. Paul had a basis for confidence and lived in hope without illusions about the unreality of evil in the world. Theologians like Barth and Maurice, while usually singing merry songs to God for his goodness, nonetheless realized with Reinhold Niebuhr that the "logic" of redemption is not fully confirmed in human experience.

The Christian disposition of hope is grounded in trust in the goodness and power of God, a goodness and power that has a vaster time-and-space span than the particular experiences of one man in one time, or a generation of men in one place. The hope of Christians points not just to a basis for renewal of life, reconciliation between enemies, and fulfillment that might be dimly discerned in even the agony of despair; it is grounded in a trust in the goodness of God who makes all renewal, reconciliation, and fulfillment possible, who secures the future as one in which men can respond creatively to new possibilities of human achievement and well-being. Ultimate despair is antithetical to a hope that is born of a trust in the goodness of God, in the God who is good, and thus in the power of newness and possibility of life of which he is Lord. The logic of the Christian life, the performance of the Christian faith, prohibits, can prohibit, or ought to prohibit Christians from falling into utter despair.

The hope of Christians in their moral activity is not the projection of an attitude out of the will of man to be an optimist, nor is it only a disposition that has been engendered by a religious *belief*. It is a confidence that man's expectations meet the reality of God's goodness, confront a newness of life that awaits our participation in it and endorsement of it. It does not equip the moral life like a mighty army, armed to the teeth with weaponry that promises a personal and historical victory, and a total surrender of some enemy discerned to personify that which is evil. Rather, it responds to marks of change and goodness that evolve and come into being in the encounters with other men and other communities. The Christian's confidence is not in man's own right not to despair, nor in the disposition of hope; it is confidence in the power of the good to come into being in each particular future, in each particular place. It is confidence in life, in the possibilities to restrain those things that are destructive of human well-being as well as the possibilities for new achievements of well-being. Hope is a disposition to meet and bring into realization in moral activity the potentialities for goodness and human value which already exist, which meet the hopeful man in his activities. Utter despair lacks confidence in any being's goodness; Christian hope is confidence in the goodness of God, whose power brings all created values into being.

The sense of fatedness is also a sin against hope. There is in it an expectation of the future, but one that breeds fear and despair more often than confidence and hope. The man who feels fated responds to the future as inexorable and unalterable in its developments, not amenable to shaping by human initiative. He views the self as powerless, unable to be other than what it is, the victim being forged or disposed of by uncontrollable forces within the self and outside the self. Fatedness can lead to despair when a person sees the future as closed, as working against human development and as destructive of human potentialities. Fatedness can lead to illusions also, if a person believes himself chosen by destiny to exert his power over other men, to be the object of glorification by others.

The disposition of hope for Christians is not based on trust in the inexorable predetermination of events, but in the emergent possibilities of life under the care and goodness of God. It is neither the sense of fate that leads to despair, nor the sense of destiny that leads to illusions. Rather, the disposition of hope is aware of the openness and newness of life, aware of the possibilities for mankind that are being made possible not only by one's own initiative, but also by the events and beings to which one responds. It leads to action; it does not wait in passivity for the good to come into being, but shapes and forms the future by human awareness and deeds. The hope of Christians does not wait for an apocalyptic victory, nor is it an opiate that enables men to endure despair. Rather, it is grounded in a confidence that the future is for man, that God enables out of his goodness new possibilities for humane life, that men are the agents of hope actualizing the good as they share in the development of history and in the building of the human community. What lies ahead is not a fate but a possibility, not of any one man's or any one generation's creation, but a possibility being given by the goodness of God.

Hope is a disposition that comes into being through faith. It is a "performative" of the Christian perspective and posture.[9] It is a

⁹ Donald D. Evans, in *The Logic of Self-Involvement* (London, 1963), demonstrates how J. L. Austin's theory of "performative language" can be used to explicate the relation between religious convictions and beliefs, on the one

manner of life, a readiness to respond and act in an affirmative manner; it is a bearing toward one another. The moral activity of Christians is in part an expressive activity, bearing witness to this hope, motivated by this hope, and enacting this hope in words and deeds.

Christians often are, can be, and ought to be inwardly free, not bound by paralyzing fears and the necessity to justify themselves in the eyes of God or man. Inner freedom of spirit is part of their bearing toward one another, part of the manner of life that is worthy of the gospel. Freedom from excessive concern with the self, from domination by the expectations of others, from crippling anxiety about death and life all correlate with confidence in the goodness of God. Freedom to give oneself in love for the neighbor, to seek the other's good rather than one's own, to identify with the oppressed and the anxious, to participate in causes that seek justice and peace in spite of their ambiguities, to make judgments that are particular and relative to complex and confused situations—this freedom is part of the Christian's readiness; it is a persisting tendency in the Christian moral life.

The interpretations of this freedom have varied in the course of Christian history, and discussions of the proper way to interpret St. Paul on the subject continue among both biblical scholars and theologians. There have been those like Augustine and Thomas Aquinas who have believed it enables one to obey the law joyously, to do in liberty what one was formerly coerced to do. There are others who have stressed the spontaneity to express oneself in love, meeting the immediate need of the neighbor in whatever way is required. As we have seen, the weight of Luther's and Bultmann's interpretations are on this side of the matter. But there is no fundamental dissent from the Pauline claim that faith in Jesus Christ brings a new freedom to the life of the Christian. Some aspects of this freedom of the Christian can best be seen by observing what life can be in its absence. I will briefly note two: cowardice and "excessive scrupulosity."

Cowardice as a disposition stems in part from fear, from the absence of fundamental confidence in the goodness of life. It is a moral paralysis that vitiates the human capacity to initiate and to act

---

hand, and attitudes and actions, on the other. Although his technical apparatus does not become visible in this chapter, I am indebted to Evans for clarification of the "logic of self-involvement."

in the course of life's events. It is sometimes given justification as prudence, or as legitimate passivity and caution. Christians have particular ways of defending passivity, some of which slip into a justification for cowardice. One can find in the First Epistle of Peter, for example, extensive evidence that submissiveness was a virtue commended to the early Christians to whom the letter was written under particular historical circumstances. Submissiveness may be an expression of fear and cowardice; it may also be an expression of inner freedom, courage, and patience. Cowardice is a form of bondage from which Christ has set men free. Freedom can issue in courage to be and to do what appears to be the right in life's experiences.

Cowardice cripples participation in the historical struggles and opportunities to achieve what is morally good. It is a readiness to secure what is and what has been, and not a readiness to move into changing conditions with an open future. Cowardice is unwilling to risk. The disposition of inner freedom, however, leads to venturing, to moving forward, to risking the good that is and has been for a good that is coming into being. This freedom for the Christian is part of a manner of life grounded in his faith, in the "sure and certain knowledge of the Divine benevolence toward us," to use Calvin's words.

Excessive scrupulosity is the disposition to be absolutely certain of the rectitude of what one proposes to do, to be unexceptionally correct in one's behavior. It is a disposition that comes from the absence of inner freedom. It can be found paraded as a virtue in rigid moralistic Christians, both Catholic and Protestant. The churches have to bear part of the responsiblity for this manner of life, for they have often given detailed instruction to their members, indicating to them what ought and ought not to be done, motivating them by fear of punitive consequences if moral mistakes are made, and leaving little room for personal discernment of the right and the good. In fear Christians have grasped rules to ensure that they do what is right, and to avoid moral guilt and limit personal accountability. Excessive scrupulosity is both the creator and sustainer of legalistic morality; legalistic morality is both the creator and sustainer of excessive scrupulosity.

This disposition can be found in a moral culture that supports an open morality as well as in one that supports a closed one. The absence of detailed moral prescriptions is no guarantor of inner freedom. Apart from inner freedom and confidence, the outwardly free man can ponder the precise moral correctness of his judgments and actions to the point of paralysis partially because of the absence of guidelines and authoritative traditions.

The perspective of the Christian, his loyalty to Jesus Christ, gives, can give, and ought to give him a freedom from excessive scrupulosity. In his confidence in God and his goodness, he ought to be able to risk the unusual word and deed when it seems to be required, to do more than or even other than the "law" requires when such deeds would restrain destructive forces or bring new good into being. He ought to be free to commit himself to the partial good that is possible, rather than passively and scrupulously waiting for some total and pure good that is probably impossible. The disposition of inner freedom is a "performative" of belief and trust in the abiding goodness of God. Scrupulosity in excess is rooted in the dread that finite mortal men will make a moral error; freedom accepts this possibility and acts with prudence and courage. The freedom of the Christian is enabling; excessive scrupulosity is crippling.

Freedom, like hope, is not the single, the total, or even the dominant aspect of the disposition of the Christian man. Even such a proclaimer of the freedom of the Christian as Rudolf Bultmann, as we have seen, ties it at least to love, hope, and obedience. For Luther freedom is to issue in deeds of love, following Christ who not only enables man to be free, but is also the example of man's loving relations to his neighbor. St. Paul had to remind the Christians in Corinth that while all things are lawful, not all things are helpful, and not all things are edifying. The freedom that faith in God's goodness, and loyalty to Jesus Christ enables, is expressed in deeds that correspond to that goodness, that endorse God's care and love, that witness to Jesus Christ. It is always a tempting mistake in discourse about the Christian moral life, especially in the struggle against legalism, to isolate freedom from conformation to that which makes man free, to proclaim freedom apart from the obligation to love, and apart from particular obligations to others.

Inner freedom is a disposition, a bearing that comes into being in the life of the Christian in response to God's love and goodness. The moral activity of Christians expresses this freedom, bears witness to it in the deeds of men in the world.

The Christian moral life, however, is not only the expression of a *many faceted disposition* or bearing. All too often this has been assumed, particularly among certain Protestants. "The man of faith is free for love, which opens his eyes to what God requires of him in the moment,"[10] Bultmann says, as we have seen. To what does "love" refer here? To a disposition, to a readiness on the part of the Christian. But there seems to be little guarantee that the disposition to love is sufficient to inform one what love requires, or to open one's eyes to what God requires. Love as a disposition needs love as an intention, as a purpose, and also love as a norm. Loyalty to Christ finds its correlates in the moral self not only in a manner of life, but in purposes and ends and intentions that correspond to the fundamental perspective and posture of the Christian man, perspective and posture evoked and shaped by faith in Jesus Christ.

MORAL INTENTIONS IN THE CHRISTIAN LIFE

The Christian's perspective, governed as it is by his loyalty to Jesus Christ, forms, can form, or ought to form certain intentions and governing purposes in his life. By intention I wish to suggest a basic direction of activity, an articulation of what that direction is and ought to be, a purposive orientation for one's life. Intention suggests cognition; one has knowledge of what his intentions are, or at least he is not ignorant of them. It also suggests the function of what men have called the will; one wills to achieve his intentions, to fulfill his purposes.[11] The intentions of a Christian are, can be, and ought to be informed by his trust in and loyalty to Jesus Christ insofar as his moral activities are the performatives of his religious faith and beliefs. They also have some conformity to his dispositions as these are also brought into being by his faith; indeed they may be specified expressions of these dispositions. Moral action is governed in part by the intentions of the actor, by his thought about the purposes he is seeking to fulfill, the ends he is seeking to achieve. Man is an intending actor, not merely an automatic reactor to external stimuli.[12] One's intentions are shaped in accord with what one values, what one

---

[10] *Existence and Faith*, p. 182. Also cited in Chapter IV of this book.

[11] I have been deeply informed in working out this section by Stuart Hampshire's *Thought and Action* (New York, 1960), particularly Ch. 2, "Intention and Action." Hampshire summarizes his delineation of the concept of intention on pp. 134–35. See also G. E. M. Anscombe, *Intention* (2nd ed.; Oxford, 1963).

[12] For a very useful treatment of this, see John Macmurray, *The Self as Agent* (New York, 1957), especially pp. 84–103.

believes to be worthy of achieving, one's convictions about what is good and what ought to be, one's basic loyalties and commitments. The moral intentions of the Christian, then, are, can be, or ought to be consistent with his loyalty to Jesus Christ, and inferences drawn from what is known in and through him.

The place of intention in the Christian moral life needs much clarification. Roman Catholic moral theologians have brought the notion to some exasperated disrepute by some of their more refined casuistry in justifying actions on the basis of the intention of the actor. One undeveloped example can make the point. Abortion is wrong because it is the taking of life, but therapeutic abortions can be induced, given certain medical conditions, such as an extrauterine pregnancy, where it is necessary to take the fetus in order to save the life of the mother. The moral justification for such taking of life rests in the intention; the physician intends to preserve the life of the mother, and the death of the fetus is an evil effect of this intention. He presumably does not morally intend to take the life of the fetus, though medically this is what has to be done. I shall not argue a case for or against casuistry here, but wish only to indicate what many Protestant writers who explicitly reject or only ignore the language of intention are afraid of in its usage. It can become a defensive device of moral self-justification, and a rationalistic device that assumes a deed is determined in its moral aspects by intentions alone.

Many current writers of ethics in the Protestant tradition avoid discussions of intention by relying on what is presumed to be the Christian's ability to be immediately sensitive to what *God* is doing in the world, or by relying on the free and loving disposition of Christians to guide into the moral target or to "open their eyes." Paul Lehmann provides an example of the first way of avoiding the issue; J. A. T. Robinson provides an example of the second.

When Lehmann writes that the difference between the Christian believer and the unbeliever "is defined by imaginative and behavioral sensitivity to what God is doing in the world to make and to keep human life human, to achieve the maturity of men,"[13] he clearly focuses attention primarily on what God is doing, and not on men's moral intentions. When he stresses "imaginative and behavioral sensitivity" he indicates his desire to have a less mediated and less

[13] Lehmann, *Ethics in a Christian Context*, p. 117.

rational character assigned to the perception of what men are to do. When he writes that the "theonomous conscience" is "immediately sensitive to the freedom of God" and "is governed and directed by freedom of God alone," he makes the same points once more.[14] The Christians' actions are to be formed by God's aims and intentions, by "his humanizing aims," not by the explication of human intentions that are shaped by reflection upon the Christian beliefs about God's revelation in Jesus Christ. When he states that the conscience is to be "immediately sensitive" to God's freedom, he seems to rule out clear man-made statements about what God's will is.

Yet obviously God has an aim, an intention, for Lehmann; namely, to make and keep human life human. And man is to act in conformity to God's intentional activity. A critical question is pertinent. Either there is a logic imbedded in "sensitivity" so that in it God's intentions are implanted in the conscience of the Christian in such a way that he *responds* to God's aims by forming intentions that are consistent with God's, or it is assumed that finite men are equipped to know, to perceive clearly what God is doing immediately and directly, and are then equally immediately determined by God through that sensitivity. If it is the former, Lehmann has short-cut the intellectually intentional character of moral action by assuming it; if it is the latter, he has overcome the "distance" between man and God.[15] My point is that it is both truer to moral experience and less presumptuous to indicate that the intention of the Christian is his own, shaped in response to his beliefs. Such explication of intention also gives it a greater objectivity, so that it can be criticized and judged by the self and by others. And unless one assumes that the self has overcome both its partiality and limitations due to its finitude, and its sin, such objectivity and criticism are important for morality.[16]

---

14 *Ibid.*, pp. 358–359.

15 Kierkegaard made a comment that is apt at this point. "That the ethical is present in the historical process, as it is everywhere God is, is not . . . denied. But it is denied that the finite spirit can see it there in truth; and it must be reckoned a piece of presumption to attempt to see it there, a reckless venture which may readily end by the observer losing the ethical in himself" (*Concluding Unscientific Postscript* [Princeton, 1944], pp. 126–127). I am indebted to Mr. Charles Powers for calling attention to this passage, in his Union Theological Seminary B.D. Thesis, "Kierkegaard and Social Ethics" (unpublished; New York, 1966).

16 See my "The Eclipse of Sin," in *motive*, Vol. 25, No. 6 (March, 1965), pp. 4–8.

In one particularly unguarded statement, Bishop J. A. T. Robinson seems to suggest that explication of intention is not necessary because a disposition to love is sufficient. It makes Robinson sound much like Bultmann's statement about love opening the eyes. "Love alone, because, as it were, it has a built-in moral compass, enabling it to 'home' intuitively upon the deepest need of the other, can allow itself to be directed completely by the situation."[17] The idioms of the "moral compass" and "intuitive homing in" seem to suggest that Robinson believes that a disposition to love is sufficient without a clarification of what the loving person intends. Here the reliance is not on God's intention, as in Lehmann, but on the love that the person has. Like a missile attracted to the heat of its target, a pigeon that finds its way home, a compass that magnetically shows the direction, love is moved by the deepest need of the other. Perhaps Robinson intends to say that love directs and dominates one's intellectually designated purposes as well as one's bearing toward others, and thus intention is part of what "love" refers to; but if that is the case it is not clear to the reader. He seems, rather, to rely upon the need of the other to direct the disposition to love to the proper moral target. But issues are only left undiscussed and not resolved by such writing. Is not a disposition to love capable of deception by the self, or by the needs of the other? Is intuition to be relied upon in moral judgment-making and action without being subject to rational criticism and direction? Is there no objectivity in moral discourse, no explication of intentions and their justifications which is subject to scrutiny and debate? Man's dispositions are by no means restored and redeemed to such presumed pristine purity that they are reliable as the subjective center of moral action. Nor is the objective world, including the neighbor who can be deceived about his own deepest need, so renewed and redeemed that I, for example, can rely on it to direct me magnetically to the morally proper word and deed. A more modest and precise approach is in order: modest in its claims for the restoration of man and the world, precise in its delineation of what proper moral intentions both are and ought to be.

How do intentions function in the moral life? When Stuart Hampshire discusses this, he interestingly uses the language of light, of illumination, for which there is precedent in the history of Chris-

---

[17] Robinson, *Honest to God,* p. 115. Robinson is not consistent in his approach to ethics, as Paul Ramsey has shown in *Deeds and Rules in Christian Ethics* (Edinburgh, 1965), Ch. 3.

tian discourse. "My intention to do something is a settled belief about my future action, a belief that illumines some part of the future, like a beam of light with a periphery of darkness, the periphery not being clearly marked. There is something that I particularly had in mind to do in the center of the beam, and on either side are by-products and accompaniments, more or less clearly thought of and intended around the central intention."[18] This language and the point it makes are suggestive for interpreting the Christian moral life. In the Christian life there are relatively "settled beliefs," not only about what one will do in the future, but about the significance of life itself, as I have tried to show in discussing the perspective of the Christian. These beliefs are shaped by the biblical story and by Jesus Christ as the symbol of them and as an object of loyalty. These beliefs, and the perspective they give rise to, function as sources of illumination even before clear moral intentions are stipulated. Events and experience are interpreted with reference to them, so that one views life, responds to others, in their light. One does not, however, determine what his actions will be in the light of basic beliefs alone.

The way one moves from basic Christian beliefs to moral intentions has not been the subject of much close analysis. The "because" or the "therefore" that joins belief and action often covers a mass of confusion. The moves from theological statements to ethical principles, and to the existential moral question are often hidden in religious rhetoric. We have come to see that the logic of the relation is not necessarily the same as that used in the syllogism. Indeed, the relation for the believer is not simply one between an objective body of beliefs and an informed objective normative prescription of action, but is more "self-involved." It is the relationship between faith as trust and as fidelity in and to God, and the action of the self. One cannot say convincingly that "Christ is such and such, as all reasonable men know," and "because of the 'such and such' all reasonable men will agree that the following moral intentions can be logically derived from the theological statements."[19]

18 Hampshire, *op. cit.*, pp. 123–24.
19 The logical problems of moving from a statement that something is the case, to "therefore I ought to be," or "therefore I ought to do . . ." is a much discussed one that has a particular context in theological ethical discourse. In one sense, this whole book is a study of this issue, but not at the level of precision that satisfies the author's curiosity. Donald Evans, it seems to me, is pointing to a fruitful way to explore these issues.

I believe that it is fruitful to say that certain intentions are *in accord with* or *in discord with* the beliefs of the Christian, or that certain actions are in accord with or in discord with his faith. Or one can use the terms *consonant with* or *dissonant with*. From a mechanical sphere one can speak of some intentions as being *abrasive* against the faith and beliefs of the Christian. Or perhaps the simple language, loosely used, of *consistent with* and *inconsistent with* is still another possibility. Most people, for example, perceive an inconsistency between faith in a God who wills to redeem and reconcile man to man and man to himself, on the one hand, and action that causes enmity and hatred between men, on the other.

The moral intentions of Christians, their settled beliefs about their future actions, are or ought to be in accord with (or at least not in discord with) their basic religious convictions, with their faith in God who is made known to them in Jesus Christ. At least a critical perspective, and at most a formative one, is given by this way of thinking. Critically, Christians can ask, "Are the moral ends we seek consonant with Jesus Christ's significance to us?" "Are our intended activities in pursuit of these ends in accord with our faith and belief?" "Are our intentions and deeds moving in the way that is illumined for us in our faith?"

Our intentions illumine the future as a beam of light, Hampshire suggests. Intentions need to be specified if they are to function as illuminations. How this takes place or can take place can be explored by looking at an example. God, Christians believe, is good, and is the source of the goodness of life. Thus in a response of gratitude to God it is proper to honor and praise him, just as it is proper to honor and praise man who does good. St. Paul can say, "Do all to the glory of God." God is worthy of glorification, men's actions ought to glorify him. The intention to glorify God is not particularly moral; he can be glorified by singing hymns of praise to him. But this basic intention to do all things to the glory of God can function as a touchstone for various moral intentions of Christians. What moral intentions would not glorify God? This is to ask what moral intentions would be dissonant with, in discord with, abrasive to what the Christian believes God to be, to will, and to do. What moral intentions would glorify God? What would be consonant and in accord with beliefs about God that inform our faith in him?

The answer to such questions would not penetrate all the darkness of one's future course of action. Indeed the Bible and the tradition have specified some more particular intentions that are in accord with the faith of believers, or, one might say, in accord with the intention to glorify God in all things we do. Indeed, in the passage from I Corinthians in which "do all things to the glory of God" is found there are other statements of what seem to be proper for Christians. They are not to seek their own good, but the neighbor's. They are to do what is helpful, what builds up. They are to imitate Christ. They are to preserve the liberty of their consciences. The teachings of Jesus also commend certain intentions and actions, show a direction along which the behavior of disciples is and ought to go. From these biblical statements and from the reflection of members of the Christian community, it is possible to form more particular intentions and purposes consonant with these. In isolation from the concrete stuff of life, and in a culture that has been to some extent imbued with the ethos of the Christian community, statements of intention at a general level sound like platitudes. "Do all to the glory of God" and "Love your enemies" sound empty, even when they become one's own stable beliefs. Yet they do shed light in a particular direction; they show the way that Christians intend to go.

Such central intentions at "the center of the beam" are not in themselves sufficient to determine what one ought to do in a specific instance. If I intend to seek the neighbor's good, an intention in accord with my conviction that God has sought my good, I do not yet know what deed will achieve his good. Other information must be in hand to know what he needs, how best to meet that need, what I must have to be of service to him, and what other consequences might occur. Specific moral intentions and judgments are never formed on the basis of a central or general intention alone. The intention to love the neighbor needs specification in the light of other considerations. One's central purpose becomes one of the norms involved in the specific moral judgment in a complex and specific situation. And even the most specific intention leaves a periphery of darkness unillumined since actions and their potential consequences are never fully anticipated by intention alone. There are latent, or unintended, consequences, of actions that are beyond the bounds of determination by the actor alone.

Even at a very specific level, such as "I intend to meet the neighbor's need for better housing by testifying before the Commission on Building Codes and Standards in favor of stricter inspection and enforcement procedures," there can be an accordance or consonance with more general and central intentions. One can ask what the central intention to seek the neighbor's good requires in a given time and place, and thus find that it is fitting to use civic pressure to upgrade housing conditions. Indeed, God may be glorified, Jesus Christ witnessed to, in such actions.

To discuss the formation and function of moral intentions in the Christian life makes it sound more objectively rational than it is or even ought to be. The self finds its identity in part by the consistency of its intentions, and the formed identity of the self is expressed in its intentions. This identity, or posture, of the self is the effect of commitments and loyalties that are affective as well as intellectual, that are personal as well as public. The Christian's identity is bound to his fundamental faith and its meaningfulness in informing his life. There are dispositions that are evoked by his trust in, and loyalty to, Jesus Christ; so also there are intentions that are evoked by, and consistent with, his faith and his bearing toward the world. Given a sense of identity as a Christian, a formation of the self so that it has some integrity in accord with one's faith, there can very well be a consistency of selfhood through consistency of intention that does not consciously ask for every specific purpose, "Is it in accord with my faith?" The self has tendencies that are formed in part by what its commitments and values are which give it a basic direction in activity. These are part of what is expressed in articulated and explicated purposes.[20]

Intentions cast a beam of light, mark the way into the future for every man. They are as much a part of being human as are dispositions. Christians form, can form, and ought to form their intentions to be in accord with their loyalty to Jesus Christ. This loyalty does not exclude other considerations and concerns, but can give through our intentions a direction for participation in all facets of human life.

[20] I suspect the point has been made too often in direct and oblique ways in this book, but I make it once more. Christian ethics as an intellectual discipline has to pay more attention to what forms the self than it has in recent history. Practically, this is important for churches for several reasons. The more that they rely on the "liberty of conscience" rather than rules to govern behavior, the more important the formation of that conscience becomes. The more cultural pluralism is involved in forming selves, the more important it is for communities to see how their particular loyalties and values enter into the shaping of persons who are rightfully conditioned by other loyalties and commitments.

But the Christian moral life is more than the formation of moral intentions in accord with one's faith. It is a matter of specific judgments, choices, and actions. In making these specific choices, our intentions are of central significance. But in the reflection that occurs, one can see how Christ does, can, or ought to be considered as an objective norm among others in the determination of conduct.

CHRIST AS NORM IN THE CHRISTIAN MORAL LIFE

The moral act is determined by more than lasting tendencies and basic intentions of the self. Particular acts result from particular judgments, and in novel or serious matters the judgment is the outcome of careful reflection. Many things are brought to bear in conscious moral judgments. There is an assessment of what is going on in the time and place in which one is moved or called to decide and to act. Part of this assessment process is the gathering of information about the matter at hand, either methodically or impressionistically. Part of it is the interpretation of antecedents and possible consequences, and of relative importance of various aspects of the matter, of where the "real issues" are and what the most effective points of action might be. There is a reference to the self involved in making moral judgments: not only to what I have become and what my intentions are, but also to what actions are most consistent with what I am, what actions least violate my personal integrity. There is an exercise of reason and imagination that reflects the self's training both of mind and of affections to make discriminating discernments of what one ought to do. There are also objective norms that are brought to bear on the judgment; one may be the expectations of a social group to which one belongs, another may be a delineation of the meaning of justice or love to which one feels committed, another may be articulated value preferences that form one's own self-image.

The self that makes the judgments in the Christian community has been shaped in its dispositions and intentions by that community, and by the faith of that community. We have attempted to account for some of this formation in developing the notions of disposition and intention in the Christian moral life. Without using the word "norm," we have shown that Christ functions normatively, particularly in the formation of intentions. To ask if one's intentions are consistent with his loyalty to Jesus Christ is to invoke Jesus Christ in a normative way. It is to assume that what he means and symbolizes has authority for me, for example, that I am obliged to consider him both when there is a conformity of my own desire and preference with what he represents, and when he is abrasive to my "natural" tendency on a particular occasion. Jesus Christ is normative for the Christian's moral purposes whether it is convenient for him to be so or not. He is a standard by which my purposes are judged, he is an authority that ought to direct and inform my activity, if I acknowledge him to be my Lord.

In this section I explore three aspects of the "normativeness" of Christ for the Christian moral life. All three bear upon the moment of specific decision and action, the first more indirectly and the other two more immediately. First, Christ provides for the Christian the normative point for the theological interpretation of what God is willing in the time and place of his life. He becomes the content-filled symbol for man's efforts to discern what God is enabling and requiring in the world.[21] Second, the figure of Christ as given in the New Testament, with all of its descriptive and theological diversity, and the teachings attributed to him are normative in the sense of being the specific instance in which trust in God, and words and deeds directed toward men find their most perfect correlation. Thus Christ is a particular paradigm to be turned to in order to shed light on what those who would follow him ought to be and do in particular instances as they seek to express their faith in words and deeds. Third, insofar as one's discipleship to Christ is to be the point around which the being and words and deeds of a person find their integrity, the Christian is obliged to consider Christ as the most important norm among others that are brought to bear in his judgments and actions. Thus, Christ is the norm for the Christian's theological interpretation of what God wills that life should be among men; Christ is the norm for illumination of what the Christian ought to be and do in his actions; Christ is the central obligatory norm for those who would order their lives in discipleship to him.

Theological ethics by definition seeks to relate the sphere of morality to God, by showing within the context of belief how God orders the world in particular moral ways, or acts to "humanize" life,

---

[21] I am here suggesting something very close to what H. Richard Niebuhr began to develop in his idea of Christ as symbolic form, and in his understanding of interpretation as part of the response involved in all moral action. See *The Responsible Self*, esp. pp. 149–78.

or in other ways enables and requires the good to come into being.
Such analytical theological doctrines become in the nurture of prophetic witness of the Church the basis of "ought" statements for
Christians. If God's will is that of humanization, Christians ought to
be doing what God does; that is, they ought to be engaged in
humanizing activity. If the moral order as created by God is an order
of justice and love, then "What does the Lord require of you, but to
do justice, love mercy, and walk humbly with your God?" Theological ethics is necessarily involved in a process of theological interpretation of what occurs in experience and in history, since the vocation of
the believer is to "so respond to all actions upon him as to respond to
God's action" in H. Richard Niebuhr's language, to be obedient to
the command of God in Barth's language, to endorse and coincide
with God's humanizing activity as Lehmann suggests, to be in accord
with man's true tendencies and ends as God has created him to be, in
Thomistic language.

All such affirmations can be made only after a process of interpretation has occurred, and interpretation is done in the light of some
specific commitments, beliefs, values, or symbols. For some interpreters Christ, as theologically interpreted, is *the unique* and *only
proper* norm for elucidating what God wills in the world; we have
seen in Chapter II how Karl Barth valiantly works to make Christ the
starting point for all aspects of Christian ethics. Catholic theologians,
in contrast, have been quite at home in considering the work of God
the Creator in a relative independence from Christological statements, and explicating proper natural morality on the basis of
tendencies found in creation. Yet they have found in Christ the
means of God's saving and sanctifying grace, and therefore also use
him to interpret what life ought to be in the world, a life of love. I
am not prepared to identify myself with Barth's way of working, nor
shall I at this point launch into a theological interpretation of
morality that I would find plausible and persuasive. The point to be
made here is more a procedural one. For Christians, Christ becomes a
norm for interpreting what God wills that men and the world
become. He is norm both in the sense that he does and that he ought
to function as a source of illumination when Christian interpretation
of what is and ought to be occurring in history takes place.

Theological interpretation of what is and ought to be going on in
the world may provide the Christian with some insight into the

meaning and significance of persons or events for each other, such as we saw in F. D. Maurice's interpretation of the significance before God and before one another of relationships in the family, in Chapter II. Theological interpretation is necessary to form the perspectives of Christians in affirming the goodness of the created world; it is involved in the convictions that nourish and sustain hope and love, freedom and trust in the Christian's disposition toward the world. It may give one a sense of the course of events, of the ongoing struggle between justice and injustice, life-destroying and life-affirming powers, the depths of inhumanity and the achievements of love and reconciling forces in human experience. But a theological interpretation, informed by what Christ represents, is never sufficient in itself precisely to determine what *I* am to do in a particular time and place. Paul Lehmann, for example, finds his understandings of what God is doing by a focus on Christology; it is from a "theology of messianism" grounded in the "christological affirmations" of the doctrines of the Trinity, of the offices of Christ as prophet, priest, and king, and of the second Adam and the second Advent that he shapes his conviction that God is working to humanize and to maturate man. For this reader of Lehmann's work, however, it is not clear that the Christologically grounded interpretation of humanization by God answers all the questions that confront the conscientious man in a particular decision that he has to make. Christ, for Lehmann, is the norm for theological interpretation, but that interpretation does not fully resolve the "ought" question that *I* must face.

In particular decisions, like every man, the Christian meets a multiplicity of things to be considered; not only are there many facets of the facts of the matter at hand, but also conflicts between the obligations that he perceives, between profound desires that he has, between ends that are possible and defensible, between loyalties and commitments that he holds, and between various moral principles that can be brought to bear on the situation. To say that *I* will act to coincide with God's action—humanizing, or creating, sustaining, judging and redeeming—does not resolve the matters of choice. And if I admit that such theological interpretation as I engage in is inevitably unclear and inaccurate by virtue of my finiteness and various natural and willful biases, I can rely even less on my Christ-informed interpretation to answer my moral question. There are no simple religious or theological resolutions to moral choices; they almost always involve choices between things that are each of some value and each of some perversity. To choose one is not to choose another, and with that choice some possibilities are irrevocably lost and others are on the way to conditioning the course of my life and its events.

In this concreteness of conscientious moral decision, I would affirm that the Christian finds Christ to be a norm that illuminates his options and, insofar as he is loyal to Christ, deeply conditions his choice. Note that this is neither a claim that Christ prescribes what the options are, nor a claim that he dictates the choice. The latter, stronger affirmations are wrong, in my judgment, for several reasons. As has been reiterated again and again in this chapter, the analyses and choices are human, made by finite creatures with various biases and perspectives, and as the effects of human agency they can never claim divine sanction unambiguously. Agency, the capacity to decide, to act, to initiate and respond, is not only our human condition, but it is such by creation, and I believe it necessarily is respected by the providential power of God. Further, there is in most instances of serious moral choice no final happy resolution in which a single loyalty to Christ, or indeed to self or nation or any other object, simply and harmoniously makes all things fall together for the good of all concerned, or for the happiness and well-being of all concerned. Too often men seek and use Christ as the resolution for a secure decision in which all elements of tragedy and suffering are supposedly eliminated. Also there are many factors in most moral choices that have their own stubborn autonomy, and are not readily subsumed under an exclusive source of insight, whether this source be Christ, or love, or anything else. It is neither Christ nor love alone that tells the conscientious youth what his vocation ought to be; it is also his aptitudes, his opportunities, his desire to achieve, his awareness of various purposes, and many more. Neither Christ nor love alone tells the conscientious physician when to cease prolonging life; his medical knowledge, his obligations to the law and his patient, and many other factors are involved. Christ does not prescribe the options and dictate the choice of the Christian.

Christ, as a norm brought to bear, does, can, and ought to illuminate the options, and deeply condition the choice of the Christian. The figure of Christ given in the New Testament with all of its descriptions and theological diversity and the teachings attributed to him provide Christians with a source of illumination and a criterion of judgment, for in him there is an integrity of trust in, and loyalty to, God, and words and deeds directed toward men. Certainly it must be admitted that conscientious Christians have somewhat different configurations of the meaning of Christ, are attracted by different "portraits" of Christ. Part of the life of the Church is the formation of such a portrait, the judgment of excessively inadequate ones, the enrichment of those that suffer a poverty of appreciation. This task of the Church and of the Christian is not without some objectivity, however, since it is done in recognition of the place of Scripture as the document that provides the charter for faith and life.

To remember Christ, and the significance of his work, is part of making moral judgments in the Christian life. This is not to revert to the question, "What would Jesus do?" as it was set forth by our American grandfathers in the most morally sensitive part of the Protestant movement. It is, however, to recall him, and to think with reference to his deeds (including his death) and his words what trust in God's care and goodness, and love for man required. It is sometimes to have the imagination provoked by a parable, with the concreteness that that form of discourse has, and to exercise one's imagination in discerning what is concretely required in the moment. It is sometimes to think analogically about the deeds we are given opportunity to do in relation to the deeds Christ did under somewhat similar circumstances. It is sometimes to think very clearly about what the command to love requires, what an "in-principled love," or love in dialectic with equity, directs us to do in a given ambiguous instance. It is to be conformed to what one discerns about Jesus' own attitude and bearing toward others, about the intentions that express and are shaped by his trust in God.

This is not to confuse faith in God with moral action; it is not to say that a man's sense of worth and his salvation are gained by making Christ a norm for his moral life. But it is to seek to bring his light to bear upon the place where one's own life before God and the world is enacted. Nor is this to say that Christ alone is sufficient as a light, a norm, to shape one's decision in a given occasion. Christ gives insight and direction; he shows something of the way in which his disciples are to follow. He helps them to see what options are more in conformity with the human good as it is understood in and through

God's work and disclosure in him. He helps them to see what choices about ends to be sought and means to be used are in accord with trust in the goodness of God who gives and sustains life, and who acts to redeem it.

Nor is this affirmation of Christ as a norm to be brought to bear on the Christian's decisions a claim for the moral superiority of a Christian. He is not to say that only Christians can perceive the good or even to say that they perceive it better than others do. Rather, it is to suggest that those whose lives are nurtured by the Christian community, who are called to faith in God through Christ, who commit themselves to discipleship to him are given illumination from Christ in their moral lives. Nor is it to claim that Christians are separated from the world by this life and this norm. Rather, they are impelled to share in the struggle of every man for whom Christ died, every man created by the Father who is known in Christ, every man under the Lordship of Christ. But to share in the struggle is to be loyal to Christ in it, to bring him to bear upon it, to have a resource in the service of the needs of every man.

Indeed, the Christian moral life is a life of discipleship to Christ. It is not to be determined by one's own powerful desires and interests, but to be under the obligation to scrutinize and direct them in obedience to him. It is not to be determined by one's loyalty to the community of family, or university, or nation, or ecclesiastical affiliation, but to find one's way in and through these in loyalty to him. It is not to be determined by the mores of one's group, but to bring them under his judgment and direction. It is not to find one's integrity in an image of oneself as principled man, or as emancipated man, or as serious man, or as joyous man, but to find one's selfhood integrated around what he is and means. It is not to be responsive to the movements of history, to the course of events as if in so doing one were doing what Christians ought to do, but to respond and participate in obedience to him, being directed by the discriminations and discernments that he enables. It is not to find perfect coincidence between my wishes and his commands, between my nation's wishes and his requirements, but to live in faithfulness to him both when there is coincidence and when there is discord between them. As one who is called into faith and newness of life through Christ, the Christian is called into faithfulness to him, and is obligated by that life and that call to turn to Christ to be the central norm, the main source of illumination for his words and deeds.

Disposition, or bearing toward one another, one's manner of life, and intention, or the settled beliefs that cast the beam of light into the future and direct the will's achievement, and decision and action with norms brought to bear on them, are all subject to the Christian's loyalty to Christ, and thus subject to Christ to whom they are loyal.

INDEX

273